GENDER ISSUES AND SOCIAL DYNAMICS

Gender Issues and Social Dynamics

LATIKA MENON

KANISHKA PUBLISHERS, DISTRIBUTORS
NEW DELHI-110 002

KANISHKA PUBLISHERS, DISTRIBUTORS
4697/5-21A, Ansari Road, Daryaganj
New Delhi -110 002
Phones : 2327 0497, 2328 8285
Fax : 011-2328 8285
E-mail : kanishka_publishing@yahoo.co.in

First Published: 1997

Second Edition: 2011

ISBN : 978-81-7391-168-1

PRINTED IN INDIA

Published by Madan Sachdeva for Kanishka Publishers, Distributors, 4697/5-21A, Ansari Road, Daryaganj, New Delhi-110 002, Typeset by Sunshine Graphics, Delhi, and Printed at Rajdhani Printers, Delhi.

Preface

Women, though not quite 50 per cent of the population thanks to the disturbing imbalance in the gender ratio, are increasingly being viewed at more than just the second sex in India. This change in perception may have much to do with politics but it is welcome nevertheless. Over the past two years, the governments of Tamil Nadu, Maharashtra and most recently Andhra Pradesh have framed policies for women, aimed at their emancipation and empowerment through social, economic, legal and administrative changes. Karnataka too has a women's development programme. All these exercises are based by and large on three documents the *Towards Equality* report brought out in 1975, the *National Perspective Plan for Women,* and the Shrashakti report. These reports had made policy and programme recommendations such as 33 per cent reservation in local bodies and joint *pattas* (which Maharashtra has now given a commitment to).

The current status of women in the country calls for similar initiatives in other States – There is a dowry death every 102 minutes, a rape every 54 minutes and a kidnapping or abduction of women every 43 minutes. The women's policies formulated so far many not be comprehensive or without flaws but the whole process is path-breaking. So far all policy pronouncements took place at the Central government level. This is one time where States themselves are taking the initiative.

A far reaching move taken by the governments of Tamil Nadu, Kerala and Karnataka has been to amend the Hindu Succession Act of 1956 in order to give co-parcenary rights to women. That is, giving daughters equal rights of inheritance. Maharashtra has also proposed to do the same. Recently, Union Law Minister said in Parliament that the Central Government was also considering such an mendment. Maharashtra, though it was the second State (after Tamil Nadu) to come out with a policy for women, deserves the credit for Framing the most comprehensive policy so far. The others could be more accurately described as action plans.

A women's Committee noted with conconern that at several places, the women workers were denied maternity benefits. They were forced to work till the last day of pregnancy, and in some cases, their services were terminated when they proceeded on leave. The Committee also found it most shocking that the Government had failed to take adequate steps to safeguard women workers against health hazards when they were exposed to chemicals and dust. In Mysore, the Committee found that because of poor light conditions at the place of work of cleaning silk yarn, women workers often got serious eye problems.

The Committee was informed by a woman engineer in Calcutta that even in organised sectors of employment, women suffered discrimination. They were denied field duty. Another woman told the Committee that air hostesses in Air-India were grounded at the age of 45, whereas men continued to be on board till the age of 58. The Committee recommended that these 'distortions' and employer's bias should be removed.

The Committee noted that women constituted about 12 per cent of the work force in the country, though they were hearly 49 per cent of the total population. It felt that in private companies, women were treated as an 'object of sex' and they were recruited exclusively for jobs like private secretaries and telephone operators or receptionists in hotels. The Committee was told that air hostesses were not allowed to wear spectacles because the male bosses thought it spoiled their appearance.

A very large number of gender issues continue to determine the nature and shape of our society. Some of the above mentioned issues are profiled and in some cases analysed in the present collection of articles, papers, excerpts and report abstracts. The intention is to provide the student as well as the researcher a framework of studies and approaches in the area of gender issues and related sociological and developmental policies and programmes.

LATIKA MENON

Contents

1

Women, Mothers and Daughters: Education and the New World

It is not within the scope of this paper to examine at length the content and methods of teaching citizenship through the school curriculum, so we will take up the thread of educational experience at that stage which comes to every mother with a daughter—when she recognizes that she has another woman in the house. First, let us consider the out-of-school and after-school activities which can be encouraged among adolescent girls and young women and then look at the leisure-time organizations for their mothers. In some cases there is no hard-and-fast dividing line. It is usually, however, better for adolescents to be on their own or with contemporaries for some of their time, away from the parental generation.

In the Western world, and wherever the impact of Western manners has been much felt, young people tend to be great joiners of voluntary organizations. For a young girl adolescence is the period when she emerges from the dependence and restrictions of childhood into a transitional stage of preparing to marry and have children of her own. Whereas in a primitive society the period of transition may be very short, in specialized societies it lengthens and becomes a time of life which is of great social significance. Training for adult responsibilities of all kinds takes place in a great variety of youth organizations. In Britain these are all voluntary associations in the special sense that no girl or boy can be compelled to join any of them. There are between twenty and thirty major youth organizations in Britain besides a great number of small bodies independent of the large associations. This variety gives a girl the opportunity to choose her group and choose how much of her time, energy and loyalty she will give to it. It is on the basis of that free choice that the youth group builds up the attitudes and habits of responsible participation in public life.

If we could examine all the organizations we should find that each one has a different experience to offer but that all aim at the development of personality and training for social responsibility. Let us consider the aims and methods of a small sample of them.

The Girl Guides Association is organized:

> for the purpose of developing good citizenship among girls by forming their character; training them in habits of observation, obedience and self-reliance; inculcating loyalty and thoughtfulness for others; teaching them services to the public and handicrafts useful to themselves; promoting their physical development; making them capable of keeping good homes and bringing up good children.... The method of training is to give the girls pursuits which appeal to them, such as games and recreative exercises, which lead them to learn for themselves many useful crafts. It is a scheme of elder and younger sisters playing games together, rather than the instruction of privates by officers in a cut-and-dried disciplinary machine, or of pupils by teachers in an academic curriculum.

The Guides wear a uniform and have a simple ritual attached to the symbols of loyalty to God and the Queen; but Guide interests and loyalties reach beyond national boundaries. The movement is worldwide. We see how much stress is laid upon developing self-reliance, largely through increasing one's range and depth of skill and knowledge. Badges which attest proficiency can be earned not only in subjects usually accepted as being proper to women but also in carpentering, building, shoe-mending and other 'manly' activities (just as a Boy Scout learns simple sewing and cooking). A special point is given to these pursuits by the important role of camping for both Scouts and Guides. Learning to look after themselves and each other away from home, in tents, with essential equipment only, is a testing experience for girls. Leaders (not only of Guides) say that a week in camp is worth a year of ordinary meetings. In a few days one sees a growth of self-reliance, initiative, common sense and co-operation—all good civic virtues.

The statistics of the association in Great Britain show that the bulk of the work is done among children and the younger adolescents. The numbers dwindle sharply in the later teens. This does not imply a failure; it is of the essence of growing up satisfactorily to be able to proceed from experience to experience. Adult members of the association not only do its normal work among young people but are especially competent by reason of their experience to help at times of international emergency: for instance in post-war relief work.

For girls in their later teens, youth clubs have great attractions. Here a girl meets boys on equal terms and in a variety of social situations. She learns how to behave in a mixed society and make friends with youths among whom or their like she will one day find a husband. In a society where young women go out of their homes to work, and are likely to meet men who are unknown to their families, a girl needs to be able to discriminate between men for herself. Also, as worker and a citizen, she can be helped to adjust herself to a relationship with men as colleagues and friends, not only as potential husbands. This is one of the functions of a youth club.

A club is a democratic association. It may be very large, running into a membership of some hundreds, or in a village it may be only a handful. It may have its own specially-built or adapted premises or it may meet in a school, community centre or church hall. Its leaders are often unpaid, but in a big club open every night or most nights the leader may be a paid professional. The essentials are that the club should be a friendly place, full of life and interest, and the leaders not only good but attractive personalities who have faith and joy in life and can impart their vitality of interest to others. The club should also provide opportunities for the development of skill, for physical recreation, for the acquisition of knowledge and—above all, perhaps—for practising citizenship. Clubs differ greatly, and some only pay lip-service to democratic ideals, for young people come to clubs for fun and friendship and have to be wooed to undertake social responsibility.

Most clubs genuinely attempt to train for citizenship. For instance, it is a principle with most that the members pay a small subscription regularly (fixed according to age and earning capacity) and do not merely pay an admission fee on the occasions when they happen to attend the club. This emphasizes that the club is an organization towards which one has a continuous responsibility, not a place of which one makes use. Again, when a new members wishes to join she may be interviewed by the leader, welcomed as a guest, told what the club does and what it offers her and then told what the club, in turn, asks from her. It is useful to have a system whereby a new member is 'on approval' by the club and the club 'on approval' by her for a few meetings. This gives importance to the decision she must eventually make and stresses the reciprocal nature of the duties of the individual and the group. If she decides to join and the club agrees there should be some simple ceremony of admission. She may repeat a 'club promise' if there is one, or sign her name on an electoral roll, or be publicly presented with a club badge. In one way or another, her accession to the club should be given social recognition and be made the occasion for her undertaking to be loyal and helpful.

Club leaders share their responsibility with a committee or committees. Often there is an adult advisory Committee, or Management Committee. These men and women are usually responsible for providing and maintaining the premises and equipment, for paying any professional staff and for any other large-scale expenditure; they raise most of the money needed and appoint staff; they are the body responsible to the Local Education Authority if the latter grants money to the club. Generally speaking they have legal and financial responsibilities and so have the right to determine the main lines of policy in the club. The young people's own committee, under the guidance of the leader, takes on the responsibilities of the day-to-day running of club life. It is they who, as the elected representatives of the members, look after newcomers and guest, take care of equipment, help organize activities, keep their ears open for criticisms and suggestions for new activities, help to raise money and keep order, and by their own behaviour maintain the club principles and traditions.

It is not easy for a girl or boy who is not far out of childhood to fulfil such responsibilities and the youth club which has a succession of really good committees is the exception, not the rule.

Usually one finds that only a proportion of committee members take a full share in the work. That is not surprising, they are only citizens in training. The committee can be helped a good deal by the method of its election. Show-of -hands elections are less useful than a ballot. Full warning of elections should be given so that the electors can consider and discuss beforehand the composition of possible committees. Candidates should be nominated and seconded and their consent to stand for election obtained beforehand. The committee should not hold office too long—six months may be plenty for youngsters—and when it retires it should be publicly thanked for what it did or tried to do, while the incoming committee in its turn is thanked for accepting the responsibility. The committee's decision on club organization should be made known promptly on a notice-board or at a general meeting and the club in a general meeting should receive reports from the committee and be encouraged to ask questions and offer advice and criticisms.

This very brief summary sounds painfully dogmatic from sheer force of compression. There are innumerable ways of running clubs; no two clubs are or should be alike. Clubs are run for *people*, not for the hypothetical 'average citizen' or 'ideal citizen'. Nevertheless they all can by one means or another give practice in democratic techniques or organization and cultivate mental attitudes of mutual respect and co-operation.

Like all youth organizations, clubs can serve in many ways the community of which they are part: visiting hospitals and singing in choirs or performing plays for the patients; inviting old people or the blind to entertainments at the club; providing a service of visitors to the homes of old or handicapped people to read aloud, or help with housework or look after the garden or go shopping. Girl members often act as 'baby-sitters', so that the parents can go out together in the evening to an entertainment or political meeting or perhaps to their own club or community centre. If a club looks round its neighbourhood it cannot fail to find needs which its members can help to meet.

A popular club activity is the discussion group which often concerns itself with current events. At times of public elections clubs may hold 'mock election' or invite representatives of the different parties to address them and answer questions on their party's election programmes. Some clubs take a more continuous interest in public affairs, especially in local matters. They may, for example, help in making a map or a social survey or the neighbourhood.

In a club for boys and girls it is sometimes found that the girls are less articulate and less active than the boys in committees, discussions and in all the organization of club life. One answer is to run clubs for girls separately and this solves the problem up to a point; for in a girl's group some members usually emerge who are relatively confident and enterprising, either because there are no boys present or because that kind of girl seeks girls – only groups, or for some other reason possibly connected with leadership.

It is however a partial solution only, for everywhere the tendency is to bring men and women together in an increasing number of social situations. We are moving away from the time when women influenced events through the men of the family into an age in which they are forced to act alongside men, known or strangers. The writer recalls vividly a large conference of 16 to 18-year-old girls and boys representing some of the grammar schools and public schools of England. They were meeting to listen to experts on public affairs. It happened that on the first day the number of boys present was negligible, and lively, intelligent questions and discussions poured forth form the girls. Next day the representation of the sexes was about equal and from then on the girls left the boys to do all the talking. Many such experiences have suggested that the ideal group for girls is one in which they share equal rights and duties with boys but where each sex has a good deal of separate life within the whole framework. The girls should have a woman leader who understands the special problems of the young girl facing unfamiliar situations. Such a leader will, to take a small practical example, make sure that a girl member of the club committee is well briefed before she goes to a meeting and has either a few notes written down or some points memorized on which she is to speak. There are of course confident, independent girls to be found in every group but we are not at the moment concerned with them but with all the others.

An ordinary youth club programme may cover anything from drama to beekeeping, carpentry to camping, dancing to debates. A Young Farmers' Club is more specialized, and concentrates its interests accordingly. Some are attached to schools and may in that case be run for members of one sex only. Most are for young people out of school or who have left school and are mixed. Their purpose is to bring together young people who are interested in farming as a way of life. Clubs tend to specialize in different branches of farming and each boy or girl member must take an active part by (for example) working a piece of ground, or keeping poultry or a pig. Members are expected to work seriously and scientifically at their farming and keep proper accounts; they are in effect, though not technically, apprentice farmers. Each club is a self-governing entity electing its own officers. Adults are invited to act as trustees for club property but the clubs do not have adult leaders. A special feature of Young Farmers' Clubs for some years now has been training in committee procedure and the conduct of meetings and in public speaking. In public-speaking contests with other youth organizations YFC's have very often been successful. A YFC may have a very considerable range of social activities in common with a youth club, but it has also the special value to its members of combining vocational training with social experience. This is exceptional in youth organizations, though pre-service training units do something of this. It is interesting that YFCs are now spreading into towns and cities from the countryside where they originated.

If we compare these three kinds of organization we can see that each has a valuable experience to offer and indeed that a girl might, with profit to herself, be a Guide, a member of a Young-Farmers' Club and of a Youth Club at different stages of her development. In a fair-sized town she might also be able to choose to be a member of the Junior Red Cross or the St. John's Ambulance Cadets, if she felt a call to serve the sick and injured; or of one of the uniformed Brigades attached to the churches; or of a club belonging to the international network of the Young Women's Christian Association—or many more. There are also the junior sections of political parties and the very numerous fellowships of young people attached to the different churches.

As we turn from daughters to mothers we must note that many women find an opening for their service in membership of a youth club committee of management or in some other capacity in a children's or young people's organization. From among the organizations run for women's own leisure-time recreation, we will choose four: the Mothers' Union as an example of many religious organizations attached to the different denominations,

Women's Institutes, Townswomen's Guilds and the Co-operative Women's Guild. All these are for women only, though a group sometimes invites men for special occasions. The Mothers' Union is one of the oldest organizations for women in Britain. It is attached to the Church of England and holds meetings in each parish, usually once a month, to which speakers are invited and at which business connected with the church is discussed. There is a religious service at each meeting and once a year a national service is held in Westminster Abbey to which women come from all over the country. The Mothers' Union is concerned especially with upholding Christian ideals of marriage and family life. The meetings tend to attract middle-aged and elderly women chiefly, whose own children are grown-up, so a young Wives' Fellowship has come into being in recent years for the mothers of young children. At their meeting talks are given, among other subjects, on the care of children, and if possible a nursery is provided where the babies can be looked after during the meeting. Most other religions denominations have women's organizations attached to them, Fellowships, Meetings or Guilds, and between them they have in the past provided a very large proportion of women's experience of group activity outside the home. They still do so, alongside more recently developed organizations.

Women's Institutes have become an important feature of life in villages and country towns since the first one was set up in England in 1915. Their aim is to give country women opportunities to improve conditions in their own homes and villages, and to increase their enjoyment of life. The institutes are grouped in counties and co-ordinated in a National Federation. Meetings are held monthly to discuss institute business, listen to a talk and, after the inevitable cup of tea to spend a short time in social activities. This is the usual pattern of a meeting but it can of course vary and many institutes develop special interest which involve their members in extra meetings; for instance, the institutes are often keen performers of plays and enter for drama competitions which require the members to travel a good deal; some arrange pageants of local history, or form choirs or run competitions in domestic crafts. Women's Institutes take a special interest in preserving local crafts and have sometimes been instrumental in saving an almost obsolete craft. They study and record the history and folk-lore of their neighbourhood. In an age in which ways of life everywhere are being drastically affected by the spread of urban, industrial influences, it is most important not to let slip the beautiful, useful and historically significant remains of one's cultural inheritance. The Women's Institute which performs dialect plays in the village hall, collects traditional local recipes for food and drink, resuscitates a local craft (of lace-making, or whatever-else it finds in process of disappearance under the flood of standardized goods) is doing something to preserve the native heritage of its community. 'A culture once dead cannot be resuscitated; let us therefore beware of lightly allowing a culture to die'.

Townswomen's Guilds endeavour "To encourage the education of women and to enable them as citizens to make their best contribution to the common good'. They are organized in a National Union. Like the Women's Institutes each holds as a rule a monthly meeting for the guild as a whole, and groups within the guilds pursue their special interests and find ways of rendering public service. Both institutes and guilds are unconnected with any religious denomination or political party.

The Co-operative Women's Guild is not a political organization in the strict sense but it has political interests. It states its aims as those of a:

> movement which exists to serve the interests of the working housewife... Democracy can only function satisfactorily if individual democrats are competent to play their part, and the purpose of the Guild is to make the ordinary housewife a democratic co-operator and an informed citizen.

Meetings may be as often as once a week. There are talks on subjects of local, national and international importance, especially on such matters as civics and politics, education, the upbringing of children, women's rights and duties and the work of co-operative movements in other lands. The guilds also undertake practical service in their localities, for instance in the welfare of children, lonely old people and disabled people, and they help many national and international charitable causes.

It can be seen that in these four organizations (which are only a sample) one has a good deal of unity in diversity. The machinery of organization is similar; local branches with their elected committees and officers; branches co-ordinated through counties or regions, or federated directly in the national organization. The pattern of meetings is similar: a time for business, a time for education, a time for social relaxation. The flavour is different however. The devotional atmosphere of the Mothers' Union and the Young Wives' Fellowship is not present in the others. The Women's Institute stresses practical activities and the bringing of 'enjoyment' into the lives of countrywomen who often live isolated lives. The Townswomen's Guilds are differently situated, within access of town entertainments and educational facilities. They tend do draw on a wide range of membership, women of different social, educational and occupational groups. The Co-operative Guild sets out to appeal especially to the working class woman and has strong political interest.

There is another way in which we can look at these bodies. Two of them, the Women's institutes and the Townswomen's Guilds, lean towards the community pattern, of organization; the others show a different principle of association; they are indeed 'associations' in a special sense. We must examine the differences between a community and an association for they have importance for our general theme of citizenship. Sociologists do not always agree precisely in their definitions of these terms but here are helpful and clear statements. A community is a group of people who 'live together in such a way that they share, not this or that particular interest, but the basic conditions of common life..... a community is an area of common living'. As association on the other hand is 'a group organized for the pursuit of an interest or group of interests in common. It is not a community but an organization within a community. A community.... is the matrix of organizations'.[1]

All four of the organizations which we have examined are obviously 'associations'. The Women's Institutes and Townswomen's Guilds, however, have purposes so widely defined that no woman in their area is necessarily excluded. A denominational or partisan group has a more exclusive membership; those who hold a different faith or belong to a different party cannot share all its purposes. Obviously each type has its advantages and both are necessary.

Just as we saw earlier that a family in modern society tends to be fragmented into individuals, so a community tends to be fragmented into associations. There are two aspects of the same process. We noted that the family does not necessarily fall apart, since its members are held together by love and a sense of responsibility towards and for each other, and, let us add, by habit, shared experience, sometimes a common inheritance of property and always the intangible heritage of the family name, traditions and status. To adopt the terms used above we can call the family the matrix of individuals.

The formation of associations as a rule brings together likeminded people in relatively small groups, where they concentrate their interests. Through associations it is possible to increase the sum of knowledge, skill and power; but what is achieved by association should in some way come back into common life as part of the common stock. Wherever people live in large agglomerations which have sprung up quickly, community feeling tends to be weak; as on the other hand it may weaken in a small, old-established neighbourhood, if there is a strong pull on the more mobile members to seek occupation and entertainment elsewhere. We will look at two methods of countering these tendencies which have been tried out in London and in a rural area of England respectively.

The first is a particular form of the familiar community centre. The Peckham Health Centre in London was conceived, planned and brought into being by a group of doctors, with a special interest in biology, who aimed at preventing sickness rather than curing it. Their biological approach to their patients' medical problems led them to regard the family rather than the individual as the unit of treatment. The family from this point of view is the 'body', the individual member is a limb only and can be treated successfully only as part of the whole. Families as such, not individuals, were accepted for membership of the centre and each family was medically examined at intervals, the examination being followed by a family consultation with the doctor. The centre had very fine premises, suitable for all kinds of activities: drama, music, dancing, swimming and crafts and so forth. The building had certain special features which helped to make the principles of the centre possible in practice. There was a minimum of sub-division and, wherever possible, partitions were made transparent; people were together and yet apart at the same time. Husbands, wives and children attended as members of the family group within the community group but in practice each could go his or her own way. They attached themselves as individuals to the different age-groups or interest groups.

The Peckham Health Centre was a specially interesting form of community centre. Nowadays we regard the provision of some sort of community centre as essential in all kinds of neighbourhood, and when a new town or a new housing estate is being planned consideration has to be given to the site and construction of its centre. Every village likewise has or hopes to have its village hall. To women—who, in spite of all social changes, still tend to stay closer to the home than men—it is of especial importance to see that there is an adequate meeting-place in the neighbourhood. We do not know how long it takes for a mushroom town to grow into a community but we must probably think of it in terms of generations and we cannot begin too soon. Finding a site and erecting a building will not of itself evoke community spirit unless the people for whom it is intended take part in the work and understand the purpose. A hut build by a handful of enthusiasts is often a better nucleus for a community centre then a superior building provided by an authority which is felt to be remote and impersonal, though one cannot remain contented with the hut indefinitely.

In the county of Cambridgeshire a successful experiment has been tried in rural areas which have a scatter of small villages. A fairly large village is chosen as the centre of a region which is treated as a cultural unit, and a village college created to serve as the cultural headquarters of the region. In the daytime, part of the premises is used as a secondary school, at night the whole building comes into use by adolescents and adults. Special buses are run by the Local Education Authority (which is responsible for the scheme) to and from the college and the outlying villages. This idea is now being adopted elsewhere, with modifications to suit different parts of the country.

Very often in both towns and villages the school is also the community centre and some local education authorities now take this into account in planning a new school and provide a dual-purpose building. Teachers take a considerable share in staffing youth clubs and in the work of community education generally, but it is one criterion of their success that the work involved in community education should be increasingly widespread among all social, educational and occupational groups.

Before we leave this question of the development and interaction of the community and its associations we must briefly refer to the great value of residential education. The Scandinavian countries led the way in this great development of adult education with their Folk High Schools, and the value of their example has been very great. In Britain we have eight long-term centres of which one is for women only. These colleges provide a one or, occasionally, two-year course of study (not vocational training) for men and women workers. Only a few working men and women can afford to leave their employment so long or have kept alive the necessary desire for study since they left school at 14 or 15; but the small stream of students is important out of all proportion to its numbers in the life of the country. Enlightened employers willingly co-operate in this scheme and education authorities and voluntary organizations also join in making it possible. The oldest of these colleges, Ruskin College of Oxford, has now given half-a-century of service.

There are also many short-term centres where people go to study a subject or group of subjects for a week or weeks or as little as a couple of days. Men and women from very different social back-ground use these centres and the programmes cover every interest: politics, civics, religion or music or the study of the countryside or a handicraft—according to the demand of the students, the enthusiasms of the staff, the nature, equipment and site of the college and so forth. No two residential centres are alike. In all of them one meets a good many women students, both housewives and women out at work. It is especially interesting to meet the middle-aged woman, whose children are growing up or have already grown up and left home, who is finding time on her hands and is looking for new interests. She is vigorous and has a great deal to give, but her occupations are leaving her and she wants to use herself and be used in a new way. As health and longevity increase in a society the pool of energy created by middle-aged women becomes more and more important.

In India as part of the monumental "Education for all by 2000" project on adult and continuing education, women as well as men are invited to attend "social education camps' of six weeks duration. These camps are part of a scheme for promoting adults literacy and at the same time raising standards of health, hygiene and citizenship. In the United States the League of Women Voters has invented the technique of the Citizenship School, lasting as a rule for one, two or three days, to which a woman can come for several hours a day to study problems of government from the elementary problems of making out a ballot paper correctly to more abstract questions of political science. In Sudan, it is a feature of some women's club meetings to listen to reading of a special column in the local newspaper and to discuss the problems of women's duties and behaviour in the community which it poses from time to time. In Yugoslavia, after the war, reading-clubs were formed at which countrywomen could learn to read and to discuss the newspapers, and this technique was found to be very useful during the earlier years of the national drive for literacy and especially for stimulating women's interest and activity in affairs outside their homes. These examples can be paralleled in many other countries.

What is the husband's attitude? The writer recollects a residential week-end course, one of a series of half-a-dozen one winter, for unmarried boys and girls of 17 to 21 years old. The series was called 'Myself and My World', and lectures and discussions dealt with health, morals, religion, work, the use of leisure and citizenship. In a discussion of marriage one boy, a factory workers, said that when he married he would want his wife to have interests outside the home for her sake and his too. He would like her to belong, for instance, to a class run by the Workers' Education Association. One of the girls asked sceptically whether he would stay at home and wash the dishes and mind the baby. He and all the other boys were emphatic that they were perfectly prepared to take their share of work in the home to release their wives to pursue other interests. The proof of the pudding, of course, is in the eating, but at least one sees here a change in the traditional attitudes of men towards women. The fact that these young people of the working class were able to come away from their homes to study and play together in a residential centre represents a social revolution in itself.

Reference

1. Robert M. MacIver, *Society, A Textbook of Sociology*, New York, Rinehart & Co.

2

Fertility and the Status of Women

Introduction

In the eyes of many demographers and development planners, women's lives consist of little more than their reproductive roles. Thus 'the role of women is conceptualized as a simultaneous system of micro-decisions regarding contraceptive use, fertility, labour force participation, education, wages occupational choice, migration, marital status, health and nutritional status within an environment conditioned by a range of government policies' (Berman *et al.*, 1978.)

Often discussions of the position of women in the Third World suggest that the only reason for taking any interest in women is in order to reduce their excessively high fertility. Programmes to educate women, to provide them with paid employment or to extend their participation in public life are put forward, not because they are good in themselves, but because it is argued that they will result in reduced fertility. To some development planners, women seem to be little more than producers of children to be manipulated by the granting of a few minor concessions in the world which is still considered to belong to men. There is very little thought that women are human individuals with rights and interests of their own independent of the family.

Thus, it is necessary to stress that women are much more than mothers and that childbearing is only a minor part of women's lives. Although this chapter focuses on the relationship between fertility and the status of women, this is not the central issue in the relationship between women and development. Equally, even if it could be shown that raising the status of women would result in a rise in fertility levels this would not be a valid reason for refusing to improve their lives. Politically it may be wise to argue that helping women makes a major contribution to development by reducing population growth rates. This is an argument which wins moral and financial support from national governments and international aid agencies alike. However, it should never be forgotten that the best reason for promoting equality of status for women is to allow them their human rights and not to solve population problems.

Women's Education and Fertility

There is a general agreement that the education of females is associated with a reduction of fertility levels. Thus it is claimed that 'the inverse relationship of education to completed family size is one of the most clearcut correlations found in the literature' (McGreevey and Birdsall, 1974).

There still remain a number of debatable questions concerning this relationship. These include:

(i) the conditions under which education does not reduce fertility, and whether there is a threshold point beyond which education will always reduce fertility;

(ii) the relative contributions of male and female education to the reduction of fertility;

(iii) just why it is that education should reduce fertility and the exact mechanisms by which it does so;

(iv) the relative impact of education at the individual level as compared with the impact at a societal level; and

(v) the extent to which the provision of female education is a cost-effective method of reducing fertility or whether there are more direct means which are equally effective.

The relationship between female education and fertility is

not always an inverse one. In poor countries with relatively low levels of literacy, education may at first serve to raise fertility (Bjork, 1971). This is because education is associated with improved health and lower levels of infertility. Also the traditional constraints upon sexual intercourse and the practice of prolonged breastfeeding are often abandoned by women who have acquired a limited degree of education and no longer observe these customs. Increased education may also be associated with more stable and cohesive marriages (Hull, 1979). Yet, at the same time, women with only a limited level of education, unlike their more highly educated sisters, have yet to adopt the practice of delaying marriage or using modern contraception. This curvilinear relationship between female education and fertility, usually, with both the illiterate and the highly educated women having lower, fertility than those with some primary education, has been reported from Indonesia, Tanzania, Thailand and West Malaysia (Hull and Hull, 1977; Ewbank, 1977; Knodel and Prachuabmoh 1973; Palmore 1969). In Tropical Africa where prolonged breastfeeding is linked with post-natal sexual abstinence and polygyny it is almost unavoidable that, at first, the spread of formal education for girls will raise fertility levels.

There is little evidence of a single threshold level of female education beyond which fertility begins to fall in every country. The exact turning point would appear to be related to the nature of the traditional cultures, the level of development, and the mechanisms through which education affects fertility. Kirk (1971) found that the national level correlation between female education and female fertility was—0.55 in Southeast Asia,—0.71 in Latin America, and—0.81 in fifteen Islamic countries. This would suggest that education has a more dramatic impact upon women's lives and fertility in Islamic countries.

At an elementary level many studies have shown a direct relationship between female education and knowledge, approval and practice of contraception (Arnold *et al.*, 1975; CELADE 1972; Chung *et al.*, 1972; Knodel and Pitakepsombati 1973; Freedman and Coombs 1974; W. Morgan 1975; Williamson 1970; WFS Nepal 1977). It is not clear how far this relationship is due to the greater interest of the more educated women in limiting family size and how far it simply reflects their greater access to information and services of all kinds. Contraceptive use is not always directly linked to reduce fertility. This is because women with above average fertility are often the first to practise contraception in developing countries. In many contexts, a more important factor linking female education and reduced fertility is the effect of education in delaying marriage (Dixan, 1971; Harman, 1970; Knowles and Anker, 1975; Nayar 1974; Palmore and Ariffin, 1969; Smith, 1977; Sundaram, 1977).

The much broader issue which remains concerns how education influences women's views on childbearing and childrearing. Many studies have shown that the number of children which women consider desirable declines with increasing education (CELADE, 1972; Chung *et al.*, 1972; Knodel and Pitakepsombati 1973; Ware 1975). A more striking finding is the sharp decline in the number of sons desired with increasing education. This holds true even in the United States (Freedman and Coombs, 1974). It is tempting to argue that women who have themselves been educated value girls more highly because they are aware that girls can adopt the same range of roles as boys, but there is little evidence on this point. Education almost certainly acts to increase women's awareness of themselves as individuals and thus to make some women less the servants of their families.

Education also makes women aware of Western patterns of childrearing: this has both positive and negative effects. Modern Western norms until very recently have strongly stressed the child's need for a one-to-one relationship with her or his own biological mother (P.Morgan, 1975). This is a very long way from the pattern in traditional societies where society in general, a range of relatives and especially older siblings, and the child's age-mates all participate in childrearing. A change-over to a more Western pattern encourages small families and the rearing of children who are motivated to succeed in a competitive world. However, this change also discourages women from going outside the home to work and increases the stress on the central importance of motherhood in women's lives.

Where education acts to reduce fertility by raising women's evaluations of their own worth and making them aware of a wide range of alternatives to childbearing as sources of fulfilment, one could expect female education to be more strongly related to fertility reduction than male education. A clear majority of the few studies which have separated the effects of male and female education have found that female education has a considerably stronger and more consistent effect than male education upon fertility levels (CELADE, 1972; Kocher, 1977). Several such studies have indeed found that female education is inversely related to fertility whilst male education reveals a positive relationship (Kelley, 1976; Khan and Sirageldin, 1975; Ohadike, 1969; Rosenzweig 1976).

Cochrane (1979) has made an extensive and rewarding survey of the literature on the relationship between fertility and education. The way in which education is believed to influence fertility are set out in Table 2.1. To give an example: the literature suggests that educations raises (+) the probability of marrying for males but reduces it for females (-). Since the married have higher fertility than the unmarried, education thus in this case will raise fertility for males but lower it for females. In individual cultural contexts it is possible to debate whether the relationships assumed should be positive or negative. For example, female education does not appear to increase the incompatibility of the wife's work and childrearing responsibilities in areas where servants are poorly paid and widely available (Safilios-Rothschild 1972).

The virtue of this model is that it shows that in any particular context there are at least twenty ways in which education may influence fertility levels. It should be noted that there are apparently thirteen areas in which the indirect effect of female education is to reduce fertility in contrast to eight areas where the impact of male education is negative. Part of the positive effect of male education would appear to act through higher male incomes resulting in healthier and more fertile wives (Jain 1979).

Caldwell (1979) maintains that the essential link between education and declining fertility is through the reversal of wealth flows within the family. Where children do not receive formal education the life-time balance of the movement of wealth is from children to parents. Parents thus benefit from having large numbers of children. Formal education reverses the direction of the movement so that parents expend more resources on their children than they receive in return. This is not so much because education is expensive as because education destroys the family 'morality' which obliges children to work for the benefit of the family as a whole (and hence, effectively, for their fathers) and make children into individuals who work for their own benefit.

From this point on, parents will benefit from limiting the number of their children who now constitute a drain upon their parents' wealth rather than contributions to it.

Table 2.1
The Effect of Education on Fertility Through Intervening Variables

	Effect of Education on the intervening variables		*Effect of intervening variables on fertility*	*Effect of education on fertility through intervening variables*	
1	2		3	4	
Intervening variable	Male	Female		Male	Female
Supply Factors					
Probability of being Married	+	-	+	+	-
Wife's age at marriage	+	+	-	-	-
Health	+	+	+	+	+
Separate location of Spouse	-	?	+	+	?
Joint family living	-	-	-	+	+
Monogamous marriage	?	+	+ (?)	?	+(?)
Taboos on sexual activity	–	–	–	+	+
Infant & child mortality	–	–	+	–	–
Demand Factors					
Desired family size	–	–	±	–	–
Husband's income	+	0	?	?	0
Money cost of children	+	+	–	–	–
Wife's income	0	+	- (?)	0	- (?)
Incompatibility of wife's work	0	+	–	0	–
Cost of alternative child minding *	0	+	–	0	–
Economic benefits of Children	–	–	+	–	–
Fertility Regulation					
Husband's power in the family relative to wife's	+	–	?	?	–

(Contd.)

1		2	3		4
Husband-wife communication	+	+	–	–	–
Knowledge of birth control	+	+	–	–	–
Attitude to birth control	+	+	–	–	–
Access to birth control	+	+	–	–	–

Source: Adapted from Cochrane (1979 : 71).

Notes: + = increases, - = decrease, 0 = not applicable, no effect, ? = debatable. In some cases, the signs have been changed from those given in the original, which also notes that Catholic education may have a pro-natalist effect.

* The cost of alternative child-minding will be strongly influenced by the proportion of adolescent girls who are in school.

However, Caldwell also argues that providing education almost exclusively for males, as in some Moslem countries, delays the beginning of fertility decline. This is because educated wives demand that more is spent on their children and no longer support the traditional family morality of the wife and children working for the benefit of the male head of the family. ..... A school child can falter in feeling part of a new wider world if the father, whether educated or not, remains completely patriachal towards him and the mother uncomprehendingly traditional. In this case, the wealth flow may not turn downward until the second generation of mass education, when mothers as well as children are educated, and may not turn down at all if fathers only are educated and the tradition of illiterate wives persists' (Caldwell, 1979). Educated wives further contribute to fertility decline because they are more likely to wish to avoid the inconveniences of pregnancy, to share decision making with their husbands, and to reject the claims of the extended family in favour of the claims of their children.

Mandelbaum has given a descriptive account of the effect of education upon Indian women:

> An educated woman is usually less closely confined, physically and psychologically, with her husband's family and its narrow familial concerns than is the woman who is brought into their home as an uneducated girl .... She is more likely to feel that she can do something about the conditions of her life, including the condition of pregnancies in close succession or conceiving during her later reproductive years

> Her horizons of information are wider, if only by being able to read a newspaper; her network of communication is likely to be broader, if only to school friends beyond the confines of household and kin. These differences are not, of course, direct results of her having studied algebra or learned to read another language, but they are potent consequences that help to shape her life and are (more) likely to induce her to limit her fertility.

This is a very vivid picture, but is also a portrait of the privileged class of women who learn algebra and foreign languages. What is still needed is a much clearer examination of the effect of education upon the village girl who only experiences a few years of primary school with a half-trained teacher, with very little to read and not enough paper to write on.

The impact of female education may be greatly reduced if it appears to lead nowhere. Around the world 'the education system seems to be geared to preparing people for civil service positions in towns and cities; a rural woman with a high school education feels she has no realistic goals or opportunities in the village. It is also clear, however, that there are not enough jobs even in the cities to absorb all the graduates of the school system. It is not surprising, then, to find that there was prevailing attitude among middle class Maguharjo (Javanese) women that the only real justification for the education of young girls is to prepare them to be better mothers' (V. Hull, 1977).

Studies of the impact of education upon fertility have almost all been concerned with the quantity of education (which is relatively easy to measure) rather than with the quality or content of education which is much harder to evaluate. There have been a few studies of population education and its effects (Viederman, 1974; Paik, 1973) but no Third World studies of what girls learn about women's roles in school. In the Western world feminists and others are now stressing the extent to which schools unintentionally serve to reinforce traditional roles. Thus, the books which teach children to read show women as mothers and housewives who stay at home and men as having interesting jobs and exciting adventures. Single sex schools may either give girls a special confidence in themselves and their abilities or reinforce their feelings of inferiority. Here too, studies in a developing country context are lacking (Women for Women, 1978).

Now there are requests for educational reforms to promote women's autonomy. For example, 'female labour-force participations could be fostered by setting up specific programmes and training schools for girls and more subtly by portraying women in productive, non-traditional roles. The sense of being able to control one's own life can be fostered by improving the individual's problem-solving capacity (as opposed to rote learning and memorization) and by projects emphasizing doing and making and then observing the consequences (as opposed to the passive absorption of information)' (Ridker, 1976). The Report of the Committee on the Status of Women in India (1974) reflected somewhat ironically that teaching rural women to drive tractors would be an excellent way to raise the status of women but that it would prove impossible to teach such skills to women before raising their status, (Boserup 1970).

Simmons (1979) has made a very interesting attempt to estimate the relative costs of various interventions designed to reduce fertility levels in developing countries. The comparison is, in order of cost-effectiveness, between family planning visits, a rural education programme for women, income redistribution and a nutrition programme. Preventing one birth through a family planning programme is estimated to cost US $ 220 as compared with US $1,600 for achieving the same goal by means of rural education for women. This assessment process is unrealistic and would be harmful if used to guide policy making. A thousand family planning visits will not persuade women to make effective use of contraception if they do not believe that they will gain by limiting the number of their children. Equally there is no reason whatsoever to believe that if, for example, eight years of education will reduce average family size by half a child, than one year of education will reduce it by a sixteenth of a child. Education is not like paint where if one container will paint a whole house a quarter of a container will paint quarter of a house. Eight years of education may provide full functional literacy, access to a whole new world, and a range of job opportunities. There is little to be gained from being one eighth or one quarter literate.

Looking at these calculations from another viewpoint, the administrator might well be impressed by the fact that for the cost of five family planning visits it is possible to provide one year of rural education, although much would depend upon the content of the education and how much could be absorbed. However, the wise administrator will also not that the choice being offered is an artificial one. If there are money or resources to spare then they may be deliberately concentrated upon family planning or rural education. In many cases, there will be no spare resources but there will be existing rural education programmes available for men (Lele, 1975). The question will then concern the cost-benefit of devoting half of the rural education programme to women. This is the calculation which no one seems to have the courage to make. Women's programmes are always seen as a minor addition to existing programmes to be given three per cent not 50 per cent of available resources.

Marriage, Fertility and the Status of Women

The timing and nature of marriage are obviously essential factors to consider in any examination of the links between the status of women and fertility levels. However, not all survey in this area do take marriage into account (Birdsall, 1974). This is but a part of the widespread reluctance to acknowledge that the 'intermediate variables' which direct the influence of fertility (Davis and Blake, 1956) are not neutral with respect to women's status. The result is that 'less is probably known about the social determinants of age at marriage and the proportions marrying than about the determinants of any other important demographic variable' (Hawthorn, 1970; cf. Karkal, 1971).

Age at Marriage and Proportions Marrying

One reason why the demographic transition, form high levels to low levels of mortality and fertility, passed off so easily in Europe was the fact that Europe had already undergone and earlier demographic transition with respect to marriage. In mediaeval times, Europe in common with many of the developing countries today, experienced a pattern of early and almost universal marriage. However, by 1600 a new pattern of delayed marriage and significant proportions of individuals who would never marry had already been established (Hajnal, 1965). This pattern was related to the fact that Western European families were already remarkably nucleated in structure (Laslett and Wall, 1972). Thus, it is necessary to be very careful before generalising from European historical experience to developing countries today.

Dixon (1978) has discussed 'Late marriage and non-marriage as demographic responses: are they similar? 'She shows that most countries either have a pattern of early and nearly universal marriage, or of later marriage with a significant proportion who never marry. Effectively because of the relationship between culture, family structure and marriage it is rarely possible to alter one factor without the other. An exception is Japan with its unusual stem family structure where the proportion of ever married women aged 20-24 fell from 69 per cent in 1920 to 34 per cent in 1955 but the proportion of women never marrying still remained one of the lowest in the world (Dixon, 1978). The social connection between age at marriage and proportions never marrying results from the fact that early marriages are usually arranged by the families who can make some provision for almost every healthy woman to marry, especially where polygny is practised. Late marriage is generally associated with the free choice of individuals, ideals of romantic love and some women who never find a mate. Delay of marriage also gives women an opportunity to learn to value their independence and thus to make a deliberate choice not to marry.

Upper Burma appears to be an interesting example of a traditional area where, owing to Buddhist ethics and a high value placed upon the state of being unmarried, there is a pattern of late age at marriage, relatively high proportions who never marry and little remarriage of the widowed (Nash and Nash, 1963). Here the expression for marriage *eindaung chabi* means either to 'build a house' or to 'make the home a prison'. However, is most traditional cultures it is the state of being married that is most highly valued and indeed is often considered an essential prerequisite for the attainment of full adult status.

Bourgeois-Pichat (1965) has calculated that, excluding the effects of mortality, whereas Latin American and European women spend some 60 per cent of their reproductive lives in formal marriages, women in tropical Africa spend fully 85 per cent of the time available in marriage. One of the clearest indicators of modernization of family structure is a rise in the female age of marriage. By 1960 the age of brides in the Philippines, Hong Kong, Sri Lanka, and Thailand was as high as that of brides in the United

Kingdom or Belgium (Dixon, 1978). Recently Jones (1980) has examined marriage patterns in Malaysia, showing that two-thirds of the decline of fertility in that country prior to 1970 was the direct result of declines in the proportions married. He argues that the rise in the median age at marriage (which has moved from 16.6 years in 1947 to 21.4 years in 1974 for Malay females) results from a combination of a change in social mores, economic developments and, to a lesser extent, a shortage of appropriate mates.

More broadly Sundaram (1977) has examined 'The literacy transition and female nuptiality: implications for the status of Asian women'. Her contention is that a woman's opportunities for development are largely determined by the options and time available to her between puberty and marriage and the birth of her first child. Her analysis relates variations in literacy in eight Asian countries to the female mean age at marriage. Grouping the data by religious orientation accounts for 66 per cent of the variance in female mean age at marriage. However, there are still consistent positive relationships between education and age at marriage within the countries studied and for the region as a whole. The variance explained in the female mean age at marriage by the literacy variable is 68 per cent for all eight countries but ranges from a low of 15 per cent in Thailand to a high of 92 per cent in Malaysia. More detailed analysis shows that the female literacy level and the literacy gap between males and females are two different components in determining female mean age at marriage. From a policy view point this means that governments who wish to encourage female education with a view to raising the age at marriage need both to raise the female age at marriage and to narrow the age gap between males and females.

There have been many discussions of the policy impact of raising the female age at marriage as a means of reducing fertility (Lesthaeghe, 1971; Yaukey, 1973). Some of these discussions have been rather unrealistic since they take little account of the effects of adolescent sterility or the possibility of women who marry later catching up by bearing births more rapidly (Agarwala, 1967; Das 1967). It is also necessary to assume that the onus of ex-nuptial births will remain at present very low levels as the age of marriage rises. Unfortunately for policy makers there appears to be a very real difference between spontaneous rises in the age of marriage and legal decisions to raise the cut-off point. It is not only that parents in countries with poor vital registration records can easily falsify there children's ages. It is rather that social change does not occur in such a piecemeal fashion.

Tunisia presents one case where it is argued that legal provisions have effectively raised the age at marriage and have thus reduced fertility (Tabutin, 1979). China, however, is a case where the campaign to raise the age at marriage has been just a small part of a far borader campaign of social change associated with the 'new democratic family'

> Since they are able to contribute to the family income (through work points), young women are now better able to persuade their families to postpone their marriages until they feel ready for them. They can and do oppose matches which will obviously bring them unhappiness. When they marry, their earning power and an increased stress on affectionate, co-operative, and equal marriage relationships ease their entry into the new family. From being her daughter-in-law's supervisor, the mother-in-law is now often relegated to the position of helpmate. When the young women go out to work in the fields, the folder women often care for their young children and do the menial tasks which were once the lot of the younger women (Davin, 1976).

All marriages in China are officially 'free choice marriages' but where tradition still forbids marriage with someone from the same village or with the same surname it is still difficult for young people to find their own partners or chose the right time to marry.

There has been some debate as to how far the availability of paid employment for unmarried women contributes to the postponement of marriage. Some say that the opportunity to be independent encourages women to postpone marriage while others argue that couples can marry earlier if they have two incomes and also access to contraception to postpone the first birth (Preston and Richards, 1975). A great deal depends upon the family context in which the decision is made. In Hong Kong, Salaff (1976) has argued that women are postponing their marriages because their parents appreciate the contributions which they make to the household budget, because they enjoy activities with their friends, and because a long romantic courtship is becoming the ideal.

It has been hypothesised 'that where subsistence dependence between spouses is strong, romantic love is unimportant as a basis of marriage, while, where subsistence dependence is weak, romantic love is important as a basis of marriage' (Coppinger and Rosenblatt, 1968). In other words, where husband and wives do not need each other in an economic sense it helps to preserve marriage if they need each other in a romantic sense. The idea of marriage for romantic love, rather than to cement the union of two families is a Western ideal, and, despite Romeo and Juliet, it is usually associated with the marriage of adult women who can make their own choices rather than with the marriage of submissive child-brides. The idealisation of romantic love is a major factor influencing almost all western women to want to get married. Non-western emancipated women are less likely to fix upon marriage as an ideal destiny (Theodoroson, 1965). A sad division sometimes emerges in non-European countries where women adopt the ideal of romantic love but men do not. Questionnaire surveys in Nigeria suggest the female students expect to marry for love but male students expect to marry a high status woman with a good character. Most traditional women in Nigeria marry to have children and almost half of one Yoruba sample said that they would not marry except to have children (Ware, 1979).

While it is almost universally agreed that delaying marriage contributes to raising the status of women and to reducing fertility levels there is at least one dissenting voice. As a result of her analysis of world Fertility Survey data from Fiji, Sri Lanka, and Dominica, together with the Rand Corporation Household Survey in Malaysia, Weekes-Vagliani (1979) has argued that in agricultural economies raising the age at marriage may have predominantly negative results. The argument is that where young couple start married life living with the husbands' parents, then the sooner the young couple leave the sooner they are likely to adopt the practice of fertility regulation. Keeping young unmarried girls at home with their parents will do nothing to change their ideas. From the point of view of women's status, educating rural girls so that they consider themselves above farm work without providing them with alternative employment is counterproductive at both the individual and the national level.

What Weekes-Vagliani's analysis does make very clear is that the differce *beween* ethnic groups in relation to any one variable was consistently greater than the variation *within* any ethnic group' Young Indian girls who remain unmarried in Fiji and Malaysia are not choosing to work rather than to marry, they are being forced to stay at home because their fathers cannot afford the dowry to marry them off. Thus in Fiji non-marriage of Indian daughters is much more common in households where the father is currently unemployed and where there are sons to be educated before the daughters can be married off.

Age Difference Between Spouses

One of the ways in which men in traditional societies maintain their control over women is by ensuring that husbands are generally considerably older than wives and can thus add the advantage of surperiority of age to that of superiority of sex. Greater age gives the husband a considerable advantage in status, experience and power. Even in a society where men and women shared complete equality in educational and occupational opportunities, men could always maintain their superior position so long as status increased with age and men married women younger then themselves.

In traditional societies, and especially in polygynous societies, the husband is frequently old enough to be the bride's father. Thus amongst the Konkomba of northern Ghana, the mean age difference between women and their first husband is 22 years (Trait 1961). In northern Nigeria, Kanuri women marry between 12 and 14 with men 'as much as two, three and even four times their own age which enhances the traditional seniority of the husband as well as taking any "romance" out of it for the girls' (Cohen, 1967). Interestingly Kanuri men do not find young girls sexually attractive, but they marry them because they are more obedient.

In all countries of the world with adequate marriage statistics, husbands are on average older than their wives (Dixon, 1971). The average gap for the 55 countries examined was 3.8 years. The greatest differences are found in the Moslem Middle East where grooms are on the average 5.3 years older than their brides. Libya, with a difference of 9 years, and Iran, with close to 7 years have the largest gaps recorded in national level data. Asian husbands are 4.7 years older than their brides, Eastern European husbands are 2.9 years older and husbands in the English-speaking countries are 2.7 years older.

In his study of Shiraz, Iran, Mòmeni (1976) used local records to confirm Dixon's hypothesis that in general, the younger the brides, the greater is the age difference between them and their grooms'. He also showed that the greater the age difference, the greater the likelihood of divorce. Although the age difference in Shiraz was declining, as recently as 1966 the mean gap was 9.3 years, with 20 per cent of brides marrying men 15 or more years older than themselves.

Several authors have suggested that the age difference between spouses is an excellent indicator of the status of women, especially where it is common for women to marry men who are younger than themselves (Safilios-Rothschild, 1972; Presser, 1975). Women who marry younger men reverse the traditional order in which brides bring youth, beauty and innocence to marriage while husbands contribute experience, wealth and authority. Safilios-Rothschild (1972) has even claimed that 'the greater the economic emancipation of women in a society, the more the option to marry a younger man becomes a reality'. This may be true in West Africa where a rich market woman may marry a university student. However, it would not appear to explain the distribution of such marriages in Western nations, where East Germany is the country with the highest proportion of women marrying younger men (19 per cent). A more satisfactory measure of women's status would be a joint index with a positive score based on the proportions of women never marrying or marrying men five or more years younger than themselves, and a negative score based on the proportions of women marrying at age 17 or younger and marrying man five or more years older than themselves.

However, there is something artificial about all such indices which assume that a relationship will always work in the same way, and that facts share a universal cultural significance. A woman may be disadvantaged for life by marrying at 13 and bearing her first child at 15, or she may require considerable authority and freedom by virtue of being the mother of a 15 year old by the time she is 30. Kanuri woman are child brides but in their 30s they can become powerful divorcees (Cohen, 1967).

Remarkably in all the hundreds of thousands of published tabulations of factors affecting the adoption of contraception there appears not to be one which examines the age difference between spoused as a contributing factor. Given the greater natural longevity of females a wide age gap between spouses contributes to the creation of large numbers of youthful widows. Customs constraining remarriage and allowing little autonomy to widows can greatly depress the status of women in such circumstances whilst also contribution to the reduction of national fertility levels.

Marriage Type, Fertility and the Status of Women

There is no simple, universally valid relationship between types (monogamous/polygynous, companionate/segregated) of marriage and levels of fertility of the status of women. Polygynous unions are not invariably less fertile than monogamous unions. Women in companionate marriages do not necessarily have higher status than women in marriages where each partner leads a separate life of their own. The literature on the relationships between marriage types and other variables often reveals the cultural biases of Western researchers who project their feelings that Western ways are best into their discussions and analyses.

It is much debated whether polygyny serves to raise or lower fertility levels (Lorimer, 1954; Nag, 1962). Those who associate polygyny with lower fertility claim that

(i) Infertile or subfertile women are selectively found in polygynous marriages because husbands with less fertile first wives are most highly motivated to marry additional wives (Page, 1975);

(ii) Infertile women who are divorced by dissatisfied husbands will normally only be able to remarry into polygynous unions;

(iii) Venereal diseases which cause a reduction in fertility are easily spread within polygynous unions;

(iv) Each wife within a polygynous union has a reduced coital frequency and a lesser chance of becoming pregnant (Musham, 1956); and

(v) Wives in polygynous unions, being generally more traditional and less well-educated than wives in monogamous unions, will be more scrupulous in observing traditional taboos on sexual intercourse, for example when breastfeeding or in mourning.

On the other hand, those who argue that wives in polygynous unions are more fertile than monogamously married wives contend that:

(i) Polygynous union will be selective of more traditional women who value children most highly and are most reluctant to adopt any form of fertility regulation;
(ii) Polygynous wives compete to have more children than their co-wives in order to secure a larger share of the resources, affection and ultimately of the estate of the husband which is often divided amongst wives in proportion with the number of their children;
(iii) Polygynous husbands take special care to have coitus with each wife at the most fertile time of the month.*

Yet a third group of researchers have argued that there is no significant difference between the fertility of polygynous and monogamous unions once other factors such as marriage duration and educational differentials are controlled for (Busia, 1951; Olusanya, 1971; Podlewski, 1975). Yet another viewpoint is that it is unrealistic to treat all wives in polygynous unions as a homogeneous group as senior and junior wives are in very different positions, and as the significance of polygyny varies greatly from one ethnic group to another (Clignet, 1970). For husbands who are polygynists the important fact is that polygyny raise the number of children which can be born to an individual male who is sufficiently rich or powerful enough to maintain a number of wives. Certainly, in the African context where the maximum number of *surviving* children is achieved by prolonged breastfeeding and intervals of three or four years between births, polygyny represents a good compromise between the male desire to have many descendents and the health of mothers and infants.

In reality, in societies where polygyny is commonplace, as in much of Tropical Africa, almost all marriages are potentially polygynous and thus it becomes quite unrealistic to distinguish between polygyny and monogamy as if they were immutable

---

* Whether this serves to raise or lower fertility will depend upon the accuracy of the knowledge of the most fertile period. A number of East African groups believe the first five days after menstruation to be the most fertile and thus polygynous husbands try to roster their wives for these days which are actually infertile (Molnos, 1972).

categories (Ware, 1979). To fully answer the question of the impact of polygyny upon fertility it would be necessary to have full fertility and marital histories for women which specified their rank as first, second wife, and so forth, and which could be classified by other socio-economic and demographic factors such as education, age and the practice of abstinence and contraception. To date no one had assembled such a data set. Analysis of the partial data sets which are available would suggest that polygyny as such has little effect upon fertility since almost all the apparent differences in fertility can be explained by differences in the characteristics of women recruited into the different types of marriage. In most cases controlling for age, the proportion of childless women and education is sufficient to destroy any significant differences in fertility (Arowolo, 1981).

It is equally true that there is no simple relationship between polygyny, or even polyandry and the status of women. Societies which practice polygyny, are often presented as attaching little value to women but it would be at least equally valid to turn the argument on its head and say that they place little value upon men. Where women co-operate rather than compete, then polygyny has a great deal to offer women: constant companionship, child-care always at hand, the sharing of domestic burdens and a considerable degree of independence and autonomy. A women who only spends one week in four being a wife has considerable free time to devote to her own interests. In polygynous societies the merits and disadvantages of abolishing polygyny are often hotly debated, with the western educated elite commonly failing to convince the mass of women that the practice should be abandoned (De Vallenga, 1968).

At a more general level it is widely claimed that effective fertility control is most likely to occur in companionate marriages where there is free communication between spouses and where the wife has an equal say in decision making (Piepmeier and Adkins, 1973). However, the evidence to prove the truth of this contention is very scanty. Most studies which claim to have shown this do not include adequate controls for education and other socio-economic factors (but see Coombs and Freedman 1979; Mitchel 1972). There would appear to be no studies which show that the nature of the relationship between illiterate husbands and wives influences the adoption of fertility control practices. However, there are circumstances where family planning programmes make a certain degree of collaboration between spouses a condition for access to contraceptive or sterilization services. In most Nigerian family planning clinics wives are supposed to produce consent forms signed by their husbands before being given contraceptives, and it is common around the world to ask the spouse's consent in the case of sterilization.

It is widely assumed that if the wife wishes to control her fertility and her husband wants more children his views will prevail. There has been little discussion of the opposite case where the husband is the only partner to want to limit fertility. Yet given that men have greater access to education and modern sector employment it might be expected that they would be the first to desire to limit the number of their children. Men also have many alternatives to childrearing as a source of personal fulfilment which are usually not open to women.

Family Type, Fertility and the Status of Women

There has also been much debate of the nature of the relationship between family type and fertility. Very broadly the argument is that extended families, where several generations and several married couples live together and share a common budget, encourage high levels of fertility:

(i) because they encourage early marriage (since the couple do not have to be capable of supporting themselves at the time of marriage);

(ii) because they give the older generation and their traditional views greater power over the decisions of the young;

(iii) because they create a situation in which the individual couple does not have to bear the burden of their fertility alone, and cannot benefit by limiting the number of their children unless others in the family will also agree to restrain themselves.

On the other hand, it is claimed that opportunities for sexual intercourse are relatively limited in the extended family setting and that the elders are the ones who ensure the observance of traditional customs, such as post-natal sexual abstinence, which limit fertility.

The debate has been bitter but not very rewarding (Bebarta 1966; Burch and Gendall 1971; Freedman *et al.* 1978; Olsen 1976, Pakrasi and Malaker 1967; Strauss and Winkelman 1969). One problem has been that although the original theory contrasted cultures based upon extended families with cultures based upon nuclear families (Lorimer, 1954: Notestein, 1948; Davis, 1975), almost all tests of the theory have contrasted extended and nuclear families within a single society. This raises a difficulty similar to that found in the case of polygyny: all families are potentially extended families, and a nuclear family at one point of time may once have been part of an extended family or may become part of one in future. Three-generational families become two-generational families when the grandparents die but can become three generational again if the grandsons bring their wives to live within the family. Thus it is necessary to have longitudinal data on family formation patterns and fertility and not simply cross-sectional data linking fertility and family type at a single point in time. Thus, for example, it has been argued that the significant factor in determining total fertility is not age at marriage as such, but whether the bride was living with her mother-in-law at the time of the birth of her first child (Weekes-Vagliani, 1979). There has been one study which examined the fertility regulating characteristics of whole cultures in an attempt to explain the variations in fertility levels between traditional societies (Nag 1962). However, the results obtained were inconclusive and certainly did not prove that there was an association between the status of women and fertility levels in traditional cultures in five continents.

It cannot be overstressed that in any examination of the causes of fertility differentials the fertility variable and the control variable must refer to the same time span. Thus, for example, children ever born should be cross-classified by the total number of years spent (or spent since marriage) in an extended family situation. Alternatively, births within the past year should be classified by family type during the period 9 to 21 months earlier (Ryder 1976). An additional complication often raised by the failure to define the meaning of the term 'extended family'. Since censuses and surveys provide data on residence patterns it is common to restrict the 'extend family' to relatives living in one household. However, from a theoretical viewpoint, mutual financial obligations are of much greater significance than sharing one residence. Is the mother-in-law living next door any less influential than the mother-in-law living in the same household?

Any study of the relationship between family structure, the status of women and their fertility needs to take into account changes over the life cycle. Fertility researchers generally concentrate upon the case of the young woman who is supposedly pressured into having more children than she wants by her mother-in-law. The matter is very rarely seen from the point of view of the mother-in-law. Yet in any examination of the status of women it has to be recognized that most women play both roles during a life time. In traditional societies it is the older woman who has the high status and every daughter-in-law looks forward to the time when she will be a powerful mother-in-law ruling over the wives of her numerous sons. With the transition to modern conditions there come a numbers of awkward transitional generations when women no longer increase in status as they grow older but are simply regarded as old-fashioned nuisances. Most studies of the status of women compare women with men; however, most illiterate women are probably more concerned with the contrast between their status and that of other women. When women have children for status reasons they compete not with men but with other mothers. This is formalized in West Africa where there are special honorary titles for the mothers of ten surviving children.

Women's Work and Fertility

In 1965, Judith Blake confidently asserted that the 'relationship between married women working and family size is generally acknowledged to be one of the strongest, most persistent over time and space, and most theoretically reasonable' of the social determinants of fertility. However, in 1975 Geraldine Terry still argued that 'the frequently documented relationship between fertility and female employment may...be due to the common influence of a number of other factors' including education, rural background and the interval between marriage and the first birth.

Whole books have been devoted to the controversy over the relationship between women's work and their fertility (Kupinsky, 1977; Dixon, 1979). Much confusion could have been avoided from the start if it had been accepted that almost all women work, irrespective of the proportion of women who are included in the official definition of the labour force. Some women work for wages, some are self-employed for profit, and some participate in the household economy receiving little more material reward than their keep, but they are all workers. Industrialization resulted in a false division between work for pay or profit which was real 'work', and unpaid work which was not. Thus, where the servant and the mistress labour together only the servant is 'working' and a man who marries his cook reduces the national labour force by one. It is more realistic to define a continuum which stretches from the work which is furthest from the domestic context: wage employment working fixed hours in a factory, to the work which is closest to the family: unpaid domestic work within the home. This makes it clear that it is not possible to draw a fixed line between working women and non-working women with conflict between childrearing and work limited to one side of the boundary. As any mother knows, there is a conflict between coping with a crying child and cooking the dinner, all mothers experience some conflict although the degree of conflict varies with the workplace, the hours worked and the level of concentration required. Grinding corn for six hours is work whether the person doing the grinding is the male owner of the corn, his manservant, his womanservant or his wife.

In its original, simple form the theory linking women's work and fertility said that women who worked (*i.e.* were employed to work for wages in institutions outside their home) would have fewer children than their sisters who stayed at home and kept house because they would experience a conflict of roles between motherhood and employment. Even at this very simple stage there was still the problem of determining whether women had few children because they worked, or whether, having had few children for other reasons, they then continued to work.

The theory was developed in the United States by demographers and economists who believed that 'it is obvious that bearing a child and caring for the infant child are normally labour intensive activities on the part of the mother' (Schultz, 1973). They had already forgotten that the working wife and mother is not a modern invention. On the contrary, the nonworking full-time wife and mother is a phenomenon that only modern affluency, that is, modern technology, had made possible (Bettleheim, 1962).

Large because the theory was developed in the context of the Western industrialized nations, it was not at first recognized that the degree of conflict between 'work' and childrearing would depend upon a multitude of associated factors such as the availability and cost of alternative childminders; whether the work was in the formal or informal sector; whether it could be performed in the home and whether mothers had been trained to feel guilty about 'working' (Jaffe and Azumi, 1960).

The writers who first put forward the hypothesis that women's workforce participation would be inversely rlated to fertility also believed that work would compete with childrearing not simply in terms of demands upon the mother's time, but also in terms of the women's interests. Perhaps because they were themselves academics, they thought of work in terms of challenging and interesting careers rather than in terms of boring drudgery. Thus they tended to ignore the probability that women might be working simply because they were poor, and the possibility that the reason for their poverty might be precisely because they had to provide for a large number of smail children. Even today, the grater part of the discussion is based upon the assumption that women (as opposed to men) 'work' because they chose to and not because they have to. This belief is linked to a large number of ideas about the liberating effect which work outside the home is supposed to have upon women. Thus it is thought that 'work' frees women by giving them money of their own to spend; by bringing them a broader knowledge of the outside world; by raising their status relative to their husbands and by improving the self-image which they have of themselves. Such ideas would probably seem very strange to an Indian women working sixteen hours a day breaking stones in a quarry, (Sengupta, 1960) or an Indonesian wife harvesting rice stem by stem (Stoler, 1977). Even where employment is associated with a greater say in decision making by women it is difficult to define the direction of the causal relationship – are more independent women the ones who choose to work outside the home or does such work make women more independent?

It must always be remembered that the majority of female (and male) workers are toilers earning their living and not career makers in pursuit of an ideal. Even in Australia less than 10 per cent of married women in the labour force have any claim to be following a career. While there are a few working wives in Australia who take time off from their careers to have children, most women are working mother who are taking time off their career of motherhood to ease the economics strains on the family (Ware, 1976). Women's employment as such only appears to depress fertility in the Third World under very special circumstances – for women in the modern, urban labour force. Such women form only a very small proportion of working women throughout the world (Birdsall, 1976).

One way of examining the compatibility of work and childrearing is by looking at the age pattern of female participation rate (Durand, 1975). If women drop out of the labour force during their peak childbearing years it is reasonable to assume some conflict between the roles of mother and worker. Frejka (1971) found two typical patterns of female age-specific participation rates (which show the percentage of women of a particular age who are in the labour force):

(i) A one peak distribution, the peak being close to the average female age at marriage (usually within the 20-24 age group), followed by a continued decline in participation;

(ii) A two peak distribution, with the first peak being close to the average age at marriage and the second peak at about 40 when some mothers return to work once their children have reached the age of relative independence.

Lucas (1977) has pointed to a third pattern found in many African and some Asian countries;

(iii) A late one peak distribution with participation rate rising until attaining a maximum at ages 45-54.

While the first two patterns are clearly compatible with childbearing the last one certainly is not in line with Western expectations (Ware, 1977). Yet in those West African societies where women engage in trade, the newly married woman either has to save up the necessary capital, or to wait until it is presented to her as a reward for the birth of her first child by her husband or mother. Data form Ibadan, Nigeria show that childless women are more likely to be just housewives than their sisters with children (Ware 1977). Older women gain increasing freedom and mobility as their oldest children attain an age to be responsible for their younger siblings. In any case, where mothers are not regarded as irreplaceable childrearers, a greater number of children may well spur the mother to make a greater contribution to the household economy. In West Africa it is not unknown for polygynous husbands to declare that they will be responsible for their children by each wife but only to a limited extent, and that if an individual wife wishes for additional children or for secondary education for her children then that is her responsibility. Alternatively the arrival of a second wife may free or spur the first to increase economic activity.

There is now ample evidence from a number of Asian countries to show that 'work' does not generally reduce fertility. Thus in urban Bangladesh very few women are in paid employment but those who are not distinguished by lower fertility since they have easy access to servants and are expected to show that they are real women by bearing many children (Chaudhury, 1978). In West Malaysia, employment and average fertility level are only in conflict for a small elite of highly educated women; otherwise there are variations in the relationship between age groups and geographical areas but no consistent evidence of lower fertility for 'workers' (Fong, 1974). The best predictor of a woman's employment status is not her family size but the extent of her employment experience prior to marriage. In the Philippines women 'workers' have higher than average fertility reflecting the fact that they seek employment because of financial problems (Harman, 1970). Data from rural Korea shows a similar phenomenon (Lee and Cho, 1976). In Thailand 'in the metropolitan centre of Bangkok, the fertility of women in the labour force is lower than that of housewives. In rural agricultural places, the fertility of employed woman is higher, although minimally so. This pattern suggests that the greater separation of work and family roles, which characterizes employment for women in the urban centres, lowers fertility. In the general absence of such a conflict in rural society, labour force participation has a minimal effect on fertility' (Goldstein, 1972; *c.f.* Debavalaya, 1977). In urban India fertility does not vary with employment status amongst the illiterate (Minkler, 1970). More sophisticated analyses suggest that where reduced fertility appears to be associated with employment the association between employment and age of the youngest child and the number of children under school age is stronger than the association between employment and the total number of living children (Darian, 1975; Da Vanzo and Lee, 1978).

The theory as to the relationship between employment and fertility has also been refined. It is argued that commitment to work is a vital factor (Hass, 1972; Safilios-Rothschild, 1972) and that the relationship between male and female incomes may be an important factor (Da Vanzo, 1972; McCabe and Rosenzweig, 1976). It is also recognized that a woman with three children only spends a small fraction of her adult life in childbearing (Dinnerstein, 1976).

One overview of a series of case studies around the world concludes 'work for women is not a panacea for the world's population explosion; but .... the worker role for women may yet prove to be an important element, lowering fertility in an industrializing economy or maintaining the existing low level in a more developed economy' (Kupinsky, 1977). It is suggested that countries should encourage fertility decline through delaying marriage by the institution of a civilian national service scheme for young people of both sexes with the obligation that service be completed prior to marriage.

In contrast, 'Rural women at work: strategies for development in South Asia' (Dixon, 1978c) is a plea for the creation of small-scale rural industries which would promote reduced fertility by only employing unmarried girls and wives with less than four children. The theoretical model shows female employment leading through income, skills and social contacts to greater self-esteem and alternative social and economic roles for females. These in turn would result in changing opinions on marital timing and fertility and greater decision-making power in the family with the ultimate consequence of delayed marriages for unmarried employees and the daughters of married workers and the adoption of the practices of birth spacing and family size limitation (Dixon, 1978c). The weak link appears to be the assumption that more alternative roles and greater self-esteem would lead directly to a desire for fewer children. Rural food-processing co-operatives would be of great assistance in helping women to cope with their problems within the existing social structure. It is not clear how they would act to reduce the value of children in high risk societies for they are unlikely to provide security in old age.

Women's Incomes and Fertility

Given the remarkable amount of attention which has been devoted to the relationship between women's work experiences and their fertility, it is very striking how little attention has been devoted to the issue of the relationship between women's incomes and their fertility (Simon, 1974). Generally, the stress is on the 'opportunity cost' paid by the wife who has to give up paid employment in order to have a baby (Mincer, 1963). The assumption is that the more highly paid the woman the more reluctant she will be to give up her job. However, there are real problems in deciding how to calculate the additional opportunity cost of the third child for the woman who has already given up employment to rear the first, two. In the developing country context where servants are widely available, the calculations are complicated by the fact that for more highly paid women paying for alternative childcare arrangements takes up a lesser proportion of their wages than for the women who have lower wages. There is a marked contrast between servants who receive much the same wages whatever the number of children to be cared for and institutionalized childcare centres which usually charge a set fee for each child with minimal reductions for a number of children for one family.

Most economists have used the woman's educations as a proxy for the income which women outside the labour force could be earning if they were employed (Snyder, 1976). Obviously this serves to confuse the effects of education and income (Ben Porath, 1970). In the Third World no one appears to have studied the impact upon fertility of the wages that women can earn holding women's education constant (but Cain and Weininger, 1972 have done this for the United States). An alternative method is to examine women's earnings relative to men's earnings , as well as the extent to which the industrial structure in a given area tends to hire women (Preston, 1973). This approach is also apparently untried in the developing countries although the expectation would be that the greater female wages as a proportion of male wages the greater the negative impact on fertility. Overall 'the evidence for a negative correlation between fertility and women's wages is extremely thin' (Loewenthal and David, 1972).

A number of Asian and African studies have now given evidence of total family income being positively associated with fertility even in urban areas (Anderson and McCabe 1978; Buck 1937; Hull and Hull, 1977; Zuidberg, 1978; Prachuabmoh, 1967; Khan and Sirageldin, 1975). However, studies which incorporate the independent effect of the wife's income have generally been restricted to the United States and Latin America (Kupinsky, 1977; Cassen, 1976 Peek, 1975; Behrman *et al.*, 1978). This neglect of Women's incomes is a part of the broader assumption that it is women's 'work' as such which has a negative impact upon fertility and the overall neglect of the actual mechanisms which might produce such an impact. In studies in the developed countries it is almost invariably assumed that the higher women's incomes, or the closer to men's incomes the greater the depressive effect of women's employment. Interestingly there is no examination of the possibility that women might be working in order to be able to afford to have a greater number of children. Very little attention has been devoted to the relationship between women's wages and marriage postponement by the unmarried, or to the relationship between women's participation in deciding how income is to be spent and the adoption of fertility regulation.

Conclusion

There are many general studies of the relationship between women's status and fertility (Chung, 1977; Dixon, 1975; Germain, 1975; Piepmeier and Adkins, 1975; Youssef, 1978). Together they contribute little new that is not already to be found in the more detailed individual studies of the relationship between fertility and women's education, women's workforce participation and women's decision making powers within marriage. Their conclusions are based as much upon liberal hopes as upon proven statistical relationships. Their ideas appear in distilled policy form in the statement in the World Population Plan of Action that one important way to moderate fertility is through

> The full integration of women in the development process, particularly by means of their greater participation in educational, social, economic and political opportunities, and especially by means of the removal of obstacles to their employment in the non-agricultural sector wherever possible.

It would appear to provide a very limited yield for a very

great amount of skilled research effort to be able to say in the last resort that there is some agreement that the position of women in society is significantly related to the level of fertility, though there is substantial difference about specifics' (Mauldin and Berelson, 1978). The truth is that there is no accepted index of women's status in developing countries and that female enrolment in school and female employment in non-agricultural employment correlate so highly with male enrolment and employment that they obviously reflect educational and industrial development rather than female status. Substituting male rather than female indicators in at least one analysis of international variations in fertility made no difference to the level of explanation (Mauldin and Berelson, 1978).

The real problem is that since all traditional societies have relatively high fertility and all industrialized societies have relatively low fertility to prove the direct link between fertility and women's status it would be necessary to prove that women's status always rises with the transition to the modern state. Life is not that simple. There was a great deal of variation in the status of women in preindustrial societies (Whyte, 1978), just as there is still considerable variation between industrialized societies (Boulding *et al.*, 1976). It is more realistic to accept that fertility declines as society changes and that changes in the status of women are only a part of the broader transition whose causative importance is still very imperfectly understood.

3

Male Migration and Indian Rural Women

In the past two decades, most developing societies have achieved a fair amount of success in technological advancement, but because of neglect to secure social justice by effectively implementing institutional measures for the equalization of opportunities to all sections of the society, development with its accompanying rapid social change has in fact been instrumental in widening the gap between the rich and the poor. Furthermore, when development introduces or increases inequality within rural societies, women—at least the poorest ones—become doubly underprivileged, first as members of the rural poor and then as women (Institute of Development Studies, 1985).

Several factors have contributed other prepetuation of this situation European colonials did not recognize women's customary land-tenure rights in South and South-East Asia and vested ownership in men (Boserup, 1970). They also destroyed the healthy balance between handicrafts and agriculture. After attaining independence, the new governments recognized the importance of revitalizing the economy of their countries, yet instead of correcting the imbalance they in fact introduced polices that contributed to the increase in social and economic disparities, first between classes and secondly between men and women (Desai,

1975). Thus, for instance, introduction of cash crops led to windfalls for the larger land-owners and to marginal benefits, if any, to those who did not control the material resources of production (Bardhan, 1974). Among the rural families, the cash returns from agricultural produce are controlled by the men, though women had fair access to, and control over, agricultural produce in the traditional economy.

A large section of rural labour is rendered surplus by mechanization. The overall planning strategy does not provide adequate employment alternatives. The general tendency for the land-owning employer is to reduce his dependence on labour. Consequently, those who do not own land have to move to the alien and hostile urban environment, where it is equally hard to make a living. Efficient transportation and communication facilities promote this mobility Furthermore, the spread of education has also been instrumental in dislocating the village population, which finds no place for its skills in the rural economy.

The overall processes of urbanization and industrialization promise better economic opportunities to the small peasants, dispossessed tenants, and the bulk of labourers swelling the stream of migrants from rural to urban areas.

In India, as in other Asian countries, the labour force continues to be dependent on agriculture. This, long with the fact of the rapid increase in population, which offsets most gains from increased production, causes a deterioration in the land-man ratio. The transfer of the surplus labour to Urban areas is often a transfer of the human-resource problem from one area to another. Poor unskilled and underemployed migrants increase the burden on the overcrowded urban areas, which are already faced with unemployment.

Nevertheless, for many people in the rural areas, the only alternative is to seek a living outside the village. The 'push' factors from the village are even more forceful than the promise of a good life in the cities. Until recently all internal migration was considered beneficent, but this is not so now (See Todaro, 1976). In the study *Migration from Rural Areas* inequality is considered the most important single variable underlying both 'push' and 'pull' factors, the former applying to the poor and the latter to the affluent in the rural society (Connel *et al.*, 1976). But the book confines itself to the migrant and his characteristics. The rural family whom the migrant leaves behind has not been studied. There are, however, some useful points mentioned in the study: the majority of the migrants are male, married, have more education, and come from self-employed or non-agricultural households. Perhaps agricultural labourers (who constitute only 5.4 per cent of the male migrants to urban areas in this study) migrate to other rural areas, where there is a high demand for labour. The villages from which they come have land shortage, low fertility, skewed distribution of land, and a high proportion of landless labour.

Existing studies of migration tell us about the destination. Occupation, income, visits home and other characteristics of the migrants. But there is hardly any concern with the village-based family. Furthermore, different patterns of migration are seen among certain castes, groups, regions, etc. From some regions only males migrate, while from others whole families do so. There are various social and cultural factors that explain the variations in the migration streams to major cities. Emotional attachment to village, home and land, sex segregation and immobility females (except migration subsequent to marriage and migration due to principles of patriarchy and village exogamy, which account for 58 per cent of the total female migration). The concepts of purity and pollution and the norms regarding work in different castes may provide part of the explanation. 'Male-only' migration has been a traditional feature of internal migration in India from regions where local employment opportunities are scarce to places with greater economic opportunities. The women remain at home. There is much more evidence in the oral tradition and folk-songs than in social-science literature of the sufferings and deprivations of the women of such families whose men have gone to earn a living in the city. (The phenomenon of migrant families dates back to the pre-industrial period, though migration has increased with industrialization). The folk-songs called *bidesia* and *birha* of eastern Uttar Pradesh and Bihar, two areas with a high concentration of male migration to cities, refer to the beloved living in a far off 'country' and reflect the unhappy and lonely existence of the women who are left behind (Saxena, 1977).

One universal feature of the process of migration in the village is that pre-established way undergo changes: there are rises in the level of aspirations and values of the members of the family, changes in the occupational structure and economic status, and a revision of intercaste relations. The outcome may be enrichment of the village due to remittances from the city on the one hand, and impoverishment of the village due to the absence of a large number of able-bodied young men, who leave the village to the very young, the very old and the women, who sometimes have to face great challenges.

The time and distance factors in migration are crucial in analysing the impact of the process on the rural family. While short-term migration is undertaken to save for the specific objective of meeting temporary crisis long-term migration means with the village-based family.

While analysing the effects of male migration on rural society it may be noted that migration is not a caste/class neutral process. There is one migration for the rich and another for the poor. A man belonging to the rural elite (which is composed of higher castes and powerful peasantry migrates to the city for advanced education and subsequently takes up an urban job, adding to the family's wealth. He provides the capitalist base for agriculture to the parent family (Rao, 1973). On the other hand, poorer peasants and dispossessed tenants, landless labourers, marginal groups and artisans whose crafts are not valued any more, migrate to the other villages, town and cities in order to avoid underemployment.

The effects of the above two types of migration are different. When a man from the elite group migrates, he maintains contact with the village, conferring cumulative gains and prestige upon his family. The money sent home is used to build a new house and buy land and agricultural equipment, as well as to educate more members (especially males) of the family. The migrant from the lower stratum sets out to find work in the city without any specific abilities. He is seldom in a position to support the village-based family, which maintains itself with whatever work is available in the village. The woman who remains behind has to assume, in addition to her own familial and domestic responsibilities, the role of sole bread-winner; the older daughter takes over the household chores and plays the role of a 'little surrogate mother' to her brothers and sisters.

It is evident that women suffer in both kinds of migration. Elite-class women suffer emotionally because of physical separation. Poor women bear; in addition to the emotional problems, the increased burden not only of looking after the home and children but also of supporting the family. Thus they suffer silently in the village. The migrating man also suffers harrowing experiences: he works hard, struggling to save something to send home to his family, but is caught in the vicious cycle of staying in the city to find a job, and doing a job in order to continue staying in the city.

With all its negative as well as positive consequences, the process of migration continues to be a social reality, and there is every indication of its acceleration in future. But as long as there is no infrastructure for a parallel scheme of employment in the village in the form of agro-industries augmenting off-farm employment for the members of the growing work force, migration alone will not solve the problem. Rural people will continue to run to the city, but the entire urban-industrial complex is not capable of absorbing this vast surplus labour force. In this study we are primarily concerned with that section of society which is being squeezed out of the rural economy and pushed into low-paid urban employment.

There is no dearth of date about the magnitude of the problem, especially in a country like India, where there is an unbroken chain of 100 years of census-taking, in addition to periodic national sample surveys and longitudinal researches. The picture that emerges clearly shows that rural-to-urban migration has been particularly male-selective and furthermore that the pattern seems to be 'rich student, poor worker' (see Dasgupta, 1978). But we have little information on the consequences of male migration on the family in the village. We do not know how male migration affects the structure of roles, division of labour between the sexes or the forms of dominance in the village production system. There is little data to show how women face the situation created by the absence of males within the family and in the larger community. Changes in labour demands, the increasing vulnerability of women, the widening access to developmental and political processes, the conflicting social demands, and the economic compulsions may all be critical factors affecting the lives of such women. While we have some idea about the economic and social deprivations of these women, we have little knowledge about the precise extent of exploitation and suffering they undergo, or about the views they have on their situation.

Some observations from a pilot study made by the author in a village in western Uttar Pradesh may be typical of a wider region (Jetley, 1979).

The introduction of advanced methods in agriculture, achieved though labour-saving mechanical technology and/or land saving biological and chemical technology, substitutes other inputs for land and labour. Thus the traditional activities performed in the subsistence economy are affected by the improved technology, rendering much rural labour surplus. In the village studied it was found, that a large part of the labour force was vitally affected by the introduction of high-yielding varieties of wheat, by assured means of irrigation and consequently a multiplicity of cropping, by commercialization and medchanization, and by legal reforms (such as consolidation of landholdings) and sociopolitical protections (such as special privileges to suppressed castes).

Some of the questions that need to be asked concern the effects of male migration on the family structures, on the authority pattern, on the decision-making process, and on the adjustment of the females within the family and the larger community. Furthermore, more information is needed on how the women manage these crises, how they cope with day-to-day problems and above all with their increased work load.

The census shows that only 12 per cent of total number of workers were female in the villages studied here. Since 94 per cent of all the women workers are in the unorganized sector, they are always liable to be grossly underenumerated. The Planning Commission worked out by adjustment that the female work participation rate is about 28 per cent. Apart from problems of underenumeration of female workers there are those of unemployment and underemployment. In addition to the burden of looking after the family in the absence of males who migrate in search of work, these women face changes in their roles, status, and responsibilities. Often they have to undergo exploitation and harassment at the hands of the affluent locals who are the sole providers of work. Efforts at self-reliance and self-employment meet with no success because of lack of capital for investment, training, marketing facilities and protection. A larger number of males migrate to find work outside the village, either in other rural areas or in towns and cities.

Legal reforms, educational and occupational guarantees, political rights and constitutional guarantees do not really affect most of the women in developing countries. Very often these women go unnoticed because of their low-paid, low-prestige, unorganized work. In India female workers are engaged in agriculture or in the unorganized sector. Their representation in the organized sector is only 12 per cent.

A global study puts the potential women-headed households in India at 18.7 per cent. This figure is based on the number of widows, divorcees and separated women and does not take into account those who are effective heads of households because of migration of men (Buvinic and Youseff, 1974). Governmental efforts do not include special emphasis on the class of women who are alone in the rural society. Only recently has concern been growing to help women achieve self-reliance through training in agriculture and the vocational crafts.

The overall movement of the population in India is low (only 3.3 per cent of the total population is migrant), but the regional variations reveal that some states are more open and thus 'gainers' in net migration while others are insulated. Delhi ranks first in the category of those which gain. Gupta (1972), calculation the hospitality ratio of different states (computed by dividing the migrant population in a state by the local population) finds Delhi having the highest ratio of hospitality and ranking as 'a metropolitan community in the true sense of the term'. In the second category are states like Kerala, Uttar Pradesh, Bihar, Jammu and Kashmir. Gupta's study shows that Uttar Pradesh is the prime exporter of men, appearing among the first-three states from which men migrate to as many as ten states in India.

All Asian societies have symbols, rituals and credos exhorting women to be submissive, obedient, subservient, humble and dutiful to their husbands and to acquire these 'virtues' by self-sacrifice. In the urban-educated female there is resentment against these traditionally prescribed roles for women, but in the rural society customs and traditions still have a firm hold on the women. The main concern of the women lies in the home; she has to work inside the house as well as on the farm. She seldom participates in the political and public life of the community. Women's organizations under the new development schemes are confined to the rural elite class. Who have the time to spare for such activities.

The rapid social changes which Asian societies have been undergoing have upset the rural-urban ratio of population, and not always to the advantage of the population which moves. Until recently the process of migration of males from rural to urban areas was applauded as a solution for the ever-increasing pressure on land. Not so now, for the industrial expansion of these societies is not big enough to absorb the streams of migration to the cities. It is being increasingly realized that Asian societies are essentially peasant and rural societies, in spite of their massive infrastructure of industrial-based scientific, technical and entrepreneurial skills. Faced with increasing population and shortage of arable land, nationwide programmes aiming at rural reconstruction are being implemented. The Community Development Programme in India, the *Seamaul Undong* in the republic of Korea, and the emphasis on sexual equality as expressed in the Balikatan spirit in the Philippines are some illustrations.

The modernization of rural society has not been an unmixed blessing. It has disturbed the traditional economy and has adversely affected the landless of the village, especially the women among them. While the male sets out in search of employment outside the village, the female stays at home to wage the battle for survival single-handed. In the newer context, female-specific traditional skills are less in demand, and thus women are deprived of employment opportunities that were previously available. A woman is generally not recognized as the functional head of the household in the absence of the male, nor is she included in the training programmes for teaching new skills. Work for the poor rural woman is not a privilege but a necessity for economic survival. This burden becomes even heavier when it has to be shouldered alongside family responsibilities in the absence of males.

Form and Content : An Approach

The cross-cultural study of which this report forms a part will try to clarify variations in the social structures, agrarian relations and value systems of the different societies concerned. Our existing knowledge about these societies covers cultural differences such as those in the family and kinship system (specifically the relation to the patriarchal and matriarchal systems of family). However, the modes of production which give more powers and control to women remain to be examined. Apparently there is more equality between the sexes in South-East Asian societies, which is sometimes attributed to the greater participation of women in wet-rice cultivation than in dry-cereal cultivation. India shares this feature in its eastern and southern states, yet sexual equality is not merely a function of the economic participation of women but is more related to the institution of property, laws regarding inheritance, pattern of landownership, valued and prestige attached to manual labour and work as a whole, demand and supply of labour, as well as the nature of the state and its relationship with the peasantry. Some of the hypotheses that could be tested are:

Socio-economic inequalities accentuated by the process of modernization lead to male migration from the poorer strata:

The females in the families, whose males migrate to the city, have to bear heavier burdens within the family by having to work harder to assure the family's economic survival, among other things.

The longer the duration of stay of the migrant in the city and the greater the distance between his home and place of work, the weaker are his ties with his rural family and the greater the insecurity of the woman at home.

The kind of work that the women of these families can get is low-paid, dull, repetitive and hazardous. These are most likely the activities that are the first to be rejected by men when simplified, mechanized operations are introduced.

The females suffer from inadequate and insecure income, uncertainty of life, and exploitation (economic and sexual), and they have no protection regarding wages (paid on piece-work basis rather then on an hourly or daily basis), working conditions, social security, etc.

Most of their earnings are likely to be spent on food, leaving little for education of children or improvement in the living standards of the family.

The self-perceptions of these females are helplessness and lack of control over their lives, as any efforts towards self-reliance or self-employment are thwarted owing to lack of capital investment, state recognition of their role and therefore absence of programmes recognizing their special needs, capacities and problems.

The state programmes for women are most likely to be welfare measures rather than schemes for increasing their earning power.

The central concern of this research is not with the process of migration as such, but with the broader objective of understanding the impact of rapid social change on the life and work of rural people , especially of rural females when the males in their families migrate because of urbanization—a necessary adjunct to modernization. The finding are expected to enrich our understanding of the sociology of the family in general and the problems of women in particular.

Selection of Place for Male Migration

To undertake the study of rural families whose males have migrated to the cities, the capital of India was selected to trace the male migrants to their rural homes. By a snowball-sampling technique, the male migrants were asked to name other fellow villagers working in Delhi. Ninety-seven migrant's families were traced to three villages in eastern Uttar Pradesh. The state of Uttar Pradesh is the most populous as well as one of the most backward states of India. It has a high density of population, a highly disproportionate sex ratio, the highest crude birth and death rates low levels of per-capita income, literacy, industrial development, female work participation etc. (Government of Uttar Pradesh, 1979). Though primarily an agrarian hierarchies are sharply defined.

With an area of 573 km^2, the Union Territory of Delhi forms only 0.05 per cent of the total area of India. The density of population is high, with 2,738 persons per km^2. The partition of India in 1947 saw a great influx of refugees from the western wing of the new state of Pakisthan. Between 1941 and 1951, Delhi almost doubled in size. Later migrating is due to the capital city's perceived opportunities and the social and economic changes taking place in the countryside. It is the fastest-growing city of the country; its population increased from 1.5 million to 2.36 million between 1951 and 1961. After another decade it stood at

3.6 million, and it is now over 5 million.

Most migrants to Delhi belong to the lowest strata of society and most of them are classified as workers in category IV, 'other services'.[1] Among those who come without their families, four larger groups can be identified along with the region from which they migrate to Delhi. These are:

Gardeners and watchmen, employed in a large number of public parks and big private houses. They come from the eastern districts of Uttar Pradesh. There are many watchmen from Nepal too.

Peons in the offices a large contingent belonging to the Kumaon region.

Road construction/repair gangs of Public Works Departments, unskilled labourers at construction sites and loaders in the wholesale market; hailing from eastern Uttar Pradesh and Bihar.

Factory workers from nearby Haryana and other states.

The sample of male migrants was taken from one state, Uttar Pradesh. They were mostly gardeners.

The technique was to talk to groups of gardeners and ask them where fellow-villagers worked. By using the technique of snowball sampling , the number decided on (*i.e.* 100) was enlisted. Although an effort was made to select the gardeners from one village and one district, this was not possible. Thus ninety-seven male migrants from three villages in three districts of the eastern and central regions of Uttar Pradesh were selected for the sample, and their women were contacted in the villages. The selected villages and districts were:

Region	*District*	*Village*
Eastern	Jaunpur	Amawan Kalan
Eastern	Pratapgarh	Bhojpur
Central	Rae Bareli	Bewal

It tales minimum of twelve hours to reach the nearest and fifteen hours to reach the farthest of our selected villages from Delhi by rail. The data were collected from secondary sources, personal interviews, observation, group discussions and case studies.

Problems in Field Investigation

The selection of male migrants in Delhi involved exploring vast stretches of the city for work sides, settlement colonies, pavement dwellers, etc. The secondary sources of information—the census data and the interviews with researchers who have studied the Delhi scene—helped to build a rough sketch of the varieties of male-only migration. Tracking down a sufficiently large number of a group from the same region proved to be rather difficult. Though Uttar Pradesh and Rajasthan account for 75 per cent of the rural migration to Delhi, male-only migration is a peculiar feature of the former state. Thus the migrants from Uttar Pradesh who work as watchmen, gardeners and labourers were contacted. They came from practically every district of the state. Three districts were selected from a long list.

Interviewing the male respondents was undertaken both at the work sites and at their homes. It was difficult to convince them that this researcher was more interested in the plight of their women than in their difficulties. Not many were keen on the idea that their families would be contacted in their absence. Being a woman researcher proved to be an asset here.

In a society where news from the outside world is always of an extraordinary nature, mention of a man's name for location of his family in the village evoked awkward situations at times. In one instance, in response to the question as to who was Mr. So-and-so's wife, the wman in question began wailing loudly, fearing that some calamity must have befallen her husband or else why should someone from the city come and inquire about his family. It took sometime to pacify her and explain the purpose of the inquiry. Taking to anyone in the village in privacy is nearly impossible. Hoards of children, women and men appear from nowhere. Everyone is keeen to answer a question, and many seem to know more about the life of the respondent than she herself does. Thus, group discussions took far more time than personal interviews, and in fact unless a study calls for deep psychological analysis, group discussion and lengthy dialogues are much more fruitful than cut-and-dried questions aiming at unconnected pieces of information. In an illiterate population, informal oral communication helps established a rapport sooner than an official team (which they detest) noting down every word they utter. It needs a perceptive mind, an excellent memory, and perhaps less obvious recording techniques to work with rural people.

Subjected to perpetual deprivation and want and helplessness in the face of a formal official structure requiring endless formalities and printed forms, these villagers are ignorant of many benefits and facilities intended for them, or else lack the resources and skills to procure them. In one community people were not aware that they could get a drinking-water well (which they did not have, and women fetched water from a brackish well at a distance) if they asked for it at the local development office. An application to get the facility was dictated to a literate boy. Now twenty-five signatures were needed to send it to the Block Office. Excepting three, none could sign their names and not more than twelve could be persuaded to put their thumb impressions instead, out of fear of the written word. There were endless requests for help in several litigation cases being fought by some people to get land allotted for residential agricultural purposes and even for a meeting with the Prime Minister—since I live in Delhi I must know her (as every one knows everyone else in their village).

All in all, it was an experience that left one highly frustrated (because of the time constraints of the research project) and with the desire to go back for a better understanding of these eternally waiting females, who not only perform the domestic roles but also work as the assistant breadwinners of the families, cramped physically and structurally and subsisting at a precarious level.

COUNTRY PROFILE : THE CHANGING CONTOURS

Geography

India is girdled by high mountains and seas. It lies in the Northern Hemisphere and extends between latitudes 8° 4′ and 37° 6' N. and longitudes 68° 7' and 97° 25' E. South of the mountainous wall are the Northern Plains watered by mighty small and big rivers, including the mighty Ganges. On the south-west of this plain is the Great Indian Desert. To the south is a tableland with narrow coastal plains, enriched by numerous rivers and their deltas. The mountains have a wealth of forests and mineral resources, while the land yields a variety of crops—rice and wheat being the major ones.

India extends 3,214 km from north to south, covering an area of 32,80,482 km^2. It is the seventh largest country in the world. Because of its vast size there are great variations in its climate (from zero to an average of 25°C) and annual rainfall (25 cm to 200 cm). Yet it is referred to as a tropical country. The yearly monsoon is an overwhelming phenomenon that determines not only the fertility and prosperity of a given region but also the daily round of activities, life-style and religious calendar of the people. India is bordered by Nepal, Bhutan and China to the north, Pakistan and Afganistan to the north-west and Bangladesh, Burma and China to the east. The Republic of India is a union of states, and its territory comprises twenty-five states and four union territories.

Social Structure

Indian civilization is ancient, and its culture is a mixture of several racial, ethnic and religious groups. Neither the mountainous walls on the north nor the seas in the south could maintain its isolation (Spate, 1969). The successive streams of immigrants from the Afrasian dry zone to the alluvial plains of the Indus and the Ganges, as well as the contacts between West Asian and Mediterranean regions and the western coast of India, produced a blend of cultures. India has a long history of invasions and colonization and had a long struggle for independence.

The great diversity in terms of geography, democracy, economy, political life and social and cultural composition obstructs the possibility of generalizations. Yet some shared characteristics can be enumerated.

India is a highly stratified society, caste being the most manifest expression of this and marking the dominant ethos of the majority community, *i.e.* Hindus, but revealing the distinct imprint of other religious groups such as Muslims, Christians and Sikhs. Almost all the major religions are found here. There are fifteen major languages spoken by the people (the total number of languages and dialects is 826) Hindu being the language of the largest group. English is widely used for official work and by the elite and the middle classes.

In spite of a sizable urban population and a tribal component, the majority of the population lives in the villages in India. The traditional social structure is dominated by a family type that is patrilineal-virilocal, with strong attachment to the palace of origin and a network of caste and caste like affiliations with principles governing status, occupation, interdining and marriage. It is common to speak of the 'joint family' in India, but jointness is a complex concept, describing various compositions or family set-ups, which depend on the particular state which a family has reached in the process of formation and fission. It is common to find an old patent or relative coming to stay with a son or a younger member of the family. Marriages, which are arranged, are really reaffirmations of the existing social structure and involve the whole family /kinship/clan. Monogamy is the prevalent practice with preference for hypergamy. The importance of male lineage, the near obsession with the sexual purity of the female the birth of a son as a passport towards salvation;: these are some of the dominant features, at least of the elite culture.

The rules of social living are derived from the religious scriptures, which are not equally accessible to all. Besides this, the Dravidian and tribal components show departures and variations, specially in the kinship systems, which may be bilateral and matrilineal, giving relatively greater equality and freedom for participation in social life. Nevertheless the general pattern of social life is derived from the ideology of dependence and the notion of the social inferiority of the female—sanctified by scriptures and supported by folklore. The denial of property and other rights contributes to an asymmertrical relationship between husband and wife. The roles of wife and mother have been glorified. Women's instruction has been confined to the learning of spiritual and familial functions, with a view to discouraging them from social and political participation. The force of tradition weighs heavily even today. Yet these norms and values are more typical of the upper classes, while the lower classes have a tradition of active participation in economic functions and of working to support themselves and the family.

Political Structure

While India chose the democratic system of government in 1947, the feudal character of its polity did not change and the traditional elite continued to retain its position. This overlap of democratic forms of government—village panchayats to delegate power to the people, linking these grass-root organisations to higher levels of administration; voting rights based on civil rather than ascriptive status—without corresponding structural changes led to widespread group conflict. Though the demand for adult franchise was first made in 1917, women did not participate actively in the political sphere. Economic dependence, lack of social mobility, and segregation have kept them confined to the family. Though there has been a rapid political change since 1937, when India had eighty legislators, fewer female voters participate in voting than men. Some of the reasons are social backwardness and the heavy demands on women's time and energy by the families. Among those who do vote, a large number act according to the wish of male relatives. In some states, women of the middle and upper-middle class consider it below their dignity to vote. The greatest mobilization of women is in the coastal area and in the Union Territory of Delhi and Chandigarh, where a long exposure to Western culture, a cosmopolitan outlook, an industrial base and the urban character of the region are favourable factors. The states showing minimum mobilization (Orissa, Rajasthan, Madhya Pradesh, Himachal Pradesh) are also those with fairly strong feudal structures, minimal industrialization and extensive restrictions on women. Women constituted in 1952 approximately half the country's population, yet the number of women voters was only 28.7 million. The figure for 1971 was 64.2 million. Women have a negligible representation in the parliament (5.4 per cent) or in state legislature. For example, in Orissa there is not a single female member in the present legislature, and in West Bengal women legislators constitute only 1.8 per cent.

It is ironical that the states with poor political participation of women sometimes have more women in positions of political power (as in the case of Madhya Pradesh). The decision to field these women candidates is often made by the political parties, depending on the local conditions and strength of the opposition parties. Often women candidates endorsed by a party are from well-to-do families or have a father/husband/brother in a strategic position in the political power structure. During the last five general elections, the number of women elected to the Lok Sabha

(Lower House of the parliament) have never been more than 20 per cent of the total seats contested and not more than five per cent of the total number of male candidates contesting for the same number of seats (Muni, 1979). While individual women have wielded informal or indirect power, the first call for total and direct involvement in the political process and the mainstream of national life was made by Mahatma Gandhi during the independence movement. The role he envisaged for women was not merely political but a part of a larger social question. Emphasis was laid on restoring the self-reliant village economy, which, with its balance of agriculture and handicrafts gave meaning and dignity to the work of all, including women. Social issues like removal of purdah and general emancipation on terms of opportunities and participation were also a part of this movement. Unfortunately, the movement tapered off, ironically, with independence. Three decades after independence the Committee on the Status of Women concluded that there seemed to be 'national neglect of women', using socio-economic indicators such as sex-ratio in population, sex-specific mortality rates, literacy and education, employment and access to health services. These indicators have shown that there is an alarming deterioration in women's status. The data complied by the committee are supported by micro-level studies.

Economy

Rural society in India used to be based on the self- sufficient village community, where balance was maintained by mutual co-operation and by dovetailing the functions of cultivation and artisans. British rule disrupted this equilibrium with its policy of exploiting the colonies and by its misinterpretation of old systems of land settlement. India was forced into the world capitalistic system, and a decadent feudal structure, based on inequality and exploitation was entrenched. These features continue today, despite several administrative reforms.

Half of the total geographical area of 3.28 million km^2 (328 million hectares) is cultivated. From the Agricultural Census Report of 1971 we learn that households owning fifteen hectares and more are considered well off, and they constitute 0.4 per cent of the land-owning population. Seventy per cent owns up to two hectares (21 per cent of the cultivated area) and are considered marginal or small farmers. Landless labour, 29.6 per cent of the agricultural population, comprises small farmers, uprooted by economic or other reasons, semi-feudal peasants, subtenants and share croppers who have no right to the land and are compelled to sell their labour. Middle farmers own between five and fifteen hectares of land.

Since independence there has been much progress in different spheres. There has been an increase in food production from 51 million tonnes in 1950-51 to approximately 115 million tonnes in 1973-74, largely owing to the doubling of the area under irrigation (from 22.6 million hectares in 1950/51 to nearly 43 million hectares in 1973/74) and the introduction of new agricultural technology. This, and also the increase in the production of commercial crops such as sugarcane, cotton, etc. has further added to the growth of the agricultural sector. The Food and Agriculture Organization's *Production Year Book*, 1972, giving comparable data, showed that India was competing well with other countries, with 1,380 kg of wheat per hectare as against 900 kg in China and 1,467 in the Soviet

Table 3.1
Percentage Distribution of Workers by Industrial Categories and Sex, 1961 and 1971

	1961		*1971*	
Category	*Males*	*Females*	*Males*	*Females*
Cultivation and agricultural hard labour	64.88	79.88	67.49	80.07
Livestock, forestry, fishery, plantation and allied activities, mining and quarrying	3.10	2.00	2.89	2.90
Manufacturing, processing, servicing and repairing				
Household industry	5.71	7.85	3.37	4.25
Other than household Industry	5.56	1.33	6.61	2.76
Construction	1.41	0.41	1.35	0.65
Trade and Commerce	5.29	1.37	6.36	1.78
Transport, Storage and Communication	2.28	0.11	2.85	0.47
Other services	11.77	7.35	9.08	7.12

Union. The social base of the agrarian structure has, however, remained inegalitarian, with the result that economic and social disparities continue to exist and have even widened at place. The average size of land holding was 2.63 hectares in 1961 (17 th Round of National Sample Survey). Agriculture employs the largest number of persons. Eighty per cent of the female work force is engaged in agriculture as against 67.5 per cent among the males (Gulati, 1975). In the 1971 census 25 million out of a total of 31 million women workers were in agriculture. The position is given in Table 3.1.

The generation, transmission and distribution of electricity have expanded to cover a quarter of Indian villages. The use of power in agriculture increase from 4.3 per cent in 1950-51 to 10.2 per cent in 1970-71; the increase in pumpsets from 0.2 million in 1960-61 to 2.4 million in 1973-74. The share of industries increased from 63.7 per cent in 1950-51 to 67.6 per cent in 1971. The per capita consumption of electricity increased from 38 KW in 1960-61 to 90kW in 1970-71.

These are not mean achievements. But, as has been mentioned earlier, social justice and equality are far from being a reality. A very large portion (40 per cent) of the population lives below the poverty line and is barely touched by the development process. The per-capita availability of food grains decreased from 200 kg in 1901 to 162 kg in 1970-71. The per-capita availability of land (0.6 ha.) is among the lowest in the world.

Demography

The major hurdle in the development of the country is the unprecedented growth in population. The population of India showed a slow increase between 1900 and 1920 (238.2 million to 251.2 million), but between 1921 and 1951 the increase was 11 to 14 per cent, and since 1951 it has been sharp; 21.6 per cent between 1951 and 1961 and 25 per cent from 1961 to 1971. The population of India doubled between 1931 and 1971. In 1971, the total was 548 million, with an average density of 182 per km^2 (with variations from 14 in the Andaman and Nicobar Islands to 2,723 in Delhi). The total pupulation in 1976 was 630.4 million. The sex-ratio is unfavourable to females. Not only does the number of males exceed the number of females in India, but their population has shown a faster increase eversince 1901, except during the decade 1941-51, which witnessed mass upheavals on account of partition. Demographers attribute the declining sex ratio to such factors as underenumeration on females in the Indian census, preference for sons, lower status, general neglect and higher mortality of females, excessive burden of work and child-bearing on women, leading to poor health, higher incidence of certain diseases, etc. There are, however, no adequate data to arrive at the exact causes of this decline. The Committee on the Status of Women in its report emphasized the fact that more boys than girls are born and that more girl children die. The death rate in the age-group 0-4 is 58.3 per thousand for males and 70.2 for females. As Mitra (1979) puts it: The comparative deterioration in female mortality vis-a-vis male mortality an all the selected ages between 1931 and 1961 hits one in the eye'.

The expectation of life at birth is 47.1 for males and 45.6 for females. Sixty per cent of the total population is below 25, while only six per cent is above 60 years of age. People marry early, men around 22 and women around 17 years of age. Though no reliable statistics are available, the estimates made for the beginning of the century, based on data on marital status distribution and age distribution, put the average age at marriage for males at 20.2 and that for females at 13.2 Child marriages are not uncommon. The census does not provide information about the marital status

Table 3.2
Percentage of Persons Aged Five and Over by Level of Education, 1961 and 1971

	All ages				*Aged five and over*			
Level of education	*1961*		*1971*[1]		*1961*		*1971*	
	Total	*Females*	*Total*	*Females*	*Total*	*Females*	*Total*	*Females*
Literate with educational standard								
Up to Matriculation	7.03	3.84	14.37	9.2	8.28	4.24	16.79	10.78
Matriculation and above	1.88	0.59	3.91	1.74	2.20	0.71	4.56	2.04

1. The 1971 figures are based on a one per cent sample.

of age-group 0-9, but the Committee on the Status of Women in India found girls already married at the age of 10. The 1971 census reveals that 13.6 per cent of girls in the age-groups 10-14 were married and 0.1 per cent in the rural areas were widows. The corresponding figures for urban areas were 3.9 per cent married and a negligible number of widows. Although the law (Child Marriage Restraint Act) prohibits the marriage of girls below 13 years of age, custom and religion deem it meritorious for a daughter to be married before she attains puberty. Early marriage and early widowhood are more common in rural areas. In the age-group 60-64, 62.5 per cent of the females are widows. Yet according to one estimate only 10.02 per cent of rural and 9.51 per

Table 3.3
Educational Enrolment of Girls and Women in India, 1950-51 to 1973-74 in Lakh (One Lakh = 1,00,000 Females)

Year	*School Classes I–V*	*School Classes VI–VIII*	*Secondary Classes IX–XI*	*Colleges and Universities*
1950-51	53.85	5.34	1.61	0.40[2]
	(39)[1]	(20)	(15)	(14)
1955-56	76.39	8.67	3.18	0.34
	(44)	(25)	(21)	(17)
1960-61	113.47	16.70	5.41	1.50
	(48)	(33)	(23)	(22)
1965-66	182.93	28.46	11.72	3.24
	(57)	(37)	(30)	(28)
1968-69[3]	199.36	34.93	15.60	4.32
	(59)	(39)	(32)	(30)
1973-74[4]	244.01	45.37	23.40	9.00
	(62)	(43)	(36)	(31)

1. Figures in parentheses indicate the number of girls for every 100 boys enrolled.
2. Figures in the last column relate to enrolments at undergraduate postgraduate and research stages in general-education, arts, science and commerce courses.
3. Figures for school enrolment in 1950-51, 1960-61, 1965-66 and 1968-69 are from the Ministry of Education.
4. Figures for school enrolment in 1973-74 are from the Draft Fifth Five Year Plan, 1974-79.

cent of urban households are reported to have a female as head of the household.

There are vast variations in the quality of population regionwise and sexwise. In Kerala, for instance, the literacy rate is the highest; Rajasthan has the lowest literacy rate. The overall picture for the nation shows that 39.5 per cent of the males and 18.7 per cent of the females are literate. But among the females 40 per cent are actually semi-literate, while a bare 1.4 per cent have graduated. Men comprise a large percentage of the literates (35.5) without attainment of any educational level. Their position is also better in the higher levels of education.

Enrolment in primary classes increased from 18 million in 1950-51 to 63 million in 1973-74. At the beginning of the First Plan, only 400,000 people were enrolled in the universities. In 1973-74, there were 3 million.

Migration

The modernization of agriculture has created surplus labour in the rural society. The overall planning strategy does not provide adequate alternative avenues of employment for this group. Increased education also disrupts the life of the village population, which finds no place or its skills in the rural economy.

While agriculture is a family activity in which men, women and children participate, the urban-industrial complex to which

Table 3.4
Migrant Population in India, 1961-71, in Percentages

	Total migrant population	*Male migrants in total population*	*Female migrants in total population*
1961	30.7	9.4	21.3
1971	29.6	8.9	20.7
(place of birth)			
1971			
(place of last residence)	30.9	9.4	21.5

Sources: Census of India 1961, Vol. l Part II, India, migration table 1966, p. 16: Census of India 1971, series I, India, Part I special. All India Census Table (estimated from one per cent sample data Tab D I 4 D.II. D.P. 130-64.

this surplus labour is pushed is hostile to the migration of the family as a whole. For women 'marriage migration' accounts for a large proportion of the migration from rural to urban areas, while males go out either in search of employment or for higher education.

There was an increase in inter-state migration from 14.6 million in 1961 to 18.5 million in 1971. The proverbial immobility of Indians is attributed to the complex structure of Indian society, which explains why, in spite of compelling reasons. Only 6 per cent of the country's population is mobile. Yet in absolute numbers this is a large mass of humanity. The movement of population from one area to another depends to a variety of socio-economic factors relating to the situations prevailing in the place of origin and destination and also to the composition of the population in these two places. Economically backward states encourage out migration (rural Uttar Pradesh accounts for a fifth of the total out migration) while more job opportunities, rapid industrialization, better social and civic amenities may lead to an upward swing in immigration (as in the case of Delhi in 1971 over 1961) (Mehrotra, 1971). Thus while during the period 1961-71 the total population grew by 24.7 per cent the increase in urban population was 37.9 per cent.

Table 3.5

Distribution of Total Migrants by Types of Movements and by Sex

Census	*Rural to rural*		*Rural to urban*		*Urban to rural*		*Urban to urban*		*Unclassified*	
	M	*F*	*M*	*F*	*M*	*F*	*M*	*F*	*M*	*F*
1961	56.2	80.8	25.4	9.6	4.5	3.1	12.9	5.8	1.0	0.7
1971	52.8	78.2	25.9	10.9	6.0	4.4	14.2	6.9	1.1	0.9

Source: Mehrotra, 1971. p. 33.

In the twenty years between 1951 and 1971, the population of Delhi nearly tripled. The city comprises three per cent of the total population and 11 per cent of interstate migrants. Rural migrants comprise between 51 and 55 per cent of the male and 41 per cent of the female migrants. Migration from other urban areas is also significant, with 40 per cent of the male and 44 per cent of the female migrants included in this category. Those born in places outside Delhi constitute 55 per cent of all the people in Delhi (Alam and Pokshi, 1976).

The 'rural push' threatens to change the economy of the developing countries. India has 21.3 per cent of its population in the cities, which may increase to 31.4 per cent by the year 2000. This may not seem significant in comparison to other developing countries. (The increase in the percentage of urban population from 1975 to 2000 is projected as 80 to 90 for Argentina, 63 to 78 for Mexico, 47 to 69 for the Republic of Korea, 35 to 49 for the Philippines). Yet in absolute numbers, it is quite large and requires study of its impact on the urban and rural society. Most migrants move towards the bigger cities rather than to the smaller towns, the reasons being economies of scale of big cities with large labour markets, increasing communication links, concentration of governmental decision-making bodies, educational institutions and the like.

With the men migrating to the cities, rural women face an increased pressure of agricultural work in addition to their domestic chores. There is no time and little scope for self-improvement in their own lives. While suffering from the drastic changes modern agricultural techniques have caused in the village economy and social structure, women have been denied access to these very techniques, which add to their burden and can even prove detrimental to the health of all human beings.

WOMEN IN RURAL FAMILIES LEFT BY MALE MIGRANTS

The male migrants selected for this study are from Uttar Pradesh, which is the most populous state in India, comprising 16 per cent of the total population and nine per cent of the total area of the country. There are only six countries in the world that have a population greater than this state. According to the 1971 census, its population was 88.3 million, and an estimated projection in March 1979 put it at 102 million. The density of population is 300 persons per km^2, which is 68.5 per cent higher than the all-India figure of 178. India as a whole has a highly disproportionate sex ratio, but Uttar Pradesh has a still lower number of females per thousand males (883 against 930 for India as a whole). A more recent development is in the state of Haryana, where the female population has dropped to 865 per 1000 males, in 1995, largely due to the relatively new factor of female foeticide. The state has a large non working population, which showed an increase of 24.4 per cent between 1961 and 1971 as against the working population, which increased by 15.8 per cent during the same period.

The state goal of universal education is not met anywhere in the country, but in Uttar Pradesh, boys in 43 per cent and girls in 60 per cent of the villages have to walk more than 3 km from their respective villages to reach junior basic schools. The state ranks twenty-fourth in order of literacy in the country, with a literacy percentage of 21.8; the female literacy percentage being as low as 10.7.

The economy of the state is largely agrarian, yet the progress in agriculture has been slow. Technological improvement is visible in wheat, though the yields per hectare are much lower than in Punjab and Haryana. Uttar Pradesh ranked tenth in per-capita income and four-teenth in per-capita product in 1977. The largest number of workers (78 per cent) is engaged in agriculture, which contributes 40.7 per cent of the total national domestic product. Agriculture is still largely dependent on rain and on the vagaries of nature. With the development of sources of irrigation (major and minor, state irrigation work and private efforts) the net irrigated area of arable land in 1977-78 went up by 49 per cent over 1960-61. Combined with the introduction of high-yielding crop varieties and the modernization of agricultural technology, the use of land has undergone a substantial change. The extent of barren and uncultivable land and land put to non-agricultural uses has been reduced by 25 per cent. The area shown more than once has increased by 27 per cent. The cropping intensity increased from 126.5 per cent during 1960-61 to 133.1 per cent during 1976-77. The crop calendar shows a marked replacement of inferior grains by wheat and paddy and a gradual shift from subsistence to commercial agriculture. Yet to the large class of the marginal farmers (with holdings of up to one hectare and constituting 69.3 per cent of the total holdings) development is meaningless. Only three per cent of the holdings are of 5 to 10 hectares or more, but they constitute nearly one-third of the total area. This high concentration of land leads to wide economic disparities.

In the state as a whole 86.5 per cent of the residential housed have *kutcha* (mud and thatch) walls. There has been a slight reduction in this as a consequence of an increase in *pucca* (cement, bricks or stone) houses from 13.3 per cent in 1961 to 22 per cent in 1971. In our selected districts most of the houses are *kutcha*, with nearly half of them having only one room. In the development of roads, the state has remained very backward, with only 14 km of surface road per 100 km^2 of area as against the all-India target of 22 km. Public health facilities are also inadequate in relation to the population. Nearly three-fourths of the villages do not have proper medical facilities within a radius of 5 km from the village. More and more villages are being provided with a piped water supply (6,670 villages in 1977-78 as against 1,437 in 1968-69). The death rate, however, came down from 24.9 per thousand during the period 1951-60 to 13.0 per thousand during 1971-75.

The future plans of action to develop this relatively backward state include local planning, special schemes for the poorest sections, housing facilities for scheduled castes and scheduled tribes, special programmes for small and marginal farmers, and new techniques in rural and small industries.

Migrants Characteristics

Our male migrants are mainly from two castes—peasants castes (58.7 per cent), and low castes (38.1 per cent)—traditionally held untouchables (but referred to as "Harijans' for 'Children of God') and listed in the Indian constitution as castes scheduled for special protection. The remaining few are from a low caste (but ritually held clean) engaged in parching grains Bharbhuja).

The peasants are from two castes—Kurmi and Koiri. The former are cultivators and the latter specialize in growing vegetables. They are very industrious and are known for their skills with land. They have small holdings, which never exceed two hectares per family, and some are even smaller than half a hectare. Almost all of them lease some land and sometimes work as agricultural labourers too. Forty-six migrants are drawn from the families that report cultivation as their main occupation.

The low castes are Chamar, Passi and Dhobi. Traditionally they have been providing agricultural and non-agricultural labour and other services, and are by and large landless. Forty-five migrants are from families whose main livelihood comes from wage employment.

Nearly 55 per cent of the migrants in our sample have been in Delhi for more than ten years (of which 43 per cent have been there for over twenty years). Those who came to Delhi five years ago number only fifteen, the remaining having migrated five to ten years ago. It may thus be observed that the first stream of migrants started in the mid-1950s and the second in the early 1970s. The two groups show wide differences in their socio-economic characteristics, the support that facilitated their migration, and in their earnings. For the purpose of analysis, those who migrated to Delhi more than ten years ago are referred to as early migrants (EM) and those who came during the last ten years as late migrants (LM). The early migrants were mostly from the peasant castes—of the 53 migrants more than three-fourths were peasants. Before coming to the city they worked on their own small holdings, their economic status being that of earning dependents. However, their small holdings did not yield enough to support the growing family. The Green Revolution was still in the offing in the mid-1960s, when some members of the peasant families started seeking work in the cities to reduce pressure on the land. They could take the risk, as there was always some land to fall back upon.

Seventy migrants have some operational holdings: but half of them have a holding as small as less than a hectare. Only twelve migrants of those who have some holding have an operational holding above two hectares. Fifty-seven per cent of the cultivator migrants belong to the EM category, while 43 per cent are L.M. of the EM, 55 per cent have an operational holding of less than a hectare. Those who have an operational holding exceeding two hectares constitute 17 per cent of the total sample, half belong to the early and the other half to the late category of migrants. Holdings above two hectares are considered viable by the state government. Such holdings do not qualify for assistance/ concessions extended to the small and marginal farmers. To the question as to why farmers from such families migrate, the unanimous response from all the migrants was that the major portion of their land holding was leased on a year-to-year basis and sometimes on a crop-to-crop basis. Moreover, the quality of the land that was given to them on a lease basis was always inferior, quite often without irrigation facilities. This did not sustain their

Table 3.6
Extent of Land Owned by Migrants, in Hectares

	Number of migrants		
Extent	*Early*	*Late*	*Total*
No Land	19	28	47
Up to 0.2	10	5	15
0.2 to 0.4	10	6	16
0.4 to 0.6	14	5	19
Total	53	44	97

families. The extent of holdings owned by the migrants is quite insignificant, as will be seen from the figures in Table 3.6.

Only fifty of the seventy migrants who have reported operational holdings own some land, the remaining twenty depending exclusively on leased land. Of the thirty-four belonging to the EM, twenty own land of up to less than 0.4 hectare. The LM are mostly from the landless scheduled castes who started coming to the city in greater numbers only in the post-Green Revolution period. Of the forty-four migrants in this group, twenty-eight are landless Harijans. Most of them worked intermittently as agricultural labourers. The planned rural development pushed them out as a result of labour-saving technological, chemical and biological changes in agriculture, which have made a large part of the rural work-force surplus.

The EM helped in providing the supporting network in the city for the LM and acted as a cushion against the initial shocks of movement from the rural homes. It may be observed here that although caste restrictions on interdining and intermarriage are strongly observed between them, this is to a lesser extent than that found between low castes and the uppermost castes. Such distance is further reduced when in the city; some of the people were found living together in the initial stages of migration.

A large percentage (85) of the EM are illiterates, some having been to school only up to primary level. The LMs have had some schooling—there are two among them who have received college education. This may be due to the state policy of special privileges for the scheduled castes comprising most of the LM. Yet education had no relevance to their economic roles in the place of their birth nor in the occupation they obtained in the city.

Before moving to the city, 37 per cent of all migrants worked on their own farms, while another 40 per cent offered themselves for wage employment as agricultural or non-agricultural labourers on a daily wages basis. Only eight per cent were students and the rest were unemployed, looking for a job. It may be noted that the EMs were neither students nor looking for a job before they migrated to the city. They were either employed on their own farms or they combined work on their own farms with work as agricultural labourers. All the twenty-two migrants who were either students or were seeking a job before coming to Delhi belong to the LM category, which would suggest that wage-employment opportunities are decreasing in the rural areas.

Most of the migrants were persuaded and guided by their family, kinship caste and village net work to leave for the city, although 26.8 per cant made the decision alone. Eighty-one per cent of the latter belong to the EM category. A village friend is a most important link with the city for an LM. A relative played this role in 59 per cent and a father in 25 per cent of the cases in respect of LM. The social network is functional, not only for advice and guidance but also for physical, moral and even financial support in the city. The new migrants stay with a caste/kinsman or fellow villager until they are able to arrange their own accommodation (caste/kin accommodating nearly 54 per cent). Some of those who decided on their own to migrate to the city sought support of castemen after reaching the city. The boarding expenses are calculated on the basis of food and paid back as soon as the new entrant starts earning. The work immediately available is head-loading earth in parks and on construction sites on daily wages. In the meantime, the fellow villagers, relatives and friends watch out for openings for watchmen or gardeners and help instal new migrants. While none of them starves or remains idle on arrival in the city, almost all have to wait a long time to get regular employment, sometimes up to ten years. Some have been working in the city for more than twenty years and still do not have a permanent job. They earn only Rs. 200-250 per month (Rs. 10 = $ 1.00.) or Rs. 7 to 8 as daily wages. Of the twenty-six migrants whose monthly earnings fall in this range, nearly one-third belong to the EM. Seventy-two per cent of those earning between Rs. 250-300 per month belong to EM. Only about one-third earn more than Rs. 300 per month, all belonging to EM. Thus, it is a hard struggle.

The expenditure on food and other essential items is reported to be Rs. 150 per month. This is the minimum that a migrant needs. The new entrants who stay with relatives/friends on arrival in the city have to pay at the rate of Rs. 2.50 per meal. They face tough competition for getting work on a daily basis on construction sites or in parks, etc. In Delhi most labourers are drawn either from Rajasthan or from eastern Uttar Pradesh. The latter are known as 'poorvias'. The migrant from Rajasthan is considered hard-working and efficient and as such has an edge over his 'poorvia' counterpart. Thus the new entrants from eastern Uttar Pradesh do get work for all the days in a month. They frequently fail to earn even Rs. 150 a month. They have, therefore to depend upon the continued support of their relatives and friends for quite sometime. During this period they are not in a position to send home any money or presents. Nor can they visit the village. Even after they manage to obtain regular work for the whole month, they cannot send money home, as they have to first pay off the amount they owe to their relatives and friends who helped them to move to the city and who sustained them through their initial period of settling down. This may take a period of two to three years or even more. During this period, the parents who do not receive any remittance from the migrant label as 'useless', inconsiderate and spoiled in the city. They begin to criticize his wife back home. Some parents may even send the migrant's wife to the city with the migrant who is returning after a visit to the village.

Before finding a regular job, a migrant has to accept any work that may be available. Work on construction sites and roads. Work in municipal parks on a daily basis, gardening on a part-time basis in number of houses for about half an hour daily in each house, security for a group of houses, head-loading, cart-pulling, etc., are some of the jobs with a migrant takes up before he manages to find a regular job. In order to get a regular job, he has to win the favours of the contractor, clerk, or the agent of the contractor or the employer with whom he works on a daily basis. This is a long drawn-out affair and in the process he has to change jobs a number of times. Nearly three-fourths of the migrants reported frequent change of jobs. The remaining one-fourths, though they have worked on daily basis for a fairly long time, were lucky to get taken on in the same job. Most of these belong to EM category.

Thus the LM category has to work at several places before obtaining a regular job. About 24 per cent of the migrants have been in their present jobs for less than a year, and in most cases it is not of a regular nature. Another 32 per cent have been engaged in their present jobs for one to three years. This includes some of the EM, which discloses the fact that it took them a minimum of seven to nine years to get their present jobs. Only 32 per cent have been in their present jobs for more than five years. With the exception of three, who belong to LM category, all the others belong to EM.

At present, seventeen migrants (twelve LM and five EM) are not in a position to send any money to their families. Another thirty-eight (twenty-two LM and sixteen EM) have been able to send home a sum of Rs. 50 per month. Most of them fail to send this amount regularly. The maximum amount that a migrant sends home is Rs. 150 per month. This, however, is done only by a few. Only twelve of the seventeen migrants who send more than Rs. 100 per month belong to EM category. Thus, in the first five years, a migrant may not send any money at all; in the next five to ten years he may send about Rs. 50 per month, and it is only after twenty years of work that he may be in a position to send Rs. 100 or more.

The primary reason for coming to the city is to obtain employment, yet a large percentage of the migrants (79 per cent) are dissatisfied (partly or fully) with their jobs. Of these, the LM form the larger category. This is understandable, in view of the fact that they are still struggling to gain a foothold in the city. Lack of job security, low wages, and poor working conditions cause frustration. At the same time, the inability to send money home, because of the above factors, further aggravates the situation. The village family, on the other hand, believes that the migrant member is having fun in the city and is neglecting the family.

The females in the village families suffer prolonged separation and live in constant anxiety about dangers to their men in the city, and when financial support does not come as a compensation they feel miserable. When a man cannot remit money home, he does not visit the village. This further increases the unhappiness of the wife. Of the fourteen migrants who have not been able to visit to their family even once since they came to Delhi, thirteen are LM. The remaining visit the village for different periods. This is linked with the purposes of the visit. Those who go home during harvest (thirty-one of the fifty-three EM, who are also mainly peasants) spend a month or more there. The next important purpose is to visit the village on the occasion of a festival (Holi) or a marriage/social ceremony in the family, which may mean spending ten to fifteen days there. An emergency, such as sudden sickness, death, etc. may summon a man to the village for ten days or less. If he holds a temporary or daily-wage job, he has to forgo wages for that period and borrow some money to reach his home. A small number pay a routine family visit once a year. It was observed that when the frequency of visits is lower, the duration of stay in the village is longer and vice versa.

In the city the majority of the migrants spend the weekly holiday at home, doing washing, cooking and other chores; a few find time to visit friends or relatives. Only four persons said they sometimes go to the cinema. Their thoughts and actions revolve around problems concerning the family in the village. Sixty-seven wish to return to the village at the end of their working lives (these are mostly EM). Those who are uncertain about future plans are in the LM category, too preoccupied with the immediate, pressing problem of regular employment and unwilling to think of a distant future. Only four said they would bring their families to the city to settle down. Their sons are studying in the village, but they have no land in the village; and a house site has been allotted to them by the government in the city.

Most of the migrants reported that circumstances in the village forced them to the city rather than the attraction of city life. Only a few admitted their personal preference for city life.

The factors responsible for migration to the city, as stated by the villagers in our sample, are discussed below.

Push Factors

First, mechanization not only reduces the number of labourers required to prepare a field (one tractor replaces twenty ploughmen) but also negates the taboo on ploughing for higher castes. Thus landless labourers are replaced by machines that can be operated by the owner-cultivators themselves (who not only prepare their own fields, but, for remuneration, prepare those of other farmers as well).

Another factor is the change in the crops and cropping patterns—inferior crops (gram, barley, etc.) have been replaced by superior crops (wheat, rice); late-sowing wheat varieties have been introduced. This shift from a subsistence to a market economy, coupled with assured means of irrigation and increasing mechanization, has reduced the dependence on manual labour. The traditional methods of irrigation—'dhekul'[2] and 'purvat'[3]—were highly labour intensive and required animal power, too. With the introduction of power-driven tubewells, they are a rare sight on bigger farms.

Labour displacement is also caused by the introduction of herbicides and pesticides, which reduce the need for manual hoeing and weeding. Winnowing and threshing are also being mechanized, and this leaves only harvesting as the employment-providing operation. The other form of employment is that of an attached agricultural labourers on Rs. 75 to Rs. 150 a month. These people have no fixed working hours, are perpetually in debt to the landowner, and work virtually as bonded labourers.

The increase in profits from agriculture has barely touched the wage structure in Uttar Pradesh. The current rate is more or less the same as it was at the beginning of the century; given in the form of food grains, it amounts roughly to Rs. 3 per day, depending on the operations performed. This is not enough to feed the worker and his family, and there is no possibility of meeting other needs. On the other hand, the demands of modern agriculture have led to stricter control and supervision from the owner-cultivators, often requiring harder labour and longer hours.

Finally, there is the social humiliation that landless Harijans have to face from the upper castes. While the older generation accepted this, the younger generation is questioning the inegalitarian and oppressive structure of caste and economic relations. The oppression and exploitation are reduced to some extent when they move from the parochial scene to other rural areas (like Punjab) or to cities and towns (like Delhi). Here they assume a new identity and are spared some of the indignities suffered by them in the village. Besides, economic opportunities are better, and they are paid in cash rather than in kind. In fact, they never starve in Delhi. As one of them says, 'With a basket and a spade we can always earn our daily bread'.

Pull Factors

The Green Revolution in the late 1960s coincided with the increased expansion of the city of Delhi: continuous building construction generated employment for unskilled and semi-skilled labourers. Besides, Delhi is a garden city, with lovely green lawns and palatial house with private gardens, all requiring gardeners, watchmen and other domestic help. The landless agricultural labourers, although not trained as gardeners, find the task of gardening closer to their previous experience and opt for it. With the help of their village acquaintances in town they learn the job and obtain employment.

The other group of migrants are petty peasants who are unable to support their families with the meagre holdings they have. Earlier they were able to get some land on lease from the big landowners, but with the reduction in the size of the latter's holdings and the increasing interest in owner-cultivation, the peasants find it difficult to extend their operational holding. They migrate to the city to supplement the family income. They are always nostalgic about the village, because of their attachment to the land. Unlike Harijan, they do not suffer from any social stigma in the village.

Thus migrants of the two caste groups leave the village because *(a)* the village economy no longer suffices to support their family, *(b)* the social oppression and exploitation of some caste groups pushes them towards more egalitarian structure, and *(c)* opportunities for work are available because of the opening up of new labour markets in the metropolis. The migrants are in the peculiar position of being tied to the city because of these push and pull factors, but on the other hand their emotional ties and even to some extent their economic security (in the case of migrants who own small amounts of land) remain in the village.

Though they live and work in the city until they retire or are unfit to work there any more, they return annually (sometimes every six months) to the village, especially at harvest time to help their families on their own land and/or earn a little extra money or grain by working for others. Because of landed property in the village, they do not sever connections with it. Besides they find it more economical to keep the family in the village home.

Table 3.7
Statistical Profile of Migrants

	Number of migrants	Years in the city			
		Up to 5	5 to 10	10-20	above 20
Caste					
Peasants	57	2	15	23	17
Scheduled castes	37	13	12	6	6
Others	3	—	2	1	—
Total	97	15	29	30	23
Principal Occupation of the family					
Cultivation	46	6	11	9	20
Agricultural labour	45	6	16	20	3
Traditional	6	3	2	1	—
Total	97	15	29	30	23
Operational holding (hectares)					
None	27	5	9	10	3
Less than 1	35	6	11	13	5
1-2	23	4	3	4	12
2 and above	12	—	6	3	3
Total	97	15	29	30	23
Age Group					
20-25	13	12	1	—	—
25-30	30	3	26	1	—
30-35	16	—	2	14	—
35-40	13	—	—	12	1
40-45	20	—	—	3	17
45-50	4	—	—	—	4
50-55	1	—	—	—	1
Total	97	15	29	30	23
Education					
Illiterate	71	6	20	25	20
Primary	18	3	7	5	3
Secondary	6	4	2	—	—
College	2	2	—	—	—
Total	97	15	29	30	23

(Contd.)

	Number of migrants	*Years in the city*			
		Up to 5	*5 to 10*	*10-20*	*above 20*
Status before migration					
Student	8	8	—	—	—
Farmer, Craftsman	36	1	7	11	17
Wage-earner	39	2	12	19	6
Jobless	14	4	10	—	—
Total	97	15	29	30	23
By whom advised to come to city					
Village friend	17	—	3	12	2
Father	11	7	4	—	—
Relative	43	8	18	10	7
Own decision	26	—	4	8	14
Total	97	15	29	30	23
With whom came to city					
Village friend	15	—	7	6	2
Father	11	7	4	—	—
Relative	50	8	18	15	9
Other person	21	—	—	9	12
Total	97	15	29	30	23
With whom stayed in the city					
Village fellow	20	—	8	10	2
Father	11	7	4	—	—
Relative	41	8	17	11	5
Own arrangement	25	—	—	9	16
Total	97	15	29	30	23
Amount earned (Rs.)					
Less than 200	6	4	2	—	—
200-250	26	9	8	5	4
250-300	36	1	9	14	12
Above 300	29	1	10	11	7
Total	97	15	29	30	23

(Contd.)

	Number of migrants	Years in the city			
		Up to 5	5 to 10	10-20	above 20
Amount sent home (Rs.)					
Nothing	17	8	4	3	2
Up to 50	38	4	12	12	10
50-100	25	3	8	9	5
100 and above	17	—	5	6	6
Total	97	15	29	30	23
Attitude towards present job					
Happy	61	15	20	16	10
Partially Happy	15	—	7	4	4
Satisfied	11	—	2	3	6
Do not mind	10	—	—	7	3
Total	97	15	29	30	23
Frequency of visits to village					
No visit	14	12	1	—	1
Once a year	7	—	—	4	3
Twice a year	19	—	5	10	4
Three times a year	57	3	23	16	15
Total	97	15	29	30	23
Plans for the future					
Permanent return to village	67	5	15	27	20
Do not know	26	10	14	2	—
Bring family to city	4	—	—	1	3
Total	97	15	29	30	23

The sons are no better off than their fathers, as education is not perceived as a means to increase economic status. Two college-educated boys, unable to procure white-collar jobs and working as gardeners, act as deterrent to others who want higher education. The two educated migrants are making use of their education by forming an association of their caste fellows in Delhi. They have even sanskritized their caste name from 'Muraon' to 'Maurya' (the founder of the Maurya Dynasty had a low-caste mother). They have been able to exert some influence and get employment for the wives of two gardeners who died during service.

References

1. *Census of India 1961, Vol. XIX Delhi—Part II-C Cultural and migration Tables;* Table D-IV Census of India 1971. Series 27, Delhi, Part II-A. General Population Tables; *Jhuggi Jhopri Settlements in Delhi Part II,* Town and Country Planning Organization, Delhi, Mimeograph, 1975. The nine industrial categories are: cultivators agricultural labourers, livestocks, mining and quarrying, industry (household, and other than household), construction, trade and commerce, transport, etc., and other services.
2. A method in which water is drawn from a well with the help of a long bamboo, at one end of which is a bucket and at the other a heavy weight. This is manoeuvred to lower the bucket into the well and to draw it out after it is filled.
3. A big leather bucket is tied to rope operated by bullocks, which move to and for, drawing out the water from the well. Manual supervision is required for emptying the bucket into water channels and for guiding the bullocks.

4

Women's Work and Migration

Introduction

Migration provides an excellent example of the way in which women's activities can appear to be almost invisible to policy makers and researchers. In many areas of the world women move at marriage to live with their new husbands, and often with their husbands' families. The husbands continue to live where they were born. Thus cultural rules prohibiting marriage with persons who are closely related or who come from the same group, result in a continuous stream of female marital migration. In many areas such marital migration actually constitutes a majority of all migratory moves. Yet marital migrations are very often neglected in the vast literature on migration in the developing world.
The main reasons for this neglect would appear to be:

(i) that women's migrations are considered to be unimportant;
(ii) that the movement of women is considered to have little economic significance; and
(iii) that much of this migration is from one rural area to another and such rural-rural migration is generally ignored in face of the overwhelming concern with rural-urban migration.

Prior to the 1970s at least nine out of ten studies of migration were restricted to male migration, although their titles rarely give any indication of this fact. Even where males form the great majority of the migration streams (as in urban India and during the colonial development of Africa) this approach ignored the vital question of what was happening in the areas where women are left on their own because of heavy male out-migration.

Since the early 1970s there has been increasing interest in female migration and especially in economically motivated women moving independently to the cities. There have also been a growing number of references to the impact of the out-migration of males upon the preponderently female populations left behind in the areas of origin, although actual research is still very rare. If the topics covered by international conferences and special issues of journals are any guide, then female migration is rapidly becoming a fashionable topic (*Anthropological Quarterly 1976; Signs, 1977; Migration Today, 1979;* Churches' Committee on Migrant Workers, 1979; East-West Population Institute, 1979). Yet it is still remarkable how many studies persist in treating women as being more passive in the migration process (see, for example, De Souza and Singh 1976; M & J Gulick 1976). However, this current fashion has provoked a sharp protest against the very idea of treating female migration as a topic worthy of study in its own right. It has been argued that female migration should only be approached in the broader context of the family or the kin group as a whole (Leeds, 1976).

While it is generally true that all human actions should be studied in a wider social context, there are three good reasons for focussing upon female migration:

(i) general migration studies usually devote less than 5 per cent of their pages to female migration;

(ii) the nature of female migration is undergoing rapid change in many areas; and

(iii) even where women do migrate to accompany their husbands or parents their experiences are very different.

Very little is known about how decisions to migrate or to stay behind are reached, or the role that women play in such decisions. There are also pressing problems in areas where food production is declining in the wake of heavy male out-migration. This creates areas with female majorities which pose unique development and welfare challenges. There is also a more general concern that the division between treating men as part of the wide world of public life but treating women only as a part of the private sphere of the family is a false and harmful dichotomy which contributes to the perpetuation of inequalities or even creates new ones.

Even without further surveys the scope for studies of female migration is certainly very great, since almost all official migration statistics are published with information on the sex, and often the age, of migrants. While there are problems in deciding from the statistics which women move independently and which women move as *associated migrants* accompanying or joining husbands or parents, this problem has been overstressed. Men may move alone or in order to join their brothers or uncles but this does not prevent the study of male migration. Certainly, whether they move independently, or as part of a family or kin group, or even stay behind, women are just as affected by migration as men.

Table 4.1 presents a basic typology of the different forms of female migration together with references to some of the more interesting studies where the individual types have been examined.

Table 4.1
Types of Female Migration

Types of Migrant and Motive	*Country*	*Source*
1. Young Girls with parents	General	Yousself *et al.* 1979
2. Girls alone for education	Ghana	Caldwell, 1969
	Ivory Coast	Roussel 1970
	Solomon Islands	Chapman 1976
3. Young unmarried women to work: as domestic servants	Latin America	Jelin, 1977
	Smith, 1973	
: as factory workers	Malaysia	Ariffin, 1978
	Oceania	Haman, 1978
: as prostitutes	Indonesia	Papanek, 1975
: as prostitutes (divorcees)	Nigeria	Cohen, 1969
4. Young unmarried women in		

(Contd.)

Types of Migrant and Motive	*Country*	*Source*
search of adventure	West Africa	Little 1973
in search of husbands	Oceania	Stanhope, and Prior, 1977
5. Unmarried mothers	Uganda	Obbo, 1975, Nelson, 1979
6. Marital Migration	Cameroon	Podlewski, 1975
	India	Majumder, 1977.; Libbee and Sopher, 1975
7. Married women moving with their husbands	India	Singh, 1978
	Iran	Bauer, 1979
	New Guinea	Oeser, 1969
8. Married women alone		
: as servants	Niger	Diarra, 1974
: as traders	Nigeria, Ghana	Sudarkasa, 1977, Nadel, 1942
: for childbirth	Papua New Guinea	Young, 1977
9. Widows and Divorcees	India	Committee on the Status of Women, 1974
	Malaysia	Strange, 1976
10. Grandmothers as child-minders	Oceania	Stanhope and Prior, 1977
11. Circulating women	Hong Kong, Malaysia	Strauch, 1979
12. Nomads	Australia	Gale, 1974
	Iran	Beck, 1978
	West Africa	Riesman, 1974
13. Refugees	General	UN High Commissioner, 1980

Female Migration Theory

One of the famous 'laws of migration' compiled by Ravenstein in the 1880s stated that, while males form the majority of those who move over long distance, females are more likely to move over short distances (Ravenstein, 1885). This is still true of rural-urban migration in areas where Western Europeans or their descendents live. Rural women are more likely than rural men to move into nearby towns. Thus there are proportionately more females in the urban areas than in the rural areas in all the countries of North and South America (except Peru). The same relative excess of females in the urban areas is found in the great majority of European countries. In contrast, the United Nations *Demographic Yearbooks* show that in most non-European societies (except the Philippines), there is a higher sex ratio (males per 100 to females) in the urban areas than in the rural areas.

Bogue (1969) has argued that the sex ratio of migration streams depends less on the distance to be covered than on the level of development. In the early stages of development males predominate because of the risks involved and the cultural traditions which restrain the movement of women. Over time migration becomes more routine and commonplace. Men move more permanently and are more likely to bring their wives and families with them, or to sent for their families to join them later. Thus the proportion of females amongst the migrants rises. Bogue's hypothesis was based upon the United States' experience and does not take into account the re-enforcing role of many colonial governments in only permitting males to live in newly developed towns, mining camps and plantations. It also fails to consider cultural differences in the extent to which pioneering activities are considered suitable for women.

There has been considerable debate over the extent to which women's traditional roles in rural society influence their migration patterns. On one side Boserup (1970) has argued that the massive migration of young women to the towns of Latin America results from the fact that 'poor farmers send their daughters to town to become domestic servants, because they are not needed at home if the mother does little more than domestic duties'. On the other side Singh (1978) has claimed that the extent to which Indian wives accompany their husbands *in moves* to the towns depends upon the wife's economic contribution in the town. Where the wife is a direct income producer at home, she expects to continue helping in the town and thus the fact that it would be cheaper for her and the children to continue to live in the village is less relevant.

Elsewhere, Boserup (1970) has stated that the 'activity pattern of immigrant women in the town is determined primarily by the customary pattern of female employment in the village, and especially by the extent to which women participate in non-agricultural activities in the village'. Yet her own classification of rural and urban activity rates disproves her claim. It is true that in the Arab countries activity rates are low in both settings (though the low rural rates often reflect the ideal rather than the reality), and that in southeast Asia both rates are high. However, in Latin America low rural rates are in conflict with high urban rates whilst the converse is true in Tropical Africa, as Thadani and Todaro (1979) have noted. There certainly are numerous cases where women migrate to the towns despite the fact that the opportunities there for women are pitifully limited (see Nelson, 1979 for Kenya; and Oeser, 1969 for New Guinea). In some cases women may be happy to escape the drudgery of work in the village (see Caldwell, 1969 on Ghana), in others they may be frustrated by the lack of work to do in the city (see Routh, 1976 for Tanzania)* . Obviously much must depend upon the cultural acceptability of the separation of husband and wife. It would appear that in many of the developing countries acceptance of the prolonged separation of spouses is grater than in European cultures, but it is difficult to tell how far this reflects different choices. Togetherness may be a luxury beyond reach for the very poor.

It has been argued that the assumption that female migration reflects family or household migration will hold true in patrilineal societies where men control subordinate women (Connell *et al.*, 1976). One interesting question is whether autonomous female migration is a cause or a consequence of the liberation of women. In the Ivory Coast, amongst the Baoule, women migrate as an act of defiance against the men and out-number them in the migration flows (Joshi, 1973). The situation in which migration is itself a liberating experience is probably more common, although one reason why domestic service is such a popular occupation for

---

* 'At home there is plenty of work while here she feels she is idle. In the country, although work is arduous, there is something to keep one busy. here she feels she is depending too much on her husband. At home she did play a part in feeding the family, but she has not got that role here' (A messenger's wife, Dar-es-Salaam, quoted in Routh 1976.

women migrant is presumably the fact that live-in domestics are under the care of their employers 24 hours a day. Very little is known about the impact of the first women leaving the village as independent migrants although there are many cases where migrant chains are set up with girls from one area entering the same firm or trade (see Hart, 1971 for the Philippines and Hugo 1978 for Indonesia). Education is a liberating factor in itself and through its contribution to migration. Often there is even less for educated girls to do in the village than for educated boys, although this will be relatively unimportant where girls are simple expected to become dependent wives.

Thadani and Todaro (1979) have recently presented a very interesting formal model for the analysis of female migration. This model takes into account employment probabilities and income differentials in the formal and informal sectors; the chances of a women improving her status by marriage to a man of superior social status; marital migration where women move in order to secure acceptable husband; associational migration where the wife moves because the husbands does; and culturally defined sex-role constraints upon the movement of females. Although this represents a great improvement on the assumptions that women only move when following men, or that there is nothing distinctive about female migration, the model still has a number of weaknesses. The authors are obviously very much impressed by the fact that whereas men can only improve their status by getting more education or a better job, women have a third option: to marry well. The result is a model which appears to be obsessed with marriage (although this is marriage defined 'to include a wide variety of arrangements and forms of co-habitation').

One of the assumptions upon which the model is based is that the greater the degree of discrimination against women in the towns in employment and wages, the less likely women are to migrate. Where women do migrate despite considerable discrimination this is said to be because their chances of making an advantageous marriage are increased by that same discrimination since is increases the number of higher status males. Essentially the model concentrates upon factors which will attract women to migrate. It takes little account of factors which may force women to leave home, such an ex-nuptial pregnancy. Again the model is focussed upon women in the 15-44 age range and does not cover the case of the young women who moves in order to secure an education or the older woman going to live with her children when widowed or divorced.

Recent developments in migration research have tended to stress the importance of circulation and general mobility rather than examining migration as a 'once-and-for-always' process (Chapman and Prothero, 1981). It can be expected that further research on women will take this trend into account and will examine all forms of movement by women. Thus, for example, in many societies where women move into their husband's homes at marriage, they move back into their own parents' homes for the first birth, and often for several subsequent births (Young, 1977). Such moves have been little studied up until now but they are very significant in a wide range of contexts from the confusion of birthplace statistics to their implications for family planning programmes.

In terms of policy the theories of Boserup and Thadani and Todaro have very different implications. Boserup (1970) has argued that governments which wish to slow done rural-urban migration should concentrate upon integrating women who are already living in the cities on equal terms so that they can take up the opportunities which would otherwise be seized upon by immigrant men. Her view is that it is much more efficient to utilize those who are in the towns already rather than to encourage new male immigrants who will bring their families with them and require considerable further infrastructural investments.

In contrast, Thadani and Todaro's model implies their governments should encourage discrimination against women as a means of slowing down rates of urban growth. They argue that women will come to marry higher status men in any case, but that if they also have good income-earning opportunities of their own they will migrate at a more rapid rate, drawing after them men who cannot find brides at home. If there is sufficient discrimination against women then women will be under cultural constraints not to move and urban growth will be composed largely of men travelling alone.

For governments which are also interested in slowing down national rates of population growth the situation will be more complex and the range of competing advice greater. In as much as urban fertility levels are lower than rural levels and the employment of unmarried women delays marriage, they should encourage female migration of the towns (Papanek, 1976; Yoursseff, 1978).

Female Migration Patterns Around the World

An examination of female migration patterns around the world will serve to make it clear that there are very great regional variations in these patterns and that these variations are not simply a reflection of differing levels of development or of different cultural traditions as to the roles of women (Connel *et al.*, 1976; Simmons *et al.*, 1977).

Latin America

Latin America is the one region of the developing world where females clearly predominate in rural-urban migration streams (United Nations, 1977). Throughout the remainder of the developing world, until 1970 at least, men formed the majority of those moving to the towns but now their preponderance is being more or less rapidly eroded. An extreme case of female predominance can be found in Chile where migrants to Santiago aged 15-24 included only 64 males for every 100 females (Herrick, 1965). In Latin America women move to the cities to take up work as domestic servants (Elizaga, 1970; Jelin, 1977; Melville, 1978).

Ravenstein's theory that women predominate in short-distance moves is confirmed in some cases but not in others. The greater availability of certain 'female' jobs in nearby areas may induce short-distance female migration, whereas males are more heavily involved in long distance migration to 'frontier' areas and to distant regions requiring seasonal farm labour. Males also often undergo along distance moves in the course of their military service; these may be followed up by permanent migration. Adams (1969) found that Colombian girls living close to large cities could easily find urban employment as domestics, Clerks or industrial workers. In contrast, in Peru women tend to predominate on the long distance moves (Allers and Applebaum, 1968). This is because the capital and the large cities are distant from the densely populated rural areas where female domestic servants are recruited. There were some 90,000 female domestic servants in the Peruvian capital in 1966-67 (Smith, 1973). These servants comprised almost 10 per cent of all women aged 25-59 and over 60 per cent of all women in the city's labour force. Thus, the distances covered by women migrants would appear to be determined more by the location of the opportunities available to them than by reduced risks associated with the advance of development, as Bogue (1969) argued.

Substantial variations in sex selectivity of migration by age can be seen within Latin America and elsewhere. Females tend to migrate at somewhat younger ages than males. Differential availability of employment opportunities by sex, culturally determined sex roles, and social limitations during the life-cycle associated with marriage and motherhood impose constraints that limit the ages at which women are responsive to the opportunities available. In Santiago women migrants predominate at all ages but the sex ratio (of males per 100 females) rises from 62 at 15-39 years to 75 at 30-49 years (Elizaga, 1970). At older ages female migration responds more to family obligations than to direct economic factors: hence at these ages the sex selectivity of migration is less pronounced (Brown, 1970).

West Africa

In colonial times migration almost always involved males who moved and woman who stayed behind. Thus one survey of migration to Ghana and the Ivory Coast in 1958-59 found that 92 per cent of the half million migrants surveyed were males (Roussel, 1975). This male preponderance reflected both the nature of the work to be done and colonial prejudices about the nature of suitable work for woman. Males were recruited to build up roads, railways and mining enterprizes, and to work on plantations, even in areas where women were traditionally more involved in farming than men. When looking for white-collar employees the colonial authorities thought largely in terms of educating and employing men.

Since independence it has been found that 'that the female propensity for rural-urban migration is rising faster than the male' (Caldwell, 1968). This represents a 'predictable response to actual or perceived opportunities for employment, education, and /or marriage in the cities' (Sudarkasa, 1977).

Even in Upper Volta, where women have made limited formal progress in education or employments, the 1975 census shows that the number of female international migrants rose by 453 per cent between 1960 and 1975 while the number of males rose only by 153 per cent (although from a larger base number). Internally, male migrants have a slight predominance in rural-urban moves (especially past age 30) but females are responsible for the majority of rural-rural migration since it is customary for women to out-marry and to move to their husbands' villages at marriage (Mair, 1969).

Amongst the Zarma of Niger there is a preponderance of male migration but this is 'explained by the fact that the man, under pressure from his wife and from the need to pay taxes, has to emigrate to where there is the possibility of actually obtaining money ... in lesser proportion, women also emigrate, to help to pay taxes' but they are much less likely to travel internationally. 'In Zarma society men and women are complementary with no relation of inferiority'. However, the introduction of Islam and the monetarization of the economy have not been of benefit to women. Women who move abroad are often childless divorcees. Women who move to the capital have no qualifications and are being displaced from their unskilled work as water-carriers and grain pounders by the introduction of pipe-borne water and mechanical grinders. In some cases, the wives of an old disabled polygamist take it in turns to go to the capital to work (Diarra 1974).

The women traders of West Africa are famous and their mobility is very important although it usually only covers relatively short distances (Bohanan and Dalton, 1962). Women traders have contributed a great deal to the widespread availability of a great range of commodities and to the introduction of new techniques and machines such as pepper-grinders and oil-extorters. Women who travel make rural woman aware of the wider world beyond and what is has to offer. Strikingly, in this case it is not so much the separation of husband and wives by migration which contributes to changes in family structure as their joint travel into new circumstances (Sudarkasa, 1977).

Other Africa

Very little is known of women's migrations in Moslem North Africa but it is generally assumed that women move only as appendages of men. Even such an interesting indicator as the proportion of women amongst those travelling to Mecca does not appeal to be available (Constatinides, 1979).

In East Africa women are noted for their major contribution to agricultural production but they engage in few non-agricultural activities and play very little role in trade. Thus the productivity of their agricultural roles in contrast to the very limited urban employment opportunities for women, even in the informal sector, restrains women from moving to the cities (Thadani, 1978; Nelson, 1979). However, here too, rising levels of female education are encouraging an increase in the proportion of females amongst rural-urban migrants.

In Southern Africa life is dominated by the absence of men who have left to work in the mines and farms of South Africa. The urban centres of Botswana and Lesotho are relatively insignificant but do attract educated women from the villages. Also in Zambia in the 1960s the migration of women to the cities exceeded that of men (Heisler, 1974). In Zaire, the colonial government (in common with a number of other colonial governments) was originally much opposed to the cost of women accompanying male migrants to the towns and mines when the women could stay at home in the village and support themselves. There was also much concern at the fact that women who moved to the towns are freed from many of the traditional constraints of village life, had little to do, and were likely to resort to divorce, prostitution and alcoholism.

South-east Asia

The general idea that migrants are usually males has come under increasing attack in Southeast Asia. The predominance of females in many migration streams in the Philippines has been attributed to a pattern of urban employment opportunities similar to that found in Latin America (Connell *et al.*, 1976). It is also true that the Filipino tradition of autonomy for woman has survived both Catholicism and Colonialism (Gonzalez and Hollnsteiner, 1976). Pryor (1977) has argued that since 60 per cent of rural-urban migrants in Southeast Asia are under 30 and females now predominate amongst migrants under 25 'the notion of male dominance is either incorrect or these has been a marked change in the late 1960s: males are now only predominate in the age group 25-34 years, and then with the exception of Manila, whose consistently low ratios are in part products of the relative equality of educational opportunities open to Filipinos'. He has also noted that in Malaysia and Indonesia the sex ratio rises with the length of residence in the city. This probably reflects recent changes in the sex ratio of those leaving the rural areas and the fact that female migrants go home if they neither marry nor find suitable work in the city. In Malaysia there has recently been a significant change in the sex composition of migration streams as a result of a dramatic increase in the number of females leaving the rural areas for work in urban industrial centres (Khoo and Pirie, 1979; Araffin, 1978).

There is a range of census and survey evidence to suggest that female rural-urban migration is increasing in Indonesia, Korea, Malaysia, positions as domestic servants. Thus in the 1971 Indonesian census 66 per cent of all female migrants to Jakarta aged 15-19 were in service occupations. In Bangkok 46 per cent of all female service workers and 70 per cent of women aged 11-24 employed in services are migrants. In contrast, only 15 per cent of Bangkok's female non-migrant labour force is employed in services (Goldstein *et al.*, 1974). Zablan (1977) found that over 80 per cent of female migrants to Cebu City in the Philippines were in low status service occupations.

In one very interesting study of 'Socio-economic correlates of female migration in North Thailand', Muecke (1979) has described some of the traditional constraints upon migration for women in a matrilineal society. Basically, women had to stay in their home villages to care for the ancestral spirits. As the importance of the ancestral spirits declined, women were able to move to the towns but they also lost one of the roles in life which gave them most status. The best predictor of successful urban adjustment is education rather than migrant status which is not surprising since many of the better-educated migrants in the northern towns of Chaing Mai have come from the capital, Bangkok.

In Malaysia, young Malay women used to be kept in the rural areas to protect their virtue and also because their labour was needed for agricultural and household work. Now the use of machines and labour saving techniques in rice-growing and rubber tapping have reduced the demand for their labour and allowed them to stay longer in school at a time when the imposition of 30 per cent Malay quotas in industrial employment has opened up job opportunities for educated girls in the urban areas. At least 30,000 women have been recruited to the cities for factory work with dormitory housing provided. The idea of young unmarried Malay women living by themselves in cities indicates a revolutionary change in Malay values and social orginazation (Khoo and Pirie, 1979; Araffin, 1978; Strange, 1976).

South Asia

Pakistan and Bangladesh: Very little information is available on rural-urban migration of women in Pakistan and Bangladesh. The small amount of data which is available suggests that the low levels of development on these countries is accompanied by a very low level of independent female migration. Researchers assume that the migration of women is all associatoinal and linked to the movement of parents or husbands (Papanek, 1971).

India: Marital migration, which is the most important form of female migration in India, especially in the rural areas of the North, will be discussed separately as a distinct and much neglected form of migration.

Looking at the overall picture there is clear evidence that sex-ratios in rural-urban migration streams are affected both by the distances involved and the size of the city. The 1971 Census of India showed 82 males per 100 females in intra-district moves, 104 in inter-district moves, and 142 in inter-state moves. In movements to smaller towns, females actually exceeded males, in medium sized towns there are equal numbers of migrants of each sex, and it is only in the movement to the four latest cities that males clearly predominate (Singh, 1978).

India is one of the few countries in the world where males outnumber females in the population as a whole. In 1901 the sex ratio was 103 males per 100 females. Remarkably, by 1971 it had risen to 108. However, while the sex ratio in the rural areas has risen from 104 in 1961 to 105 in 1971, in the urban areas it has declined from 118 to 109. This is because females are increasingly likely to join males in migrating from rural to urban areas, (but are decreasingly likely to be married out of the towns and to men living in the villages) and because of the growing impact of women bearing their children (of both sexes) in the towns (Joshi, 1976).

Data on the causes of migration from the 1950s showed that 46 per cent of females but only 0.6 per cent males migrated because of marriage. Only three per cent of females migrated for employment reasons in contrast to 40 per cent of males. Males also greatly out numbered females amongst those moving for studies, business, transfer or political reasons. While 28 per cent of females migrated with a wage-earning spouse or as a dependent of the parental household, only 19 per cent of males were in this position. The male preponderance in movements to the four largest cities reflected the importance of employment and political reasons in influencing moves to these destinations (Premi, 1979).

Husbands in most cultures are likely to report that their wives' moves were made in order to accompany their husbands. This tends to obscure the extent to which the whole family shares in the economic motivation for migration. In her study of the squatter settlements of New Delhi, Singh (1977) found that 81 per cent of women cited poverty or other economic reasons as their primary reason for moving; but family, kinship and caste considerations were more important in deciding where the destination of the move should be.

In the urban areas of India females exceed males at ages 0-17 and over the age of 45. Males predominate at ages 18-44 because they are most likely to migrate during these their most economically productive years, while older women who have been widowed or deserted 'find the city a place of last refuge' (Singh, 1978). The Indian Committee on the Status of women (1974) stressed the substantial proportion of widows, divorcees or deserted women amongst female migrants.

Some regions have very low rates of female migration to the urban areas. The highest sex ratios in nearly every city are to be found amongst migrants from Uttar Pradesh, Bihar, Orissa and Kerala, while the proportion of woman is consistently high among migrants from Madhya Pradesh, Maharashtra, Gujarat, Bengal and the South Indian states (except Kerala). This is still true regardless of the distance to be covered. This reflects the fact that it is the localized cultural norms defining the roles of women which determine the proportion of females in outmigration streams and not simply the distance to be covered nor the level of development in the areas of origin (Singh, 1978).

Saxena (1977) found that among those leaving the four villages he studied in Uttar Pradesh there were only 21 females for every 100 men. He attributed the lack of female migrants to 'the insecure and difficult housing conditions in the urban centres', but other migrant groups face the same problems yet include higher proportions of females. Variations reflect the relative values attached to enclosed housing and protection for women as oppose to keeping the family together in one place. Migrants from Northern India, where purdah is more prevalent, perceive the city to be more dangerous and women to be more vulnerable than do migrants from the freer South (Singh, 1978).

Levels of female migration also vary with caste. Where women work openly in the villages, in those castes such as launderers and construction workers, they also join the work force in the cities. Husbands and wives are more likely to migrate together where both can earn money in the city. Recruitment to migrate is often through villages based caste and kinship networks which will recruit husband and wife as a team in those cases where it is traditional for the labour of males and females to be complementary. Thus amongst launderers women wash and men iron, and couples normally migrate together.

Singh (1977) found that amongst the New Delhi sputters 'the overall percentage of women employed in the city was exactly the same as those employed prior to migration, although the type of employment differed'. The relationship between fertility and workforce participation amongst these women migrants positive since they were driven to work by economic pressures which increased with the size of the family and the age of the children. Yet 'despite the long hours they worked and the economic motivation for working, women earned on the average less than half of men per unit of time worked' (Singh, 1978). Part of the reason why women are so badly paid is the very restricted range of occupations open to woman in India. This is not because women are specifically refused employed employment or legally excluded from particular kinds of jobs but because women look for sheltered employment preferably working with other women. A basic problem is the fact that there are almost no jobs considered suitable for women those which require no education at all and those which require graduate training or even post-graduate training. There is almost no vocational training for women in modern occupations. Tailoring is the one overcrowded exception. 'Semi-skilled and skilled occupation usually involve personal apprenticeships and degree of independence which are possible for men but not for women in such a highly sex-segregated society, (Singh, 1978).

The 1971 Indian Census showed that 72 per cent of male migrants were literate, whether they were working or not, but only 47 per cent of women migrants who were working were literate as compared to 65 per cent of women migrants who were not in the formal labour force (Mehrotra, 1974). Taking all urban women, both migrants and non-migrants, together, illiterate women were twice as likely to be in the workforce as literate women below matriculating level (7 per cent to 3 per cent) but the small elite with matriculation or above were the most likely to be in the labour force. (This was in part because labour force definitions largely exclude part-time work underestimate the contribution of illiterate workers (Joshi, 1976). Except for teachers, clerks and nurses, who together only comprise 20 per cent of the urban female workforce, the vast majority of women are found in occupations which require no education at all.

Given the occupational structure, neither literacy nor sewing skills are very useful to women. Thus education for girls is neglected by migrant parents who fear that if they educate their daughters beyond standard 5 they could not afford the dowry for an appropriate husband with equal or higher educational qualifications. Education is also associated with immorality. The lowest caste girls are the best educated among the poor slim dwellers because their parents are less concerned about their sexual purity. Girls are also handicapped by their share of household responsibilities which is grater than it would be in the village because tasks are no longer shared among the female members of the extended family.

Poor women often have to work harder in the cities than they did in the villages before migrating. They have to work all year found rather than in seasonal peaks and there is much less chance of sharing domestic tasks with older women. Thus the value of having daughters to share part of the household burden rises. For the women who are left behind in the villages while their husbands migrate the situation is easier since they are usually left within the care of joint families where tasks are shared.

The Committee on the Status of Women in India (1974) stressed that although the fact that there are twice as many female as male migrants in India is usually attributed to a combination of marriage migration and associational migration this is far from being the whole story. Massive female predominance in short distance migration is in part due to the severe under-employment of women as agricultural labourers. 'While they are deeply rooted in village life, and do not welcome moving out of the familiar boundaries, the low level of employment available to women agricultural labourers, drives them to seek short term, casual employment in nearby areas, during the non-agricultural seasons .. in construction-road building, stone breaking, major irrigation or flood control projects'.

They also stressed the impact of broken marriages, widowhood, desertion and abandonment of women on migration, as well as the frequency with which male migration results in desertion. For a women with a young family the options are '*(a)* to return to her natal family which is becoming increasingly difficult with the break down of the joint family and the rising costs of living; *(b)* to continue on her own, risking starvation and other, social dangers, for herself and her children; or *(c)* to link up her life with some other men'. Their contention was that the preponderance of females amongst migrants reflected 'the grater degree of helplessness and insecurity that affect the status of women' in India. This is reflected in the fact that while there are only 76 unmarried women for every 100 unmarried men, there are 163 divorced and separated women for each 100 divorced or separated men and 277 widows for every 100 widowers (1971 Census of India).

Marital Migration

Although this fact is usually ignored by almost all migration researchers (who are themselves predominantly males), in many traditional cultures, including India, the clear majority of all those who migrate at least once in their lives are women.* In cultures

* Connell *et al.*, 1976 justify 'leaving aside migration of women because of marriage — usually rural-rural, short-distance, balanced by movements of other brides the other way, and little influenced by policy–' on the ground that it is *not* 'sex-selective'. That is to say sex selectivity is only worthy of study when it is males who are in the majority.

where women must marry into their husbands' group as outsiders, marriage by definition entails migration for women. Marital migration is simple that migration which occurs when one (or, less commonly, both) of the partners to a marriage change their place of residence at marriage. Thus, in Cameroon ' the members of a same clan are usually united in the same villages, and as the wife usually goes to live in the husband's clan ... female mobility is everywhere more important; than male mobility' (Podlewski 1975). Equally 'in the Indian context (especially in rural areas) where occupational mobility is low, marriage migration is the major cause of total migration' (Majumder, 1977). Although in the great majority of cases wives move to join husbands, in some matrilineal societies, as in Northern Thailand, it is the husband who moves in with his wife's family.

Marital migration provides a classic example of a phenomenon which has been gravely neglected because it affects women much more than men. To date, most of the interest in the topic has come from population geneticists concerned to study how inherited variations are distributed through human populations (see the bibliography in Majumder, 1977). Apparently there are no studies of the ways in which women's lives are influenced, firstly, by always knowing throughout childhood that they must leave their home community and, secondly, by having to start all over again in a strange new place at marriage. Very young ages at marriage are often found in societies where marital migration is the normal practice, such societies believe that if a girl must inevitable have to learn to adjust to a strange place and new customs, then the sooner she moves the better. In the case of the Australian aborigines it has even been argued that if a girl did not 'marry' into a new area at the age of 7 or 8 she would be too old to learn to forage for food in unfamiliar country, although this argument has been contested by Kaberry (1939).

Marital migration is certainly yet another factor which tends to reduce the wife's status within the family. As a young stranger, sometimes even from a hostile community, the wife is never completely accepted and her advice is always open to doubt. Thus, in New Guinea, Meggitt (1976) has described the constant watchfulness of the Highland Enga who intermarry with enemy groups. He argues that there is a link between this fear of 'enemy' wives and the Enga's extreme concern with the polluting effects of menstrual discharges, for hostile women cannot be trusted to keep their husbands safe from harm. The disadvantaged position of the young stranger bride in the traditional Chinese household was proverbial, as was the contrast between a mother's kindness and a mother-in-law's harshness. In recent years the Chinese Government has encouraged late marriage and tried to reduce son-preference because of its pro-natalist impact. Thus it is laid down that where an only child who is female marries, the husband has to move in to live with his wife's parents so that the old people will not be left alone in their old age even though they had no son.

In India, Libee and Sopher (1975) have estimated the median marriage distance and the percentages of married females who were born in their village of enumeration from both the 1931 and the 1961 censuses. They found that the proportions of women engaging in marital migration had remained remarkable constant but that the median marriage distance had risen by 50 per cent. For much of Northern India the median marriage distance in 1961 was 30 kilometres and over, and less than 21 per cent of wives had been born in their village of enumeration. In general, only is Southern India had as many as 45 per cent of the wives been born in the villages where they were enumerated. In Northern India brides are generally taken from a set of villages which are different from the set of villages into which girls are given. Further, if one daughter is given into a certain family of a certain village, a second girl is not normally given into the same family or village within the next two generations (Majumder, 1977). In this system a single village may be linked by marriage with 200 to 400 other villages, and little solidarity is found amongst the women who come from such a large number of different villages. Female marital migration acts to cement solidarity amongst men while greatly weakening solidarity amongst women. At the same time stranger brides do not, at least in the early stages of marriage before the birth of children, have the alternative resource of solidarity with their husbands.

Where parents know that they will lose their daughters to stranger at the time of an early marriage they have very little motive to invest in the education or training of their daughters, unless such training is associated with a lesser dowry or a higher bride-price. In Uttar Pradesh, Roy and Kapoor (1975) found that for poor women the most frequently given reasons for quitting school were: 'My in-laws did not approve of my going to school'; 'my husband told me that I did not require any more education'; As a daughter-in-law I had too many duties at home'; and 'village people do not like a daughter-in-law going to school'. Thus the fact that at marriage a daughter ceases to be a daughter and becomes nothing more than a daughter-in-law greatly restricts the options open to women.

Motives for Migration

Since it is generally assumed that females move either in association with their parents or with their husbands, few researchers have seen any need to study female motives for migration. Even in the case of unmarried women who move independently it is considered that male economic models will cover them equally well. As has been discussed above, Thadani and Tadaro (1979) have designed a model of female migration which largely revolves about the marriage market. Very few studies appear to have asked women why they chose to move, and none appear to have posed questions such as 'Who played the most important part in the decision to move, you or your husband?' or 'Did you consider the possibility of your husband moving along, why/why not?'.

Accounts of the motives for female migration are often very schematic and restricted to the 'respectable' reasons for migration which are predominantly associated with family moves, economic betterment or education (Pryor, 1977). Also it is often assumed to be sufficient to state that wives are following husbands, although, since not all wives do follow their husbands, wives do have some degree of choice in the matter. Married women are rarely shown as moving in search of employment, yet the availability of income earning opportunities may be the factor which determines whether the wife accompanies her husband or stays behind in the village. It is sometimes implied that women are influenced to a greater degree than men by the attraction of the bright lights and amenities of the city (Little, 1973), yet no one appears to have put this theory to the test (Smith *et al.*, 1979).

One small scale survey whose results still preserve some of the flavour of the reasons for migration given by women themselves relates to a low-income unofficially settled area of

Kampala, the capital of Uganda (Obbo, 1975). Some 38 per cent of the women said that they had come because their husbands had moved; 21 per cent to the city to escape from unsatisfactory marriages; 12 per cent had been pregnant in circumstances which were strongly disapproved of in the village; 6 per cent had wanted to escape from the hard work and boredom of village life; 3 per cent were childless and could no longer bear the villagers' suspicions of the witchcraft potential of barren women; 3 per cent had thought that the city offered better economic opportunities than the villages and 2 per cent were widows who did not inherit from their husbands. The remainder gave a variety of other personal reasons. There appears to be a great gap between the neat motives of the Asian respondents recorded in Table 4.2 and these African women. In part the difference is simply one of interviewing style, but it probably also reflects the extent to which African women are prepared to stick out on their own and make a new life for themselves even after marriage (Sibisi, 1977).

Migration Decisions

Much more would be understood about the motivation of married women migrants if more were known about the process in which migration decisions are made. Despite a vast amount of research on migration very little is known about how individuals and families arrive at the decision to migrate or to stay put. There is a widespread tendency to assume that male household heads are the decision makers and that their families simply follow their lead. In Africa there are certainly some situations in which the women decide when the men should leave the rural areas to go and earn a cash income. Thus among the Zarma of Niger women grinding millet sing verses telling their men that they must go and earn the money for taxes and new clothes for if they stay behind they will not be fed (Diarra, 1974). In other cases, as amongst the Mossi of Upper Volta, the young man who has not been away to work in the richer coastal countries will be unlikely to be able to find a wife (Capron and Kohler, 1979). Again, some attempts at resettling overcrowded rural population originally failed because the Mossi wives refused to stay in new areas where there were no markets and no schools. It was only after the authorities had begun to provide the basic facilities that the women finally agreed to stay and that the new settlements began to achieve some degree of permanency.

Once again the examples are drawn from Tropical Africa where dissatisfied women are likely to vote with their feet and leave. There would appear to be a clear need for Asian studies to examine the process of decision making and the role which women play. To give but one example what role do women play in Indonesia in motivating families to join the transmigration movement?

One way in which migration may contribute to improving the status of women is by cutting the links with the husband's family in patriarchal and patrilocal societies where old men control resources and newly married couples live with the husband's father. In these cultures women and especially young brides are in a singularly powerless position because they are strangers in their husbands' families and are cut off from their families of origin. While the couple stay within husband's extended family there is often little opportunity for the couple to develop a close marital relationship. Migration away from this setting often gives the wife a much greater degree of intimacy with her husband and a much greater influence in family decision making. She may even be able to re-enter into contact with her own kin because in a strange setting men are much more willing to make use of all their kin-networks whether the relationship is through the wife or not (M and J Gulick, 1976).

One Indian study of the status of women in one largely traditional town showed that education alone was not enough to give women a degree of freedom, but that education in combination with migration so that the couple were away from the influence of the husband's parents was a liberating factor. For women who were natives of the town, the least educated were the most free to act independently because the poverty of the family meant that they were either in the work force or taking a big share of the responsibility for stretching the family budget. One study in the Philippines suggests that moving to a medium sized town contributes more to improving the status of women than does movement to the big city (Bulatao, 1979 but cf. Rengert, 1976).

Restrictions on Female Mobility

Women's mobility is subject to a great number of cultural restrictions. In the extreme case of societies which practise purdah, women do not appear in public except in veils and clothes which cover their entire bodies. In such societies males usually choose to migrate alone, leaving their women in the care of the extended family. They are very fearful of the threat posed to their women by all strangers, and will only take their women with them when they are certain of being well-established. This is the pattern found in the Middle East and the northern areas of the Indian subcontinent (Singh, 1978). Women brought up in this tradition learn to be extremely anxious when out in the streets because the expectation that they need to be protected serves in turn to justify strange men in attacking them, at least verbally (Jeffery, 1979). Independent migration becomes unthinkable for such women (Kim, 1974).

At the other extreme are those societies which allow broad freedom to unmarried women to move as independent individuals. Examples are found in Latin America, the Caribbean, the Philippines and Tropical Africa (Gugler, 1972; Melville, 1978; Mowat, 1977; Uhlenberg, 1973).

Prostitution and Migration

In many parts of the world there is an association between female migration and prostitution. A major reason for opposing the independent migration of women without husbands is the fear that they will become immoral women. Thus in Ghana 83 per cent of rural households thought that urban migration was good for men whilst only 52 per cent thought it was good for women. The main reason for discriminating between the sexes was the fear of 40 per cent of the rural households that unsupervised women would become prostitutes. Interestingly, this fear was only shared by only 27 per cent of urban households (Caldwell, 1968).

While the authorities are almost always officially opposed to prostitution, local reactions may be more tolerant. Cohen has described Hausa migrant community in the city of Ibadan in Nigeria where of the women over the age of 15, 950 were housewives, 250 were prostitutes and 70 were old widows or recently divorced (Cohen, 1969). However, there is no immovable barrier between prostitutes and respectable women and at least 14 per cent of the wives had formerly been prostitutes. Indeed, in 1931 when the government declared that the prostitutes must all marry or leave town within a week, all succeeded in finding husbands. This community maintains two female ideals. One is the prostitute who 'is a women freed from the ties of her natal community who is thus rendered mobile and capable of following male migrants to their new settlements'. The other is the 'settled housewife who maintains the household, bears children, and renders important services within the economy'. In this Moslem merchant setting, trading wives are rich in money while prostitutes are rich in independence.

Prostitution is often associated with rapid urbanization because of the excess males in the growing towns and the lack of alternative employment opportunities for women with limited education and training. Prostitution is also often associated with the growth of the tourist trade as in Fiji, Bangkok and Manila. Local attitudes towards prostitution may determine the extent to which women migrate with the intention of becoming prostitutes. Certainly there are some villages in Java which appear to specialize in sending a stream of prostitutes to the city in a regular form of chain migration (Hugo, 1978). Where governments are very hostile to prostitution the position of single women migrants may become very difficult since they may all be subject to harassment. In many cases, the level of wages paid to young woman is so low as to leave those who have migrated and have not the economic support of their families open to a constant temptation to supplement them by selling their favours (Papanek, 1975).

Women Refugees

Refugee movements represent a very special kind of migration. Men usually predominate in refugee populations. Thus a recent study of Chinese refugees from Vietnam arriving in Australia showed that 75 per cent were males (Christopher *et al.*, 1978). The special fears of former soldiers might account for some of the male excess, and it is also possible that slightly fewer females survived the journey. However, the fact that even amongst the young children 75 per cent were boys suggests that the Chinese cultural preference for boys extends to the selection of those who will try for a new life in a new country.

The sex ratio of refugee streams would appear to depend upon both the conditions which drive the refugees to flee and local cultural traditions. In Africa, where there are probably almost a million refugees in total, Gould (1974) has noted that refugee migrations involve whole families. In fact, the striking contrast is between the predominantly male and youthful rural-urban flows and the much more balanced refugee flows. This is a continuation of past patterns of African migration in which whole ethnic groups would move in search of new land under the pressure of other expanding groups.

Women Nomads

Most reviews of migration show remarkably little interest in nomads who are effectively life-long migrants. However, there have been a number of anthropological studies of surviving nomadic groups which have presented very sympathetic portraits of the role of women in these societies. Examples are Kaberry's (1939) study of Australian Aborigines, Riesman's (1977) study of freedom in Fulani social life in West Africa, and Beck's (1978) examination of the status of women amongst the Qashqa'i nomadic pastoralists in Iran. In contrast to many more conventional studies, these three works all emphasis the degree of autonomy enjoyed by nomad women which is closely related to their productive roles in the subsistence economy.

Women's Adaptations to Urbanization

Recently there has been increasing interest in women's adaptations to urban living. There have been two related areas of concern: one focussing upon the extent to which towns make sufficient provisions for immigrant and local women, and the other upon the issue of the extent to which urbanization contributes to raising the status of women.

At a very broad level some writers have argued that, in the long run, urbanization and industrialization will serve to liberate women, even in areas such as the Muslim world where the existing constraints upon them are very great (Goode, 1963; Yousseff 1978).

On the other hand, Denich (1976) has used Yugoslavian data to argue that urbanization and economic processes alone are not enough to liberate women who move to the cities. Boulding (1972) has gone further to argue that improved access to information is the additional factor needed since women's failure to participate in urban life is the result of 'the extent to which the poverty-trap catches the poor rural in-migrant and impedes the working of the urban-based communications network model of development.

From a different approach White (1978) has claimed that the problem stems from a failure to bridge the gap between reforming legal provisions and reforming reality. Just as rural areas in a country such as Bangladesh only take up those aspects of legal reforms which suit the purposes of the local elite, so sections within the towns can remain quite remote from the modernizing influences affecting the elite. Thus, in Tehran little significant change in women's participation, roles or behaviour has resulted from immigration from the rural areas. 'Manipulated by threatened male members, family networks continue to define the context in which urban women must behave' (Bauer, 1979). Since their respectability continues to depend upon male acceptance, women still find that they need their husbands' permission to go out in the street.

Papanek (1976) has reviewed the problems of women in the cities in relation to social and economic status, work, education and training, geographic and social mobility, and women's groups and associations. Interestingly, she makes few references to specific studies in the developing world: most of the works which she cites consist of broad generalisations or refer to the United States (McAllister, 1973). Yousseff's (1976) programme for integrating urban women into development includes pleas for research into how women themselves feel and how to help both those women who remain trapped by restricted stereotypes of women's roles, and those who are brave enough to step outside the stereotypes. She emphasises the importance of investigating situations such as Dahomey, where 30 per cent of adult women in towns have moved there independently, or Ethiopia where there is a majority of women in the towns due to the influx of divorced women. Little (1976) has examined the dilemma of urbanization for African women, arguing that the new-colonial economic structure, in which African economies are dependent upon the developed countries, contributes to the marginalisation or down-grading of urban women who lack the opportunity to produce goods for local markets. He holds that the marital problems of African towns women are simply a reflection of their loss of the economically productive roles which they held in the villages.

In India, De Souza and Singh (1976) have shown that women carry the limits imposed upon them by caste and religion with them into the squatter settlements of New Delhi. Females still find it hard to get an adequate education and occupational choice is heavily restricted by caste origins and values which women bring with them. In Malaysia, village women have discovered new options through mobility, aided by the local belief that women are superior to men in the management of money. Childless women have pioneered the move to paid employment in the urban areas (Strange, 1976).

In Bolivia, both migrant women and the non-migrant women left behind in areas of high male out-migration gain increased control over economic resources which is followed by greater access to public life in general (Bucelhor, 1976b). Dominican women migrate to the United states as domestic servants, prostitutes or garment workers, but whatever their occupations the opportunities available for autonomy are much greater than at home in unemployment-ridden Dominica (Gonzalez, 1976).

In Isfahan in Iran the Gulicks (1976) designed a study to examine the differences between native-born wives and those who had moved in from the rural areas. For most characteristics the two groups were remarkably similar, Migrant wives moved with their husbands from a domestic, female-secluding, sex-segregated environment in the rural areas to a protected domestic environment in the city which was similar both to the atmosphere at home and to the atmosphere in which the native born women lived. Cities have been a major feature of life in the Middle East for centuries and thus there is no inevitable link between movement to the cities and the adoption of more modern forms of family life. In fact, in this case the average age at marriage for migrant wives was 15.5 years for migrants and 14.3 for the native-born.

Migration and Fertility

Much of the debate over women's adaptation to urban conditions has concentrated upon the impact of migration upon fertility behaviour. Many researchers have tried to measure the extent to which, over time, the fertility of immigrants from the rural areas becomes closer to the fertility levels to be found amongst life-time city dwellers. A typical example is Goldstein's (1973) study of 'Interrelations between migration and fertility in Thailand' which is an analysis of the fertility levels of migrants, recent migrants, and non-migrants, based upon census data. Its conclusion is that, regardless of migration status, fertility levels are markedly lower for those living in urban place as compared to those living in rural areas.

A central problem with such studies is that they give no information about why migration should be associated with reduced fertility, or indeed about whether the causal link moves from reduced fertility to migration or from migration to reduced fertility. What is needed is life cycle data which will distinguish between women who move before marriage and at various different stages of family building. It seems plausible to suggest that unmarried women who migrate independently of their parents may practice different fertility behaviour from other unmarried women who migrate with their families. Yet studies generally do not get down to this fine level of analysis. The assumption seems to be that the reasons why migration should lower fertility are so obvious that all that is needed is to measure the extent to which it is effective. Migrants who persist in their high fertility behaviour are considered to be traditionalists, allowing their beliefs to overrule their economic interests (Martine, 1975; Hendershot, 1971).

There are many relevant issues which are rarely discussed in studies of the impact of migration upon fertility. Thus there have been few attempts to measure the effect of the migration of married men upon the fertility of their wives left behind in the villages. In some cases, husbands deliberately make annual visits home, perhaps in association with some religious festival, in order to maintain fertility levels, thus indicating a very clear demand for additional children. In some of the more traditional areas of tropical Africa, it is the duty of the brother of the absent migrant to ensure that the wife becomes pregnant at regular intervals.

Other issues concern the extent to which the differential impact of migration upon males and females affects fertility behaviour. Do return migrants take favourable attitudes to birth control back to the villages with them? Do women who migrate to the cities with their husbands but are little integrated into urban life have different fertility attitudes to their more highly integrated husbands? Do they lack information about family planning clinics and other medical services? Does the distance from their families of origin and their friends lead them to place a greater importance on links with their children, and does this result in a demand for greater quantity or quality in childrearing? Is the vital element in fertility change rural-urban migration as such or the transfer from an agricultural to a non-agricultural occupation?

It is often assumed that migration will be associated with a lowering of fertility levels but this is not always the case (see for example Nag, 1979). In areas where medical conditions are very poor and sterility is prevalent fertility may well be higher in urban areas where medical facilities are better. Equally where there are some traditional constraints upon fertility, these may be related in the urban areas and the result may be an increase in fertility with migration. Examples can be found in those areas of Tropical Africa where prolonged post-natal sexual abstinence is customary and is supported by the practice of polygyny. Women who move to the towns are less likely to be in polygynous marriages where other wives offer alternative solace to their husbands, and they are also less likely to accept prolonged periods of abstinence for themselves. The result is shorter birth-intervals and rising fertility levels (Ware, 1974). In many extended family households in rural India husbands and wives do not regularly sleep together, migration to the town may change this and may also result in a less rigid observance of the many religious and other occasions on which the couple are supposed to practise abstinence.

Almost all discussions of the impact of migration upon fertility link the issues of migration and urbanization. Very little is known of the effect of rural-rural or urban-urban migration upon fertility (see Zarate and Zarate, 1975). On study currently underway is examining the fertility of Javanese transmigrants before and after migration in contrast with the fertility of villagers who stay behind (Oey, 1980). The chief impact would appear to be on the timing of births rather than upon overall fertility levels, understandably women do not like to be pregnant at the time when they have to move. Additionally, it would be useful if future studies clearly distinguished between the short-term effects of the actual move and the longer-term effects of urban living.

Women Who Stay Behind

The impact of the departure of large numbers of men from the rural areas is a topic which has received surprisingly little attention. It has often been assumed that there is a permanent labour surplus in the rural areas and that the men who move are not needed at home. A broader view is that the men are moving into areas of rapid development. In recent years the women who are left behind have received more attention, partly because of concern over stagnating or declining food production, and partly because of a feminist interest in how women cope while their men are away.

Most studies of rural-urban migration in India emphasize the positive gains to the villages from the remittances sent back by the male migrants. However, women's traditional songs and stories suggest that they share much more negative view of the process (Saxena, 1977). Common themes include the wife's objection to her husband leaving for a job in the city, her fear of wasting her youth and her beauty, and her concern for her husband's health and faithfulness. Levels of venereal disease amongst lone men in the cities suggest that such fears are not without cause (Desai and Pillai, 1972). Although the migrants do send money back to the village it is customarily sent to the head of the extended family who is usually the migrant's father, and most of it is spent on debt repayment, agricultural investments and marriages. Thus the wife and her children may gain very little benefit from the money (Singh, 1978). In Saxena's (1977) study at least 10 per cent of the out migrants from the sample villages eventually divorced their wives, while an even greater proportion simply deserted them. A study of women's farm labour in Haryana found that their load of agricultural work increased when men went to work in the city, but that the men usually returned at harvest to sell the crops and thus maintained control over the agricultural income (Chakravorty, 1975).

Indian women are usually left behind in their husbands' villages when the men migrate. Often this leaves them in a very weak position in the extended family with no husband to protest at their being over-burdened with work or to support them in family quarrels. Conversely, Lipton (1977) argues that urbanization may improve the status of women in the villages. He cites Indian examples of women running farms which their elder brothers or husbands had left behind when they moved in search of urban employment. Such managerial work raises women's status except in Muslim and very traditional areas where women cannot command respect. However, other male members of the family are usually available to take over the responsibility and when the male migrants returns they resume the authority they have temporarily delegated to the women. In Latin America where urban migrants are usually women, very few women ever have the chane to manage a farm even temporarily. Overall Lipton argues that out-migration to the town means that overall 'inequality in the village is probably increased, although this may be modified in Asia and Africa by net improvements in the position of rural women as a result of selective male migration' (Lipton, 1977).

Migration steams that are predominantly male or female have implications for the organization of sex roles in both communities of origin and of destination. For instance, in areas such as Botswana and Lesotho where heavy out-migration of men from the rural economies to the mines and farms of South Africa involves up to a quarter of the total adult male labour force, the demographic composition of the rural areas is necessarily dramatically affected with a subsequent impact on the activities of women who are left behind (Fox, 1978). Essentially, the woman's role expands to carry the full weight of responsibility for domestic, economic and civic affairs. As Dixon (1976) suggests, this may increase the status of woman by increasing their power and giving them experience in leadership and decision making. Yet, at the same time, it entails the cost of a double burden for the women left behind and an increased competition for the remaining males. In those communities which are the destinations of the migrants, there are often high proportions of males, and a consequent disruption of marital patterns together with a limited experience of domestic life for many married men.

In Botswana, the international migration of the men leads directly to the internal migration of women. Owing to the absence of the men and the collapse of polygyny, women and, especially unmarried women, face a heavy burden of child-rearing. They move in search of jobs and modern housing and to improve the future prospects of their children. Unfortunately, their has been little evidence of women's common problems resulting in women's organizations to take collective action for collective needs (Bryant, 1977). For the continent as a whole, the Economic Commission for Africa has laid great stress on the fact that 'rural women's work doubles when men migrate to the cities'. Thus amongst some ethnic groups in Upper Volta there are traditionally family fields and separate men's fields and women's fields. The food and income from the family fields is shared amongst the extended family and is controlled by the older men, but women and young men can do what they choose with the produce of their own fields. However, under conditions of heavy out-migration by the young men, women are left to cultivate the family fields alone and thus have no time to cultivate their own fields and thus lose their source of independent income.

Conclusion

Rihani (1978) has somewhat optimistically summarized the findings of recent studies of women and migration as follows:

(i) due to the migration of rural men to the cities, rural women's roles are changing; their family decision-making roles (with the attendant burdens) are increasing and women frequently become heads of households;

(ii) many female migrants also experience changes in their roles and their access to decision-making, often du· to the monetization of their work;

(iii) the greater participation of migrant women in economic tasks and the public sphere leads to the development of complex networks of communications and politicization (cf Baechler, 1976));

(iv) migration to the cities has affected the structure and content of kinship relations. In addition to the generally recongnised evidence of family break-up, some new

positive kinship support systems have been noted amongst migrants (cf. de Souza and Singh, 1976).

Making world-wide generalization is inevitably a dangerous occupation, especially in the area of female migration. Some of the papers which Rihani herself quotes contradict her bright outlook. In Iran, where seclusion remains a very powerful ideal in both urban and rural areas, movement to the city implies very little change for women (M and J Gulick 1976 cf Baurer, 1979). The same would be true of much of India and Bangladesh: neither movement nor urbanization necessarily entails greater liberation for women. In some cases migration destroys customary means of avoiding traditional restraints such as the fiction that all fellow villagers are kin. Similarly the assumption that if the husband is away, or if the woman has a money income she thereby gains greater access to decision making, is unduly simplistic in regions where the extended family is the standard. The Indian bride who stays with her in-laws whilst her husband goes to work in the town loses rather than gains in autonomy.

In contrast, Buechler (1976a) has concluded that research shows that 'migration, per se, does not account for major differences in the position of women unless it is accompanied by changes in her reproductive role through family planning, and productive role in terms of control of strategic resources and education .... Without a doubt, the migration of women is an important avenue for upward social mobility for certain individuals but it is too soon to predict whether this process will result in major socio-economic or ideological changes, for ironically, migration may serve to prevent change by reducing discontent at home at the same time that it provides an avenue for new modes of belief and action'. Women who move may or may not find the world opening up before them, it depends upon the circumstances in which they move, and upon the cultures in which they live (Arizipe, 1977; Demich, 1976; Ebihara, 1974; Piampiti, 1977; Social Research Laboratory, 1977). Similarly, women who stay behind when their men move are very likely to find that their responsibilities increase, but whether they gain in overall autonomy also depends upon the culture (Clark and Ngobese, 1975; Hayano, 1979; Kolenda, 1978; Mueller, 1977; Murray, 1976).

5

Waiting for Returning Menfolk : A Study from South-east Asia

Bangkok is by far the most urbanized area of the country. As the capital city, it is the only large political, commercial and industrial centre. Its population numbers 4,178,000 and it ranks fifteenth on the list of the world's most populous cities. Studies made in the early 1970s in six slums in Bangkok strongly suggest that the North-east Region is the second most important source of migrants into Bangkok, exceeded only by the provinces immediately surrounding the city (Keyes, 1977). In the North-east, Rio-Et is one of the provinces with the highest out migration. Among the net losers of five-year migrants Roi-Et ranked second, with a rate of 48 per cent 1,000 population for 1955-60. In 1965-70, the rate went up to 57.6 per 1,000 (ESCAP, 1976).

Roi-Et is one of the sixteen provinces in the North-east. The region is a flat limestone plateaus, with poor soil, often salty and with insufficient irrigation. About 80 per cent of the farmers in this region still subsist on rainfed or partially supplemented rainfed agriculture (Asian Institute for Technology, 1978). Mono-cropping is generally practised in the area, using traditional technology. While glutinous rice is the predominant crop, other upland crops and vegetables are grown as well, mainly for household consumption. However, low productivity is common, because of poor soil, water shortages and natural disasters. The per-capita income of Rio-Et province in 1976 was the second lowest of the region, *i.e.* 2,235 Baht, whereas that of the whole kingdom was 7,237 baht (NESDB,1978). Migrants from the region are obviously in search of better economic opportunities.

The Sample

We began with the selection of employed male migrants in the city of Bangkok. Care was taken to ensure that they were from the same or nearby villages of the same subdistrict in a North-east province. They were identified mostly at their eating places. The 100 migrants selected come from villages in the Boh Pan Khan subdistrict, in the Suwannapoom district of Roi-Et province, which is about 508 kms from Bangkok; the villages are about 90 kms east of Roi-Et provincial town. The selected male migrants and their corresponding families back home form the sample of the study.

One of the villages was finally chosen for intensive case-studies of five families of migrants. Data were collected through interviews and observation.

Difficulties Encountered in Field Work

A first attempt to select employed males at their places of work failed, although an effort was made to contact them through the manager, the employer or the business owner. It seemed that they were suspicious of the researcher. This may be due to the fact that during the same period a labour union in Bangkok was bargaining about minimum wages. The second attempt, therefore, was aimed at those male migrants whose occupations enjoy relatively more freedom, *i.e.* the taxi or the pedicab drivers. Their eating place served as contact points. Efforts had to be made to select 100 male migrants from contiguous villages in the same subdistrict of Roi-Et province. Once addresses had been obtained form the male migrants, their families in the villages are contacted.

During the village field survey, the researchers met some of the male migrants who were at home visiting their families. A few of them became suspicious about the two-step investigation, since they had not experienced this kind of research before.

Some of the women had gone to visit the migrants in Bangkok during the survey and had to be interviewed later.

COUNTRY PROFILE

Geographical Background

Thailand is situated between 5° and 21°N and between 97° and 106°E. It has an area of approximately 514,000 km^2, and it is divided into four natural regions: the Northern Mountain Region, the Northeastern Korat Plateau Region, the Central Lowland Region or the Chao Phraya Basin and the Southern Peninsula Region. The countries bordering on Thailand and China and the Lao People's Democratic Republic of Viet Nam on the east, Malaysia on the south, and Burma (now Myanmar) on the west.

Thailand a tropical country, is warm and humid. It has three seasons: a hot and relatively dry season from March to June, a rainy season from June to October, and a cool season from November to February. Temperatures are the highest in March and April and the lowest in December and January: the average is 27°C. The rainfall distribution pattern is based on the monsoon winds and the location of the mountains. Average yearly precipitation in most of the northern mountains, the central lowlands and the interior of the Korat Plateau is 100 to 150 cm; it is 200 to 300 cm in the western mountains and most of the Southern Peninsula Region (Henderson *et al.*, 1971).

Population

As of December 1978 the total population of Thailand was about 45 million and the estimated population growth rate during the 1960-70 intercensal period, 3.0 per cent per annum. The largest percentage of the population lives in the Northeast Region. Next in terms of population size are the Central and the Northern Regions respectively, while the smallest proportion of population is to be found in the Southern Region. The population density of the country in 1970 was about 70 persons per km^2; the areas of greatest density were the lower Chao Phraya river basin of the

Central Lowland Region, the Chi and Mun river valleys of the Northeast Region, the Ping river valley in the North, and along the Gulf of Thailand in the Southern Region (ESCAP, 1976).

The Thais are of Mongol stock and are an ethnic majority whose ancestors migrated from China southward along the Yangtse valley to the area known as Thailand. They speak different dialects according to the regions, although the official Thai language is widespread throughout the country. The ethnic minorities are Chinese, Malay, Tribal, Indian, Pakistani, Kampuchean and Vietnamese (Keyes, 1977).

In 1970, 95.3 per cent of the population was Buddhist, 3.8 per cent Muslim, and 0.6 per cent Christian.

Age Structure

About 45 per cent of Thailand's population in 1970 was under 15 years of age and a relatively small proportion (3 per cent) was 65 or older. Males outnumbered females in the younger age groups (*i.e.* below 15 years) while the proportion of females was higher than that of males in the age-group 50 and above. A longitudinal study conducted in 1972 shows that the proportion under 15 years for both of sexes was largest among rural population, while the working ages 15 to 64, were off the smallest proportion. In contrast, Bangkok had the largest proportion of the 15-64 age groups and the smallest proportion of population under 15. In both rural and urban areas, however, there was a small proportion over the age of 65 (Prachuabmoh *et al.*, 1972).

Economy

Agriculture is the most important sector of the Thai economy. In 1971 agricultural products formed a little over 70 per cent of the total experts. These included rice, maize, cassava and sugarcane products, rubber and kenaf. Trade and manufacturing are the second and the third most important sectors respectively. The growth of the economy as a result of diversification of agricultural production has been accompanied by structural changes: a decline in the share contributed by agriculture and a rise in the shares contributed by trade, manufacturing, construction, electricity, water supply and services.

Government System

Thailand's Government is a constitutional monarchy. The Cabinet, headed by the Prime Minister, is responsible for the formulation of national policy. Administratively, the country is divided into seventy-two provinces (*changwad*), and the provinces are subdivided into districts (*amphoe*). The districts are subdivided to subdistrict (*tambon*), and the subdistricts are further subdivided into villages (*muban*). The chiefs of provinces, districts, subdistricts and villages are called governor, *Nai Amphoe, Kamnan* and *Phu Yai Ban* respectively.

Marriage and Kinship System

As with most other societies, the family (either nuclear or extended) is the basic unit of Thai society. Marriage is prohibited between siblings and between those who have lived together in the same household. Generally, the Thai are free to select their own spouses. Marriage usually takes place earlier for both males and females in rural areas. The average age at first marriage of the rural male population is 23.5 for, compared with 25.5 for provincial urban males and 26.1 for Bangkok males. The average age at first marriage for the rural females is 20.6, and those of provincial urban females and Bangkok females are 21.3 and 21.7 respectively (Prachuabmoh *et al.*, 1972).

After marriage, the rural as well as the urban ethnic Thai couples tend to live with the wife's family, following the traditional practice of uxorilocal residence. The foundation of a couple's new household (neolocal residence) usually takes place prior to marriage of the wife's younger sister or after the birth of their first child. The new house is preferably built in the compound of, or next to, the wife's parental household. Usually the youngest daughter or the last married daughter is expected to live with the parental household. However, more than half of the households are nuclear families; the average household size is approximately six (Prachuabmoh *et at.*, 1972). It may also be mentioned that while the residence is uxorilocal, the descent is patrilineal.

Prior to marriage, all young men are expected to assist their parents in their work. It is also quite common for young men in tneir twenties to leave their home villages for urban centres for unspecified periods of time, partly from a need for cash income and partly from a desire to see the outside world (Henderson *et al.*, 1971). If an unmarried man goes away to work elsewhere he is expected to remit some of his earnings home to his parents. Ideally unmarried men should enter manhood for a period of time. After marriage, a man has to fulfil his obligations to his parents-in-law: his responsibilities towards his own patents are transferred and considerably diminished (Skinner and Kirsh, 1975).

The Thai kinship system is characterized as bilateral: it is not based on a principle of descent that stresses either the male or female side. Both sons and daugthters have the right to inherit land from their parents, and the last married daughter inherits the parental house (matriarchal ultimogeniture). In the case of a man living initially with his wife's family, he still has the right to claim land from his own parents, but this can take place only when he moves back to his parental household (Skinner and Kirsh, 1975). On marriage, a woman takes her husband's surname, but there is no rule that prohibits the maintaining of her own surname inherited from her father, or from using both her own surname and that of her husband. In the case of divorce, however, a woman changes back to her father's surname.

Traditional Values Associated with Women

During the period from the thirteenth century to the early nineteenth the formal education system in Thailand was exclusively for men. Knowledge and skills for women at that time are basically passed from mother to daughter. These included cooking, embroidery and home decoration. The ideal woman is described as a good wife and mother, respectful, obedient and helpful to her husband, a wise manager of the family purse and a devout Buddhist' (Henderson *et al.*, 1971). Most parents formerly thought that literacy was not important for women, and they were afraid that their daughters would exchange love letters with their suitors if they became literate (Tapingkae, 1973). Women were not encouraged to participate in political, economic and social affairs or to get in touch with the outside world.

It was in the nineteenth century that a writer under the pen-name Tienwan first wrote on the social equality of Thai women. He proposed the practice of monogamy and advocated women's education. Later, a school for women was started by Queen Saowapa Phong Sri, wife of King Chulalongkorn. However, education at all levels was opened to both men and women only during the reign of King Rama VI (1910-25). During his reign, he persuaded the women to wear Western hair-styles, dress in Western clothes, with hats, socks and shoes, and use Western cosmetics. Attempts were also made by King Rama VI to raise the status of Thai women; he encouraged them, especially in the royal house, to participate in social affairs (National Council of Women, 1976).

In fact, the laws and regulations regarding the status of women have gradually been reformed since King Chulalongkorn's reign. After the revolution in 1932, the first constitution of Thailand granted equality to men and women in social and political matters. Following the norms of Western culture, allowing one wife only, a marriage registration law was initiated in 1935. Despite the traditional idea of women being inferior to men, a number of Thai women at present play an important part in economic and social activities. Since the International Women's Year, the woman's role has been recognized and women have been encouraged to involve themselves in the development of the country, especially in rural areas. In August 1980, Parliament approved the bill indicating that women as well as men may be selected as either heads of the subdistricts (*kamman*) or heads of the villages (*Phu Yai Ban*).

As a result of the rapid growth of urbanization, women play increasingly significant roles as wage-earners in the commercial, service, manufacturing and government sectors. A number of women with university qualifications find places in government service. Women, classified belonging to professional, technical, administrative, executive, managerial or clerical groups increased from 1.2 per cent in 1960 to 2.5 per cent in 1970 (ESCAP, 1976).

In 1975 three out of sixty-nine women candidates were elected as members of the House of Representatives, and eight out of a hundred members of the House of Parliament were women (National Council of Women, 1976). Although the proportion of women politicians is small, women in urban areas are more politically and soically aware than those in rural areas. The National Council of Woman is an organization designed to unify and improve welfare activities of women's organizations. Its work includes sponsoring conferences, seminars and workshops, where members meet and exchange ideas and experiences concerning social problems and services (Henderson *et al.*, 1971). The Women Lawyer's Association has initiated action to demand a revision of the Thai legal system, to drop those provisions that discriminate against married women and female workers. Red Cross Societies and Women's Clubs are organized in every province and are led by the wives of the provincial governors. These units provide health education and services, medicine, medical treatment and other emergency needs to the people in the area. A number of voluntary organizations have been established to help improve the socio-economic status of women, especially in the lower-income bracket. One such programme relates to the provision of service and occupational training. These organizations include the Girl Guides Association and the Wives Associations of the Armed Forces Officers.

Thai rural women, on the other hand, have had a long history of participation in economic activities as well as in domestic tasks. In both 1960 and 1970, proportionally fewer males than females were engaged in farming. Nearly 87 per cent of females were unpaid family workers and 67 per cent of all unpaid family workers in agriculture were females (ESCAP,1976). In the villages of northern Thailand women earn between 20 and 60 per cent of the household cash income and contribute as much time as their husbands to income-earning activities. It is also indicated that the time women contribute to both housework and occupational work is much longer than that of men (Tang Yong Noy and Tan Kin Yong, 1976). In the Northeast, woman in the villages contribute 2,061 hours per year to housekeeping and 2,044 hours to economic productivity. Women are engaged in farming as much as their husbands, particularly in transplanting, harvesting, threshing and storing (Kittasangkha, 1979). Although men do most of the heavy work, one work alongside and as hard as men during the busy months. After rice harvesting, women in the Northeast are usually engaged in cloth weaving or mat weaving or making pillows and mattresses, mainly for the household.

A report on the study of the role of women in agriculture indicates that women in irrigated areas play an important role in year-round rotational cropping. In the wet season, all housewives in the Northeast are engaged in rice farming, while more than half earn additional income by vegetable cultivation and only a few are engaged in the cultivation of other crops. In the dry season, most of them earn their living by planting vegetable cultivation and only a few cultivate other crops. Women are engaged in almost all farm activities, especially when their husbands go to the town centre or are away from home to earn supplementary income. When their husbands are dead, women become the household heads and undertake both domestic and agricultural work until their children are grown up (Paranakian, 1978).

In the households in the North the husbands play a major role in most decision-making, and wives take the supportive role. Equal husband-wife decisions are indicated for matters such as marriage of children, family planning, the time when children start working, taking trips and choosing a radio programme. However, household expenditure and saving, and the buying of household necessities are areas in which wives make the decisions. Housewives in the rural areas are supposed to cultivate plant vegetables, raise poultry for household consumption and spend a small amount of money. On the other hand, the decisions concerning the household business, such as selling products, buying a house and land, and the working hours of household members as well as the decision to move belong to the husband (Tang Yong Noy and Tan Kin Yong, 1976).

With regard to the adoption of agricultural innovation by the villagers in the Northeast, decisions are made equally by husbands and wives in getting a loan for investment, buying agricultural tools, buying or renting land, using farm labour, and particularly in transplanting, harvesting, animal husbandry and selling products. Decisions to increase farming efficiency and to adopt new practices are, nevertheless, made solely by the husbands (Kittasangkha, 1979).

The study of participation in development shows that, in the North the wife's participation is low and limited to the women-oriented programmes such as family planing, health care and household management (Tang Yong Noy and Tan Kim Yong, 1976). As for women in the Northeast, the proportion of wives engaged in activities outside the households is very low, and some development programmes have not yet that introduced into the villages (Kittasangkha, 1979). It is likely that women are expected to play their traditional roles as wives and mothers. Wives usually participate in side activities upon the approval of their husbands or when their husbands are absent.

Modernization

Although Thai society underwent a number of transformations prior to the nineteenth century, the modernization process was greatly accelerated during the reign of King Montage, from 1851 to 1868. The process reached its peak from 1868 to 1910, during the reign of King Chulaongkorn. Later King Rama VI initiated the policy of modernizing the country along Western lines in order to preserve the independence of the kingdom. The singing of the Bowring Treaty and similar treatise resulted in Thailand's increasing participation in international trade (Skinner and Kirsh, 1975). Foreign experts were invited to give technical assistance for such activities as the construction of roads and the digging of canals.

Westernization continued during the reign of King Chulalongkorn. He requested princes and officials as well as their spouses to dress in Western style. The King sent his own sons and the sons of princes and noblemen as well as those of commoners on scholarships for further studies in Europe, and they gradually replaced the foreign experts on their return and participated actively in the improvement of various services. Slavery was abolished. Chulalongkorn promoted the construction of many public utilities and the water supply, railways, bridges, electricity, the irrigation system and the postal and telegraph services. Modern education was provided for the people instead of education in Buddhist monasteries. During his reign central and provincial administration, including the financial system and the collection of taxes, were also improved.

To further the modernizing policy of his father, King Rama VI (1910-25) actively promoted schools at all levels and introduced compulsory education in 1921. The first Thai university, named Chulalongkorn University in memory of King Chulalongkorn, was established in 1917. The King created the Wild Tigers Corps, the Boy Scouts' organization to promote nationalism, and wrote works under the pen names Asavapahu and Ramchitti. He also created surnames to identify the people and abolished gambling houses.

During the reign of King Prajadhipok (1925-35), Thailand was transformed into a constitutional monarchy by the People's

Party. As a result of the revolution in 1932, the policy of the government to make all the people literate was implemented. The extension of primary education to four years, vocational education, and the transfer of the last two classes of secondary school to pre-university schools were some measures taken in this respect. The Public Information Bureau was established to disseminate information to the people. Besides railways and waterways, roads connecting towns throughout the kingdom were constructed. The government encouraged the people to participate actively in local administration and to engage in trade and banking, which were formerly in the hands of foreign merchants.

After King Ananda Mahidol, successor to King Prajadhipok, was assassinated, King Bhumibol Adulyadej was proclaimed the sovereign in 1946. A little later Thailand was admitted as a member of the United Nations and began to participate in the activities of the Specialized Agencies. Later in this reign, dissatisfaction with the deteriorating economic and social condition of the country led to some political crises, such as the coups d'etat of 1947 and 1957 and the revolution of 1958 and 1971. However, the National Development Plan has been implemented since 1961.

National Development Plan

Thailand's First Six-Year National Economic Development Plan for the period 1961 to 1966, included the development of economic products and the building of infrastructure such as highways, power-distribution systems and telephone services. Community facilities and social welfare, public health and education were also promoted.

During the First plan, compulsory education was extended from four to seven years and the standards of many vocational schools were raised. Universities, colleges, and schools outside Bangkok were established. The government increased budget allocations for the development of public health. The community development programme, the self-help settlement projects and the hill-tribe development programmes were initiated.

In the Second National Economic and Social Development Plan, from 1967 to 1971, a number of regional development programmes, including the construction of rural roads, urban development, land-clearing, village water supply, medical services and rural education, especially in remote areas, were promoted. In the improvement of education, priority was given to the development and expansion of the teacher-training programme. For urban development the programmes included the extension of welfare services to the helpless and under-privileged, the promotion of employment and the protection of the labour force and fostering labour relations, city planning housing and slum clearance.

In the Third National Economic and Social Development Plan (1972 to 1976) emphasis was put on the harmony of economic development with that of human development and special attention was given to rural areas. To reduce the population growth rate to about 2.5 per cent, a National Family Planning Policy was initiated. The government created programmes for the conservation of environment, the preservation of cultural and artistic heritage, and the promotion of youth activities. Attempts were made to increase agricultural production and to keep rural people from seasonal migration to the urban areas (Chavalit, 1974).

The Fourth National Economic and Social Development Plan, covering the period 1977 to 1981, was aimed at improving economic condition and the creation of social justice. An attempt was made to reduce the population growth rate to 2.1 per cent. Special attention was given to integrated rural development at the farm level, small-scale water resource development, and rural employment. Improvement in education was aimed at meeting the demands of the labour market. Compulsory education was reduced from seven to six years, and secondary education was extended to six instead of five years. Public health and medical care were expanded, and a nutritional programme was initiated with the focus on children and women in the poor areas. One noteworthy result of the Fourth Plan was that women were encouraged to participate in social development by the promotion of continuing education and adult education, in both rural and urban areas. Women were given equal opportunities with men to earn their living, and laws imposed severe punishment on those who exploited women.

Overview of Social and Cultural Change

As a consequence of modernization, Thailand has undergone a number of changes.

Education

The proportion of the population aged six years and over who have some level of education or other increased from 62.3 per cent in 1960 to 74.1 per cent in 1970. The level of educational attainment is higher among males than females, as is shown in Table 5.1

Table 5.1
Percentages of Population Aged Six and Over by Educational Attainment and Sex, 1960 and 1970

Education	1960			1970		
	Both	Males	Females	Both	Males	Females
None	37.7	31.1	44.3	25.9	21.0	30.7
Completed school	62.3	68.9	55.7	74.1	79.0	69.3
Lower primary	54.6	58.2	51.0	62.3	64.2	60.3
Upper primary	3.2	4.3	2.2	4.3	5.2	3.4
Secondary	3.0	4.2	1.8	4.8	6.2	3.5
Higher	0.4	0.6	0.3	0.7	0.9	0.5
Other education and unknown	1.0	1.6	0.4	2.0	2.4	1.6

Sources: Economic and Social Commission for Asia and the Pacific, Country Monograph Series No. 3, *Population of Thailand,* Table 121, p. 129.

Literacy

According to the National Statistical office, literates are defined as persons aged 10 years and over who are able to read. The literacy rate was 70.8 per cent in 1960. And by 1970 it had increased to 81.8 per cent. The proportion of literates for males was higher than that for females. And the proportion of literates for both males and females decreases with increasing age (ESCAP, 1916).

Labour-force participation

Thailand's population is predominantly rural, and it has a relatively high female labour-force participation rate. In 1960, 77.2 per cent of all females of 11 years of age and over were recorded as labour-force participants, and the proportion was 69.8 per cent in 1970. This is partly due to a growing tendency among young females to prolong their schooling as a consequence of the government's programme of expansion and improvement of compulsory education. In 1970, proportionally fever males (74.6 per cent) than females (82.8 per cent) were engaged in agriculture. About 67 per cent of all unpaid family workers in agricultural were also females.

On the other hand, the proportion of non-agricultural employment increased significantly from 16.9 per cent in 1960 to 21.2 per cent in 1970. This was due to a combination of factors, such as the rapid population growth in the rural as well as in the urban areas and the changing levels of social and economic development in the country. A higher proportion of females than males was engaged in commerce and in the manufacturing industry. About 80 per cent of urban females were sales workers, craft workers and service and transport workers: and the rest were professional, administrative, and clerical workers, or unclassified and new workers (ESCAP, 1976).

Transportation

Modernization of all types of transportation facilities was incorporated as a goal in the national Development Plan to meet the demands of a changing economy and to facilitate spatial mobility of the population (Henderson, 1971). The inland waterways, the railways and the highways were improved and expanded to provide an adequate transportation network. The creation of modern systems of transportation has made it possible for the villagers to travel back and forth from their homes to local urban centres and to Bangkok.

Electrification

Rural electrification has been accelerated in all regions. In 1978, the customer growth rate increased to 18 per cent, compared to 10.9 per cent in 1974. Electrical energy consumed for lighting in 1977 increased to 24.8 per cent, while that consumed by industry increased to 19.6 per cent over 1976.

Communication

Radio is the most popular mass medium in rural Thailand. It is a major network for dissemination of news, modern popular music, soap operas, and religious programmes. In 1976, there were 100 radio stations and about 4,111,235 radio receivers in the country (Sankatiprapa, 1979). Films in the open air are often shown in the villages; the villagers in some parts of the country have the opportunity to watch television. New messages have also been introduced into the villages in printed form such as posters, booklets and other literature with graphic illustrations (Keyes, 1977).

Urbanization

As of 1972 the urban population, defined as the population residing in the municipal areas of Thailand, constituted 16 per cent of the total. The average urban growth rate during the 1960, was 6.5 per cent per year (ESCAP, 1976). The Central Region of which Bangkok is a part was the most urbanized; the Southern Region came second, while both the Northeast and the North were less urbanized. The growth of a number of urban centres is due to many economic and social factors. The rapid expansion of the country's infrastructure, and internal rural-urban migration for education or for employment, for example, have accelerated the process (Prachuabmoh and Tirasawat, 1974).

Migration to Bangkok

For the country as a whole, the number of life-time migrants increased from 10.8 per cent in 1960 to 13.1 per cent in 1970, and the number of five year migrants during the period 1965 to 1970 was more than double that of 1955-60. The city of Bangkok is the central attraction for migrants from every region, and while the Northeast experiences the highest loss migrants.

Between 1965 and 1970 the number of immigrants to Bangkok was more than twice that between 1955 and 1960. Males outnumbered females among the migrants from the Central Region as well and from the southern Region. In contrast, the proportion of female migrants from the North and the Northeast is higher than that of the male migrants.

For both males and females from every region, the peak age of migrants to Bangkok is 20-29. The female migrants are more numerous than male migrants at ages of 5-9, 10-19, 50-59, and 60 years and over. It is noted that from 1955 to 1960 male migrants outnumbered female from every region except the North, whereas in the 1965-1970 period, more males than females moved from the Central and the Southern Regions.

Meinkoth, in a study of migration from the Northeast to Bangkok in 1957 (Menkoth, 1971), reported that 90 per cent of the migrants were males and only 10 per cent of the married ones were accompanied by their wives. As of 1978, the largest proportion of immigrants to Bangkok came from the Northeast with females being more numerous than males. The number of male migrants is 42.8 per cent while that of the females is 50.8 per cent and a majority of them moved from the villages.

The most important reason for migration to Bangkok is economic. Meinkoth indicated that approximately 80 per cent of the 415 migrants studied gave economic reasons for migration and that about 15 per cent moved to Bangkok because of inability to grow rice or lack of food. According to a survey of immigration in Bangkok about 63 per cent of the total came to find work. Approximately 83 per cent of them were identified as seasonal migrants who moved to Bangkok during the agricultural slack season, particularly from March to May, and their number declined from July to September (National Statistical Office: 1978). However, there is sometimes and increase in the number of immigrants during the planting season, which is probably due to natural disasters (either droughts or floods). In 1974, 19.5 per cent of the immigrants to Bangkok cited drought as the push factor. A study in four villages of the northeast in 1978 found that 41 per cent of the migrants gave drought as a migratory motive, and more than 64 per cent came to link for a job in Bangkok (NESDB, 1980). Almost a quarter of the migrants studied by Meinkoth stated that they had relatives in Bangkok, and about a third had come to join friends or relatives. The successful male migrants who had come to Bangkok alone doubtless sent for their wives and children, and probably persuaded other friends or relatives to join them.

MEN IN TOWN

All of the selected 100 male migrants were either pedicab or taxi drivers, and their average age was 32.7 years. Most of them had four years of primary education. As many as 67 of them had entered into manhood at sometime for the sake of their parents. Some gaining prestige and respect because they had acquired either the first-grade certificate of Buddhist studies or the second or third grade. Eighty-three were married, with families back home in the villages, and seventeen were still single. Before earning their living in Bangkok, ninety-five had been engaged in rice-farming. The duration of their stay in Bangkok ranged from one to twenty-two years.

The main reason for migration was the need for money for household expenditure. Usually, there is very little opportunity for local employment in the villages. When starvation looms, particularly in the dry season or in case of crop failure caused by either drought or flood, a large number of men in the villages are forced to seek a better life elsewhere. The decision to migrate is in half of the cases taken by the males themselves; the rest are persuaded to go by others. The migrants came to Bangkok, rather than going to the town centre in Roi-Et province or other towns in the Northeast, primarily because there has been continued migration from their villages to Bangkok for generations. Besides, it is very likely that coming to Bangkok is a dream for young people in the villages. At present, a daily bus from Suwannapoon district and a weekly local small truck from Boh Pán Khan subdistrict facilitate migration to and from Bangkok.

Upon their first arrival in Bangkok, most of the migrants stay with friends or relatives. Usually the male migrants coming from the same village live together in a rented house, which they occupy with approximately twenty or thirty persons sharing the rent. The rent varies, according to the number of occupants, from 30 to 300 baht per month per person. The house is occupied day and night in shifts. The first group of occupants works from 6 a.m. to 4 p.m. and the second from 5 p.m. to 5 a.m.

Sixty-two persons in the sample reside in the Prathuwan area around Hua Lampong railway station, in districts Sam Yhan, Suan Luang, Soi Wat Duang Khae, Trok Phut, Soi Sab and Sapan Ohn. A little more than one-fourth live in the Bangkapi area, particularly in Lad Prao Soil I, and a few live in other areas, including Phayathai, Huai Khwang and Pomh Prab. Some do not seem to live anywhere; they usually sleep in their pedicabs or taxis. Generally the male migrants meet each other at their eating place near the place where they rent the pedicabs or the taxis. They normally eat their local food, served by women from the same village who are the wives or relatives of some of the migrants.

The male migrants have been working off and on in their present jobs as drivers for an average of about ten years. Most had to wait some months before they could actually start working as drivers. This time was needed to learn how to drive, to acquire the official licence and to locate a taxi or pedicab available for rent. Driving lessons are given by friends or relatives during one or two weeks for an hour or two a day–only the patrol has to be paid for. While waiting, some of them went back and forth to work in the villages. During this time they were supported by friends, relatives or parents.

A little more than three-fifths of the male migrants reported that they had changed their jobs, from one to eight times before obtaining their present occupations. They changed mainly because of low income, and hard work, whereas driving provides them with a higher income, greater freedom, and an opportunity to live close to their relative. The previous jobs mentioned were as factory workers. Construction workers, petrol station attendants, restaurant helpers, garage workers, carpenters, and tricycle drivers (who are now prohibited in Bangkok). Some of them worked in sugar-cane plantations in the provinces east of Bangkok.

Table 5.2
Income Per Day of the Male Migrants (22.9 baht = $1)

Baht	*Migrants*
200-299	6
300-399	13
400-499	14
500-599	28
600-699	12
700-799	11
800-899	8
900 and over	8
Total	100

The male migrants earn, on an average, 580 baht a day. From this amount they have to pay for petrol and rent, and meet their personal expenses. The average daily expense for petrol is 156 baht. Usually the pedicab rent is either 85 or 90 baht, while the taxi rent is higher, *i.e.* between 100 and 120 baht per day. The rent, however, varies according to the state of the engine. Besides petrol and car/pedicab rent, food is the major expense. While living in Bangkok they usually eat out every day, spending 38 baht on the average per day. Other expenses of a more luxurious nature, such as smoking, drinking and entertainment, vary according to the total income earned, and the sense of responsibility towards the family back home. The same applies to the amount spent on laundry and transportation. Only 40 per cent of the respondents paid for commercial entertainment, 30 per cent entertain themselves by visiting friends or relative, and the rest mostly stay at home, reading newspapers, listening to the radio or doing personal chores.

Table 5.3
Monthly Expenditures of the Migrants

	Items						
Baht	*House rent*	*Laundry*	*Liquor*	*Trans-portation*	*Enter-tainment*	*Cigarettes*	*Food*
<50	28	18					
50-99	37	18					
<100			10	36	13	11	
100-149	25	6					
150>	9	12					
100-199			13	8	12	11	
200-299			6	6	14	41	
300>			8	2	10	9	
300-399			8				
400-499			5				
500>			16				
<500							3
500-999							26
1000-1499							57
1500>							13
Total	99	54	58	52	49	72	99

Most of the male migrants (70 per cent) reported that they occasionally give money to their families back home. Normally they take it with them when they visit their families, but in case of urgent need they send it through relatives or neighbours who visit the villages. Since there is always somebody going, there is no need to send it by mail.

6

Women and Social Change Under Law

More and more in recent years an awareness of the rights of women under the law is growing. Increasingly so, one of the main characteristics of modern society is a heavy reliance on law to bring about social change. This is particularly true of countries which had for centuries been under foreign rule and attained independence after a long struggle. Inequalities and exploitation, generated or intensified by colonial regimes, cannot certainly be eliminated by freedom from foreign rule only. The tasks of social reconstruction, development and nation-building all call for major changes in the social order, to achieve which legislation is one of the main instruments. It can act directly, as a norm setter, or indirectly, providing institutions which accelerate social change by making it more acceptable. One example is the introduction of compulsory education.

Like other colonial countries, independent India also relied heavily on legislation in its effort to usher in a society where there will be no discrimination or inequality. It has sought to protect the interests of those who suffer from social and political disabilities by penalising the practice of untouchability, eliminating caste distinctions and so on. By clearly emphasizing the principle of equality and removing all legal discrimination *inter alia* between sexes, our leaders have shown their acceptance of the view that to achieve liberty there must be complete liberty for women "all legislative traces of the inequality of women without exception must be removed".

Stress on the removal of discrimination and special protective legislation for women was necessary, because the British policy in the field of family law had a crippling effect on women. Whatever the motivation, the British adopted a policy of letting Hindus be governed by Hindu Law and Muslims by Muslim Law in matters of family relations. This policy of relying on age-old personal laws has been described as "another act of enlightened policy," but the result of it was to encourage the feeling of separateness and prevent the unity of the two communities. The policy achieved such success that modernisation of most of these laws has proved difficult even today. Coupled with this policy was another one of non-interference or rather non-intervention (in family law) on the plea that 'as the British legislature cannot make Mohammedan or Hindu religion, so neither can it make Mohammedan or Hindu Law'. This resulted in stagnation with the result that the two systems could neither absorb nor adjust to socio-economic changes. Social tensions inevitably arise in situations when 'law does not in fact answer the needs arising from major social change."

In the early part of the 19th century, due to the efforts of our social reformers some marginal adjustments were made in response to humanitarian considerations and social demands. Although female infanticide had been banned earlier, the most significant was the legislation which penalised the practice of Sati. The groundwork for this had been laid for a very long time and this was an example where legislative legitimacy was given to an accepted social norm. The then Governor General, Lord Bentink, in referring to the proposed legislation, said that the government would be following and not going ahead of public opinion.

The prevalence, in 18th and early 19th centuries, of child marriage leading often to early widowhood was one of the major concerns of the social reformers. Their tireless efforts to curb this social evil finally resulted in 1856 in 'The Hindu Widows' Remarriage Act. But even such social legislation stopped after 1857. The social reformers realised that in the face of the Governments refusal to legislate on social matters the only way open was to try and spread education more widely among the people particularly women, in the hope that this would help to eliminate some of the inhuman practice and also act as an incentive to women to organize and demand legislative changes.

As the national movement gained in strength, the early 20 century showed some activity in the legislative field. The plight of widows without any means of their own, depending entirely on the family, led to the Hindu Women's Rights to Property Act in 1929 followed by another in 1937. These laws, while they made the widow less dependent financially during her lifetime, stopped short of giving her any substantial rights of ownership since her right to property was only for life.

The success of the policy of division can also be seen from the fact that though demands for changes in the Muslim Law to improve the position of women where also building up, the reformers of the two communities did not work together. The significant change that was made as a result of all the agitation for improvement among the Muslims was to give the right of divorce to Muslim women in 1939.

A by-product of the policy of non-intervention in family law had been the diversification (due to customs) among the major personal laws in different parts of the country and varied interpretations of the sacred texts. These differences had hardened over the years. Among the Muslim schools of law—there were others besides the Sunnis and Shias. This was partially remedied by the Shariat Act 1937 which brought all Muslims under the Act and practically abrogated the customary practices which had grown over the years. Among the Hindus where there were two major schools—Mitakshara and Dayabhagi—and other sub-schools, lack of uniformity posed a serious problem.

The demand for major changes, no longer marginal ones, grew as a result of the untiring efforts of Gandhiji, who wanted women to suffer from no social or legal disabilities. The inferior position of women in all matters, guardianship, inheritance and divorce, had an effect on the personality of the women. Under Gandhiji's leadership the demand for improvement and modernization of the law grew and ultimately the Government was compelled to move. A committee was constituted under the chairmanship of Sir B.N. Rau, whose terms of reference included the suggestions for change and the Codification of Hindu Law, so that all Hindus would be governed by the same. Even though the report was ready and Gandhiji's exhortation that 'women must suffer from no disability or discrimination' had influenced India's national leaders, the resistance to change was so great that no effective steps could be taken for a number of years.

Only after independence, under the leadership of Pandit Nehru could this matter be taken up. Even so that law had to be passed piecemeal owing to resistance from those who believed in the status quo. It is significant that the same body which, sitting as the Constituent Assembly, adopted the equal rights clauses in the Constitution without any debate, while functioning in its capacity as the Central Legislature, blocked the Hindu Code Bill which attempted to provide only partial equality to women.

The participation in the freedom movement had greatly helped in the acceptance of the idea of women's equality and the need for their emancipation. As a result, Indian women achieved political and same social rights easily with independence, and did not have to struggle for them as women in many other countries.

But legislation cannot by itself change society. To translate these rights into reality is the task of other agencies. Public opinion has to be moulded to accept these rights. The judiciary and the executive have a major role to play in this. This effort has not always been forthcoming. Sometimes the judiciary has interpreted new legislation strictly and failed to give effect to the principle underlying the legislation, as for example in dealing with cases of bigamy or the right of women to work. The executive branch of the government has seldom made an effort to set up the machinery to educate the people about the socio-economic changes. The mass media used for publicity for certain measures taken by government, has been conspicuously silent about social legislation. If legislation reflects the social values of a country 'the degree of women's emancipation is the natural measure of the general emancipation in any given society'. It is, therefore, necessary not only to legislate but to see that it is implemented. In the following sections an effort has been made to point out the areas where the law is lagging behind the principles which have already been accepted by our Constitution.

I. POLYGAMY

General

Full equality of sexes can hardly be possible in legal system which permits polygamy and a social system which tolerates it. Though the institution of polygamy has prevailed traditionally in India, in the last five or more decades it is on the wane and most marriages are today monogamous. The spread of Christianity with its concept of marriage 'as a union for life of one man with one women' marked the first step towards the legal recognition of the principle monogamy. The advanced communities in the country like the Parsees and the Brahmos opted for the principle. The Parsee Marriage and Divorce Act 1865 provided that any marriage during the life-time of his or her wife or husband was void. The Indian Christian Marriage Act, 1872 lays down the condition that neither of the persons intending to be married shall have a wife or husband still living. With the enactment of the Hindu Marriage Act, 1955, which lays down the principle of monogamy for all Hindus, 88 per cent of the Indian population are legally governed by the principle of monogamy.

The only personal law, which has remained impervious to the changing trend from polygamy to monogamy, is Muslim Law. Most Muslim countries such as Turkey, Iraq, Iran, Syria, Tunisia, Indonesia, Pakistan (including Bangladesh, which was then a part of Pakistan) have introduced reforms of varying degrees to correct the abuse of polygamy, but no legislative effort has so far been made in India to ameliorate the hardship caused to the Muslim women by the continuance of the institution of polygamy. According to an extract given by a Urdu Editor:

> ".....the law of polygamy is not an invention of the Muslims, but a part of the comprehensive religious code granted to them by God. And the Muslims have been exercising this right of theirs since the time of the holy Prophet to this day. To tamper with it would definitely amount to interference in religion. If some Muslim or non-Muslim administration forces monogamy on Muslim, it would be a case of gross injustice; and the Muslims will oppose it as a religious duty."

During its tours, the Committee met with three different types of reaction. In U.P. we found a positive hostility to any reform in Muslim Law particularly in the educated middle classes. Among the poorer classes of the same State we found a desire to have monogamous marriages and blunt denunciation of the inequities of polygamy. In Kashmir the women uniformly and emphatically demanded that polygamy must be banned.

The seeming indifference on the part of the Government in leaving only one section of the citizens to be governed by a law permitting polygamy and other inequalities was sought to be explained by the minister for Law and Justice, Mr. Gokhale, when he said, "We believe that while we should do everything possible to build up and cultivate the consciousness for reform, the urge and the demand for the reform must come from the community itself."

Standardized Contracts

Marriage is regarded as a contract under Muslim law for the purpose of procreation and legalizing of children. Therefore, some eminent jurists like Fyzee and Danial Latifi advocate the device of standard contract of marriage which would provide *inter alia* for stipulation like, "The husband shall not take a second wife while the first marriage subsists and if the husband has married or gone through a form of marriage with another woman after the date thereof" the wife shall have to power to divorce. As in Islamic Law marriage is regarded as a contract, the prevailing opinion of the jurists is that generally such contracts become enforceable in courts.

Two subsidiary views exist as regard the technique: *(i)* to propagate the standard form of contract and leave it to the volition of the parties to enter into such contracts, and *(ii)* to provide an amendment to Section 2 A of the Shariat Act *inter alia* that "every contract of marriage shall be deemed to include, unless otherwise expressly provided , the terms set out", which would contain a provision that the husband shall not take a second wife during the subsistence of the marriage.

The critical question for consideration is: What are the consequences of a breach of the contractual stipulation on the part of the husband that he would not contract a second marriage during the subsistence of the prior marriage? Fyzee says that:

- *(a)* restitution may be refused to the husband;
- *(b)* certain rights as to dower may arise; or
- *(c)* the wife may have a right to divorce; or in an extreme case
- *(d)* the marriage itself may be dissolved.

Thus the effective right of a Muslim wife having a standard contract is to get the isolation of marriage or a right to live separately from the husband. This fails to provide a substantive relief to the first wife with children. As the second marriage is not invalidate, the position of the husband is not prejudicially affected but for the financial implications arising out of the step. The deterrence of the criminal sanction when a person intends to contract a second marriage is absent. Further, the solution of standard contracts is ineffective, in cases of fake conversions to Islam from other religions to circumvent the prohibition against bigamy. The remedy is out of step with the position in the other personal laws in India and should be rejected.

Reforms to Correct the Abuse of Polygamy

The first approach to reform Muslim Law relating to polygamy is to abolish it altogether. In Turkey polygamy was abolished by law. The Turkish Civil Code lays down that no person shall marry again unless he proves that the former marriage has been dissolved by death, divorce or by a decree of nullity. The Turkish Family Law of Cyprus also provides that a marriage shall be declared invalid where at the date of the marriage one of the parties is already married. The Tunisian Code of Personal Status in Article 18 provides: "Plurality of wife is prohibited. Any person who being already married and before the marriage is lawfully dissolved, marries again, shall be liable to imprisonment for one year or for a fine of 2,40,000 Francs or to both even if the second marriage is in violation of any requirements of this law. The Muslims in the U.S.S.R. and the People Republic of China are also governed by the rule of monogamy.

It deserves to be emphasized that in Tunisia the justification for the abolition of polygamy had its basis on a re-evaluation or re-interpretation of Islamic principles. Professor Anderson points out the following distinctive grounds:

> "The first was the broadly based argument that there were certain institution, such as slavery and polygamy, which were acceptable at a certain stage in human development, but which were repugnant to the civilized conscience today......
>
> The second argument was.....that the "Verse of polygamy" itself allows plurality of wives only on two conditions, one of which is that the would-be polygamist should have no fear whatever of treating them with less than equal justice. But experience, had proved that no man other than a prophet was capable of such a feat especially in contemporary conditions"

The second approach is to regulate the husband's right to contract a second marriage by rendering it necessary to obtain judicial or official sanction for a bigamous marriage. In most countries where Muslims constitute a majority of the population this approach, with variations, is favoured. Iran, Iraq, Singapore and Syria provide that the permission of the court is necessary for a bigamous marriage of the husband. The laws provide that in granting the permission the courts should satisfy themselves about the financial capacity of the husband to maintain more than one wife. Some of these laws provide for additional grounds to be fulfilled like the capacity to do equal justice to the co-wives.

On the other hand, Pakistan, Ceylon and Indonesia confer the power to regulate bigamous marriage on institutions other than the regular courts. For example, Section 6 of the Muslim Family Laws Ordinance of Pakistan states that no male can contract another marriage during the subsistence of an existing marriage except with the previous permission of the Arbitration Council. The Arbitration Council may grant the permission if it is satisfied that the proposed marriage is necessary and just. If a person contracts another marriage without such permission, upon a complaint being made, he is liable for punishment which may extend to one years' simple imprisonment or a fine of Rs. 5,000 or both. The legislation in Ceylon prescirbes for the prior notice of the intended marriage and the display of the notice in the mosques and at the residence of the parties, that is, the husband, the first wife and the prospective second wife. In Indonesia the family Law Regulations of 1947 enjoin the marriage officials to clarify and explain the position of a bigamous marriage under Islamic Law and legal conditions and obligations relating to it, to the person intending to contract a bigamous marriage.

David Pearl studied the impact of the Muslim Family Laws Ordinance (1961) in Quetta (Baluchistan), Pakistan. Two points relevant for our consideration emerge from his study. First,

> "many men risk the penalities inherent in Section 6(5) (a) and (b) of the ordinance, and marry a second wife without bothering to apply to arbitration council for its approval."

The second relates to classification of marriages in the Muslim Law. A marriage is valid *(sabih)* if all the conditions and formalities relating to marriage have been properly fulfilled. A valid marriage confers on the wife the right to dower, maintenance etc.; and creates reciprocal rights of inheritance between the husband and wife. Among the Sunnis, a marriage that is not valid may be either void *(batil)* or irregular *(fasid)*. A void marriage does not create any rights or obligations among the parties. The children of the union are illegitimate. An irregular marriage has no legal effect before consummation and it can be terminated by words showing intention to separate. The children of the union are legitimate but the irregular marriage does not create mutual rights of inheritance between the husband and wife. Pearl points out that the distinction between valid, void and irregular marriages was not eliminated and, therefore, "it was remarkably easy... for a girl under 16 to be married, or a man to ignore Sections 6 and 7 of the ordinance".

While the desirability of reform in Muslim Law is generally acknowledged, as mentioned, the government has taken no step towards changing the law for over two decades on the view that public opinion in the Muslim community did not favour a change. But this view cannot be reconciled with the declaration of equality and social justice. We are, therefore, of the opinion that ignoring the interest of Muslim women is a denial of social justice. The right to equality, in our view, like the right to free speech, is an individual right.

An Analysis of Polygamous Marriages Among Muslims

An analyses of polygamous marriages among Muslims in India classifies them into four groups:

(a) the largest number of cases are of husbands who abandon their wives (and frequently children as well) and go off and marry somebody else. Frequently, the second wife remains ignorant about the earlier marriage and the children;

(b) where the wives, finding the marriage unbearable have left their husbands who, in order to avoid paying the deferred Mahr, refuse to divorce them;

(c) wives who because of economic dependence acquiesce in the second marriage;

(d) where a person of another religious persuasion deliberately adopts Islam to contract a marriage which could not be permitted under his own system of law.

Regulated Bigamy

The adoption of monogamy as a rule among the Hindus under the Hindu Marriage Act, 1955 has been criticized and an opinion has been express in favour of "carefully regulated bigamy."

> "It is a serious question whether the sympathy which the public and courts seem to harbour for bigamous unions has not solid basis which we ought to recognize. It is argued that a carefully regulated bigamy *i.e.* popular marriages in cases of infertility, mental instability of the wife, and other cases where the good sense and humanity of the husband and his family recoils from divorcing her or annulling the marriage would not only be in accord with traditional Hindu religious sentiment and practice, but also much more realistic. It would savour less of "shop-window-dressing" with which the Hindu Code is charged. There is a small part of India which at present has controlled bigamy for Hindu husbands, namely the former Portuguese India (Goa, Daman & Diu).... This appears to work extremely well, and the Parliament has had the good sense not to interfere with the modified Hindu Law still in force in those territories..... Moreover, it was the opinion of Mahamahopadhyaya Dr. P.V. Kane, that polygamy should be tolerated for some classes on purely economic grounds.....It is the health and happiness of Hindus that counts, and the rash abolition of polygamy in a euphoric moment is not working out satisfactorily."

As this view gives a misleading impression of being in the interests of women and as it is likely to be advanced in the context of Muslim Law also, it needs to be rebutted in fall. We are not aware of a sympathy for bigamous unions or an opinion in favour of them in the absence of a systematic survey. A survey made some years ago showed 85 per cent of the men and 96 per cent of the women to be in favour of compulsory monogamy. While judical decisons have rendered the enforcement of the penal provision against bigamy in Section 17 of the Hindu Marriage Act, 1955, difficult, it would only be fair to say that this stemmed not from a sentiment in favor or bigamy, but from a deep seated judicial attitude that penal provisions should be construed strictly. The 'economic grounds', in our considered view, equate women with beasts of burden and cannot be accepted. It is doubtful whether the advocates of controlled bigamy will also favour controlled polyandry as a general rule on the same grounds.

Long before the passing of the Hindu Marriage Act, monogamy in preference to controlled bigamy existed under the Marumakattayam Law in the State of Travancore – Cochin and in the Malabar District of the Madras province. It was introduced in the province of Bombay in 1946 and in the province of Madras in 1949.

We are of the firm view that there can be no compromise on the basic policy of monogamy being the rule for all communities in India. Any compromise in this regard will only perpetuate the existing inequalities in the Status of women.

Enforcement of Provisions Against Bigamy under the Hindu Marriage Act

While bigamy has been made an offence and the second marriage should be void, bigamous marriages are still prevalent among Hindus. Apart from the figures available, during its tour in many of the States the Committee came to know of a large number of such marriages. In Manipur even though the women were very bitter about the wide prevalence of this practice, they were compelled to accept it as divorce or prosecution of the husband resulted in social ostracism. The Government had failed to enforce the law. Even Government servants, who are forbidden under the Government Servants' Conduct Rules, were practising polygamy. The Committee was also informed that a Resolution in the Legislative Assembly calling upon the Government to enforce the law had been defeated by an over-whelming majority. It is interesting to note that most women of Manipur earn to support their families. In spite of their economic independence they have been unable to assert their social and legal right. Quite a few of them were living with their co-wives some had separate establishments but all of them contributed a part of their incomes to their husbands. Little social stigma seemed to be attached to such a situation. In West Bengal a training centre in Sriniketan for promotion self-employment had a number of women discarded by their husbands who had married a second time. We met two co-wives taking the training whose husbands discarded them for a third wife. Similar cases were brought to our notice in some parts of Andhra Pradesh, Bihar, Uttar Pradesh and in the rural areas of Madhya Prâdesh.

Under the present law, only an aggrieved person can initiate proceedings for bigamy, which means the husband or the wife. In the case of the wife the complaint may be made on her behalf by one of her family members. Quite often an economically dependent woman who is also uneducated has neither the knowledge not the means to go to court. Many of them are reluctant to appear in court and face social, criticism as brought our very clearly by Justice Sachar:

> "We also cannot shut our eyes to the practical difficulties and problems faced by an Indian girl.... Instances are numerous where Indian women have gone through a literal misery of marriage for years rather than go to a court of law and expose themselves to public gaze. The irradiate of the parents and relations in most for these cases is also unsympathetic."

Where social customs prevent a woman form appearing in public, the law permits some other person to make the complaint with the permission of the court. The question to be considered is whether the right to initiate prosecution for bigamy should be extended to persons other that the girl's family in all cases, in view of the general reluctance of her family members to lodge a complaint against the son-in-law or brother-in-law. The necessity of obtaining prior permission of the Court would provide adequate safeguard against undue harassment. In small towns and villages a social worker could fulfil this role admirably.

In our opinion such a provision is necessary to prevent the current wide-spread violation of a most salutary provision of the law which very clearly lays down the social policy of the country.

The existing penal provision against bigamy is further defeated in a considerable number of cases because of a technical construction placed on Section 17 of the Act. The Supreme Court *in Bhaurao vs. State of Maharashtra* held that the offence of bigamy was not proved unless it was established that the second marriage was celebrated with proper ceremonies and due form. This conclusion was arrived at on the basis that the section used the word' solemnized'. They observe.

> The word 'solemnize means, in connection with a marriage, 'to celebrate the marriage with proper ceremonies and due form' according to the Shorter Oxford Dictionary. It follows, therefore, that unless the marriage is 'celebrated' or performed with proper ceremonies and due form it cannot be said to be 'solemnized'. It is therefore essential, for the purpose of Sec. 17 of the Act, that the marriage to which Sec. 494, I.P.C. applies on account of the provisions of the Act, should have been celebrated with proper ceremonies and due form.

As the law requires no specific ceremonies but recognizes ceremonies of marriage according to custom it becomes extremely difficult to determine which ceremony or ceremonies were really essential. Whether the construction pure by the court will subserve the policy and purpose of the Act or the social objectives of the legislation was never in their contemplation.

The result of this interpretation is that a difficult burden is cast on the prosecution to show that the second marriage is performed with all due formalities. This burden in many cases cannot be discharged owing to the fact that second marriages during the subsistence of a prior marriage are seldom performed with the usual pomp and show.

Even if it is not so, this judicial interpretation facilitates widespread evasion of law. As pointed out by Professor Derrett, the existing position will give rise to two types of devices being followed to evade prosecution for bigamy. First, a person intending to take a second wife may deliberately undergo a defective form of marriage, to defend himself against a prosecution launched by the first wife or her relatives. Second, the relatives and friends of the second "wife" may commit perjury and say that the marriage is not properly solemnized and the first wife or her relatives would not be in a position to rebut it.

Shri M.B. Majumdar suggested that the word, "soleminized" may be replaced by the words "contracted". But given the contemporary judicial attitudes, inherited form the English legal system, whereby the polity and purpose of an Act often are sacrificed to a literal construction of the Act, it is doubtful whether the suggested amendment will change the situation materially.

We recommend that the words 'solemnized' should be esplaced by the words "goes through a marriage." Further, an explanation should be added to the section that an omission to perform some of the essential eremonies by parties shall not be construed to mean that the offence of bigamy was not committed, if such a ceremony of marriage gives rise to a de facto relationship of husband and wife.

Injunction

As already mentioned there is often an inhibition against prosecuting a husband for his second marriage in the present social context. The easier remedy is to prevent such a marriage taking place, if there is prior knowledge of its impending celebration. The following two cases will show that though bigamy, including the attempt and abetment of it is an offence, the position is not as clear cut as we would like it to be .

In *Sankarappa vs. Basamma* the Mysore High Court held that a Hindu wife is entitled to a perpetual injunction restraining her husband from contracting a second marriage; that the suit is clearly permitted by section 54 of the specific Relief Act, 1877 (Sec. 38 of the Specific Relief Act, 1963).

On the other hand, a Division Bench of the Patna High Court in *Uma Prasad Singh vs. Smt. Radha Devi* takes the view that a remedy by way of injunction against a second marriage is not available under the provisions of the Hindu Marriage Act.

The case seem to have been argued only on the basis of the Hindu Marriage Act, 1955 and the question of remedy under the

Specific Relief Act, 1963 was not referred to by the parties or by the court. "The only point for consideration is ....where the suit as framed and filed by opposite party 1, could be maintained under any provision of the Hindu Marriage Act, 1955.

Though the two cases can be clearly distinguished and there is no real conflict, it is desirable to clarify the matter. *We recommend that a provision be introduced in Section 6 of the Hindu Marriage Act to the effect that nothing contained in the Hindu Marriage Act shall prevent a court from granting an injunction against a proposed bigamous marriage under Act or under the provisions of the Specific Relief Act, 1963.*

Laws in Former French and Portuguese Territories

After the merger of the former French and Portuguese colonial possessions with India, the laws in force prior to merger in these territories have not been abrogated and therefore they continue to be in force. A reference will now be made to these laws insofar as they affect the status of women.

A. Laws in Pondicherry

Prior to the merger, three different systems of personal law were applicable in Pondicherry. First, the Hindu Laws and customs applicable to Hindu and native Christians, (other than *renoncants*). However, in matters relating to marriage, divorce and allied topics the Christians were governed by the French Civil Code. Second, the Muslim Law, which was applied to the people of French origin and *renoncants.*

After the merger with India the categories of laws applicable increased and consequently the applicability of the Hindu Law became complicated. David Annoussamy categorizes the application of Hindu Law thus:

(A) Hindu Law prevailing in India applicable to migrants from the rest of India. *(B)* Hindu Law applicable to Hindus of Pondicherrian origin consisting of Indian statutes Applicable to Hindus). *(C)* Hindu Law consisting solely of the Hindu local customs adhered to by Hindus who remained French nationals. *(D)* Hindu Law consisting of customs of Pondicherry except in matters of marriage and divorce. This category has been further

sub-divided into two groups, viz: *(1)* Indian Christians who are governed according to their choice in respect of marriage either by the French Civil Code or the Indian Christian Marriage Act and the Indian Divorce Act, and *(2)* Indian Christians who are exclusively governed by the French Civil Code.

B. Laws in Goa, Daman and Diu

Even though these territories are now a part of India, no effort has far been made to extend the Hindu Marriage Act to them. The result is that a section of Hindu today continues to be governed by a law which permits polygamy.

(1) Districts of Goa and Diu

In the districts of Goa, polygamy is permissible among Hindus under the following circumstances:-

(i) when the previous wife is childless upto the age of 25 years;

(ii) when there is no male issue from the previous wife till her 30th year or when the previous wife who is below 30 does not conceive for ten years after her past conception;

(iii) in cases of judicial separation by wife and when there is no male issue.

(*Note:* In the case of Goa, previous wife's consent is required for the cases mentioned in (i) and (ii) above).

(2) District of Daman

According to the Code of Customs and Usage of Non-Christian inhabitants of Daman, the male individuals are allowed to have many wives but Bramos of Modd Caste cannot have more than two wives.

However, there is no polygamy among Dhobis, Morai-Machines, Barbers, Capris. Salvia, Betelas, Porobias and Bramos except those belonging to Teloquia and Modd caste.

(*Note*: For an individual to marry or re-marry more than twice – when his previous wives are living, an express previous consent of all of them is required which shall be drawn by the 'Chief of Rancho' or by the Notary Public in the Presence of four witnesses).

Judical justification of any of the circumstances mentioned above is a condition precedent for polygamy.

In our opinion, the continuation of such diverse laws contradictory to our social policy, in these territories is totally unjustified. *We recommend therefore, the immediate replacement of these laws by the Hindu Marriage Act 1955.*

II. AGE OF MARRIAGE

Legal Provisions

Another major social evil which was sought to be curbed by legislation is child marriage. The disastrous effects of such marriages have been discussed already. One of the few areas where our social reformers had taken the initiative, even in the 19th century was to curb this evil by legisiation. The first legislation was the Civil Marriage Act which laid down the age of marriage to be 14 years. But as only a very small section of the people married under this Act, the problem continued.

One of the adverse consequences of child marriage, as realised by the reformers, was early consummation, with disastrous effect on the health of the young wives and their children. An effort was made in 1891 to prevent early consummation by the Age of Consent Act which prohibited consummation before 12 years. Due to lack of publicity and propaganda, there was no impact of this provision. In 1925, the Age of Consent was raised to 13. This was the forerunner of the Sarda Act of 1929.

Perhaps the realisation that legislation, while one of the major instruments of social change, is not sufficient by itself to fight against deep rooted prejudices and traditional practice made the legislators compromise by leaving the validity of child marriage untouched but making such practice a penal offence. Parents of children, those 'performing, conducting or directing' as also the adult bridegroom, were all liable to punishment in varying degrees.

The Act was further amended but left untouched the structure of the earlier Act. The impact of this legislation and the present position regarding child marriages have been discussed already.

Apart from the Sarda Act, the various personal laws have their own minimum age of marriage. Not only do they vary in regard to the minimum age but also in the consequences of violation of the law.

The Hindu Marriage Act lays down as one of the conditions the completion of 18 years and 15 years by the bride-groom and the bride respectively. Though passed in the post-independence era, the Act remains silent about the effect on the marriage and continues the earlier penal policy in cases of violation. Most writers hold the view that the validity of the marriage is not affected and this is also supported by judicial decisions.

The Parsee Marriage and Divorce Act 1936 on the other hand lays down that no suit shall be brought to enforce a marriage between two parties or any contract connected with the marriage if at the date of the institution of the suit the husband has not completed age of 16 years and the wife 14 years. The Christian Marriage Act, 1872 provides that for a valid marriage under the Act, the age of the male shall exceed 16 years and that of the female 13 years. For a valid marriage under the classical Muslim Law the parties should not be minors, this is, the parties should have attained puberty. Puberty is presumed in the absence of evidence to the contrary, at 15 and 19 in the case of girls and boys respectively.

Only the special Marriage Act, 1954, a post-independence legislation which provides for a secular marriage irrespective of the religious affiliation of the parties, contemplates the solemnizations of marriage between adults under its provisions, as it fixes the minimum age at 21 and 18 for males and females respectively.

The legal position noted above brings forth an important feature, namely, a lesser age of marriage is prescribed in the case of girls. No doubt through the world, the laws generally provide for a lesser age in case of girls. For example, in the U.S.A. only eleven states prescribed the same minimum age for boys and girls. The remaining thirty-nine states permit girls to be married at a lower age than boys. As pointed out by Konowitz: "It (early marriage for women) can lead to premature removal from socially productive enterprise or lost opportunities."

When the legal age of marriage in case of a female is below the age of discretion she cannot be expected to form an intelligent opinion about her partner in life. The policy of law which permits the marriage of a girl before she is physically and mentally mature is open to serious question. As reported by the Pushpaben Committee, child marriage is one of the significant factor leading to the high incidence of suicide among young married women in India. Therefore, increasing the marriage age of girls to eighteen years is desirable.

In this context it is necessary to point out an anachronism that exists in the Muslim Law that governs some sects. After arranging puberty, a Muslim male in all sects and a Muslim female belonging to the Hanafi and Ithana Ashari Shirte sects can marry without a guardian. But "a Maliki, Shafi, or Daudi or Sulaymani Bohra virgin cannot marry without a guardian and her only remedy is to change over to the Hanafi School and marry according to its tenets."

In two recent decisions, viz. Muhammad Hazi Kammu *vs.* Ethiyumma and K. Abubukker *vs.* Marakkar (The Kerala High Court) struck a different note which mitigates this hardship. The parties in both cases were Shafis. In Abubukker's case, the mother who was divorced, sought the consent of her ex-husband to the daughters' marriages which he refused. On the marriage being solemnized, the father filed a suit for a declaration that the marriage was invalid as his consent was not obtained. The lower Court declared the marriage to be invalid even though the girl was already pregnant. Reversing the decision of the lower Court, Justice Pillai stated that under the Maliki and Shafi law the marriage of an adult girl is not valid unless her consent is obtained, and communicated through a legally authorised *wali* (guardian). As the father refused his consent, she could constitute any other relation or Kazi (in this case the Kazi) to act as her agent. *In our opinion a change in the law to remove the existing disability in these sub-schools and to bring them in conformity with the Hanafi law is necessary.*

Aspects Relating to Prevention of Child Marriages

As mentioned earlier the policy of the Child Marriage Restraint

Act or other statutes is not to invalidate child marriages but to punish their solemnization. The offences under the Act are, however, non-cognizable, and no woman is punishable with imprisonment.

There are large scale violations of the Act particularly in the rural areas. The non-cognizable character of the offence is a serious hindrance to the effective enforcement of this law. The State of Gujarat amended the Child Marriage Restraint Act by making it a cognizable offence. Provisions have also been made for the appointment of a Child Marriage Prevention Officer. These changes have been welcomed by the Pushpaben Committee. *We recommend that all offences under the Child Marriage Restraint Act should be made cognizable, and special officers appointed to enforce the law.*

Another effective approach to this problem is to tender such marriage void. But in the present social and economic conditions such a rigorous measure may create more problems than it seeks to solve. We suggest, that it should be envisaged as a future goal.

As immediate measures to deter child marriages and to alleviate their consequences we suggest the following:

> *(a)* to provide the girl the right to repudiate the marriage on attaining majority on lines similar to the "option of puberty" under Muslim Law;
>
> *Note*: A muslim girl married during the minority is entitled to a dissolution of marriage if the following facts are established : *(i)* that she was given in marriage by her father or other guardian before she attained the age of 15; *(ii)* that she repudiated the marriage before she attained the age of 18; *(iii)* that the marriage was not consummated.

In our view the right to repudiate the marriage on attaining majority should be made available to girls in all communities whether the marriage was consummated or not.

> *(b)* A general legal provision analogous to Section 38 of the Parsee Marriage and Divorce Act, 1865 which provides that "no suit shall be brought in any court to enforce any marriage between Parsees, or any contract connected with or arising out of any such marriage, if, at the date of the institution of the suit, the husband shall not have completed the age of 16

years, or the wife shall not have completed the age of 14 years." Under the Egyptian Civil Code, a marriage in contravention of the rule relating to age of the parties (completion of 18 years and 15 years in case of males and females respectively) though not invalid *per se* will not be registered. Under Article 99 of the Code such a marriage will not be recognized by the Court for the purpose of granting any relief, except a claim relating to legitimacy of issues.

We recommend legislation prohibiting courts from granting any relief in respect of a marriage solemmized in violation of the age requirements prescribed by law unless both the parties have completed the age of 18 years.

Compulsory Registration of Marriages

Compulsory registration of marriages operates as an effective check on child and bigamous marriages and also offers reliable proof of marriage. It ensures the legitimacy and inheritance rights of children. Section 8 of the Hindu Marriage Act, 1955, enables the State Governments to provide for compulsory registration of marriages, and any person contravening the rule may be punished with a fine which may extent to twenty-five rupees. However, it has been stated that failure to register a marriage will not affect its validity. Laws which provide for the voluntary registration of Muslim marriages are in force in the States of Assam, Bihar, Orissa and Bengal.

Table 6.1
Number of Marriages Registered Under the Special Marriages Act 1954

	Bombay	*Rajasthan*	*Delhi*
1968	601	11	148
1969	621	8	194
1970	766	13	229
1971	705	11	235
1972	816	6	212
1982	830	8	231
1992	893	7	238

Among the Parees and Indian Christians the registration of marriages is compulsory. Registration is also compulsory for marriages solemnized under the Special Marriages Act, 1954. Section 16 of this Act permits voluntary registration of marriages celebrated under other laws. The figures given (in Table 6.1 & 6.2) illustrate that the appeal of this secular law, though it ensures better legal protection to all parties, is still limited to a very small minority. Neither has the permission for voluntary registration attracted much response.

The ultimate object should be to recongnize registration as the sole and conclusive proof of marriage, irrespective of the religious rites under which it was solemnized. It may be mentioned here that India has neither signed nor ratified the United Nations Convention on Consent to Marriage, Minimum Age for Marriage and Registration of Marriage. Explaining the position of India on ratification, the Indian delegate stated "the Convention would impose an obligation to introduce legislation, and since that might not be feasible at the present time he must reserve his Government's position on the question of ratification."

Table 6.2
Number of Marriges Celebrated Under Other Laws but Subsequently Registered Under Section 16 of the Special Marriages Act

	Bombay
1968	19
1969	18
1970	43
1971	36
1972	26
1982	27
1992	33

We regret that for over a decade no attempt has been made to introduce legislation to implement the objects of the U.N. Convention. This attitude indicates a casualness and lack of concern on matters affecting the status of women. *We recommend that registration should be made compulsary for all marriages.* We have a clear precedent for a uniform measure in the Registration of Births and Deaths Act.

III. DOWRY

We are compelled to record our finding that the Dowry Prohibition Act 1961, passed with the ostensible purpose of curbing this evil, if not of eradicating it, has signally failed to achieve its purpose. In spite of the rapid growth of this practice there are practically no cases reported under the Act. During its tours of all the States, the Committee was informed of only one case that was pending before the court in Kerala, in which the father had fild the complaint only because of the ill-treatment meted out to his daughter.

During the debate on the Dowry Prohibition Bill, on MP observed, "But I feel the whole problem will be solved – very easily and more quickly, not by legislation, but by rousing social conscience. As soon as our women get economic opportunities and economic freedom, as soon as avenues of employment and other opportunities are opened to them, as soon as they become independent of their families, possibly there would not be any occasion for this low to operate."

The eradication of this evil by rousing social conscience is seemingly an attractive approach. The Committee's findings, however, indicate that there is hardly any evidence of social conscience in the country today. In Indore, at a fairly large meeting, the Committee was told of the case of a girl who was burnt in the legs and in the back by her in-laws as she had not brought an adequate dowry. The acceptance of this situation was indicative of society's indifference to this social evil. No one at the meeting mentioned the need to report the case to the police or even of socially boycotting the family. Many such cases were brought to our notice, butnow here did we hear of any social censure being exercised.

An increase in economic freedom and job opportunities for women, to the extent that the practice of dowry becomes obsolete, under the existing economic conditions, will be a very long process. The educated youth is grossly insensitive to the evil and unashamedly contributes to its perpetuation. In our opinion, therefore, a stringent enforcement of the policy and purpose of Act may serve to educate public opinion better. *A very small but significant step could be taken by the Government, by declaring the taking or giving of dowry to be against the Government Servants Conduct Rules.* Such a lead was given earlier to prevent bigamous marriages and giving or taking of dowry should be similarly dealt with.

The major cause for the failure of the Dowry Prohibition Act, 1961 is that an infringement of the provisions of the Act is not made a congnizable offence. That the offences under the Act should be made cognizable was in fact suggested during the debate in Lok Sabha.

But the offence was not made congnizable, as it was apprehended that this might result in the harassment of citizens by the police and lead also to undue invasion of the individual's right of privacy

In our opinion the policy of making the offence noncognizable completely nullifies the purpose of the Act as it is unrealistic to think that the father of a girl who had paid the dowry (and who done is in a position to adduce evidence of the fact that dowry was stipulated and given) would prefer a complaint against the interests of his daughter after her marriage. *We recommend, therefore, that the offences, under the Act, should be made cognizable.* We are fortified in our conclusion by the recommendation of the Pushpaben Committee. To overcome the fears regarding harassment by the police and encroachment on the right of privacy; *it is suggested that the enforcement of social laws like the Dowry Prohibition. Act, the Child Marriage Restraint Act, should be entrusted to a separate administration with which social workers and enlightened members of the community should be associated.*

In addition, two ancillary provisions should be incorporated in the Dowry Prohibition Act, 1961. It has been pointed out that one of the 'major loopholes' in the existing legislation is that anything is allowed in the name of gifts and presents.

Therefore, *any gifts made to the bridegroom or his parents in excess of Rs. 500 or which can be so used as to reduce his own financial liability should be made punishable.*

The practice of displaying the dowry by parents of the bride of the bridegroom, as discussed earlier, is prevalent in some parts of India. This naturally tends to perpetuate the practice as others follow sult. To curb this evil we recommend legislation on the lines of the West Pakistan Dowry (Prohibition of Display) Act 1967 which penalises such display.

We suggest that *an evaluation of the impact of the amended Dowry Prohibition Act should be made after five years.* It will help in plugging loopholes which facilitate the evasion of this law. *The next step should be to set a ceiling even on the gifts that may be made to the bride.*

This will help to improve the situation further because we have found that gifts given to the bride are often only a guise for dowry since generally she has little or no control over them.

IV. DIVORCE

A monogamous marriage without the right of divorce would cause great hardship to both parties to the marriage. The concept of 'union for life' or the sacramental nature of the marriage which renders the marriage indissoluble has gradually been eroded and through legislation the right of divorce has been introduced in all legal systems in India, but the same various and unequal treatment of sexes characterizes this branch of law also.

According to the Census of 1971, the total number of divorced or separated women in the country is estimated to be 8,17,700; of which 7,43,200 are in the rural areas and 1,27,500 in urban areas. The ratio of divorced or separated woman is 1963 per thousand males.

A survey undertaken by the Census in 1961 in 587 selected villages with a sample of 1,33,775 marriages covering a period of 50 years, had indicated wide acceptance of divorce by the village community and some variations of incidence among the religious communities. Incidence of divorce was highést among Muslims (6.06 per cent), followed by Hindus (3.21 per cent). Among the Buddhists it was 3.07, among the Jains 1.69 per cent and among Sikh 0.91 per cent. The incidence of divorce among Christians was considerably lower (0.41 per cent). The causes for divorce show that adultery and barrenness are the commonest grounds for divorce in most of the villages studied. Extreme poverty is also found to be cause for divorce. In Rajasthan: sexual incompatibility and incapacity are recognized as grounds for divorce.

Hindu Law

According to traditionalists, divorce was unknown in Hindu Law. Even today divorce is not a socially accepted norm among many sections.

"We can take judicial notice of the fact that even today considerable sections of the Hindu society look with disfavour on the idea of dissolving a marriage."

Polygamy, without the right of divorce, caused, in many cases, tremendous hardship.

Customary Divorce. Contrary to the general notion regarding the indissolubility of Hindu marriages, a large section of Hindus among the lower castes have traditionally practised divorce. These customary forms of divorce were recognized, both socially and judicially. The usual customary forms are:

(a) by mutual consent;
(b) unilaterally—at the pleasure of the husband or by the abandonment of the wife;
(c) by deed of divorce (Char—chitti);

(a) By mutual consent. The custom of obtaining divorce by mutual consent is prevalent among certain castes in Bombay, Madras, Mysore and Kerala. In Madhya Pradesh it has been held that divorce by mutual consent is a valid custom among the Patwas of that State. A customary form of divorce by agreement (chuttam-chutta) amongst the Barai Chaurasiyas of U.P. has been declared valid by the Allahabad High Court. These are only a few illustrations to indicate the existence of divorce by mutual consent.

(b) Unilateral divorce. According to the custom prevailing in Manipur (Khaniaba), it has been stated that a husband can dissolve the marriage without any reason or at his pleasure. Among the Rajpur Gujaratis in Khandesh, and in the Pakhali Community marriage is dissolved if the husband abandons or deserts the wife. Among the Vaishyas of Gorakhpur in Uttar Pradesh a husband may abandon or desert his wife, and dissolution takes place even without reference to the caste tribunal.

(c) Divorce by Deed. This form is prevalent among certain castes in South India, also in Himachal Pradesh and the Jat community. Recently the Supreme Court has upheld a deed executed by the husband divorcing his wife.

Usually customary divorce are through the intervention of the traditional Panchayats of caste tribunals. Therefore, in states where this has not been customary, the courts have not permitted Panchayts to take upon the themselves the right to dissolve a marriage. Once the custom is proved, however, the courts will not interfere.

The courts have exercised a lot of judicial scrutiny and discretion in upholding or rejecting such customary divorce practices. In doing so they have applied the strict test for the validity of such customs. When the existence of a custom was not proved, or where the custom could be regarded as running counter to the spirit of Hindu Law, or was against public policy or morality, courts have declared such customary forms of divorce as invalid.

Under customary law there is no waiting period after divorce to remarry. But if divorce is obtained under the Hindu Marriage Act, then either party to the marriage can lawfully remarry only after a lapse of one year after the decree of divorce (Sec. 15). Retention of customary forms of divorce under the Hindu Marriage Act is advantageous because this process of dissolving the marriage saves time and money in litigations. The only difficulty that may arise is if the divorce according to customary law is brought at some stage to the notice of the court and the latter decrees that particular form of divorce to be against public policy or morality. If one or both parties have remarried, such a marriage will be void and the status of the children will be affected. To minimise this, it has been suggested that the Ministry of Law should prepare an exhaustive record of customs relating to divorce found in different States and set up a panel of social-legal experts to determine if any of these customs are invalid. Copies of the record should be made freely and easily available to the people and the Panchayats.

With the enactment of the Hindu Marriage Act of 1955, divorce became a part of the law governing all Hindus. The ground for this had been already prepared by the passing of the Hindu Women's Right to Separate Residence and Maintenance Act in 1946, which *inter alia,* permitted the wife to separate from her husband on the ground that he had married again. Following this, some of the States took the initiative and as with monogamy, legislated to permit divorce for Hindus.

Divorce Under the Hindu Marriage Act, 1955

The various grounds on which a husband or a wife can obtain divorce are:

(*a*) living in adultery,
(*b*) conversion to other religion,
(*c*) insanity,
(*d*) incurable form of leprosy,
(*e*) venereal disease,
(*f*) renunciation,
(*g*) where the respondent has not been heard of as being alive for a period of seven years or more by persons who would naturally have heard of it,
(*h*) failure to resume cohabitation for a period of 2 years after the decree of judicial separation, and
(*i*) failure to comply with a decree for restitution of conjugal rights. Two additional grounds have been given to the wife: (*i*) to obtain a divorce if the husband has more than one wife living, and (*ii*) if he has been guilty of rape, sodomy or bestiality. The former has a retrospective effect in the sense that when the marriages took place (*i.e.* before the Act), polygamy was legally permissible. This right can be exercised by either of the wives, and has obviously been provided to strengthen the social policy of monogamy. From the cases reported, it appears that many women have benefited form this provision.

Adultery: Since adultery is a very grave matrimonial offence, a very high degree or standard of proof is required. The Courts have insisted that the offence of adultery should be proved beyond reasonable doubt. A husband or wife can ask for divorce only if at the time of filing the suit, the other party 'is living in adultery'. A single act of extra marital intercourse in not sufficient to dissolve the marriage, thought it is sufficient for a decree of judicial separation. The Bombay High Court, therefore, rejected the petition of a husband as at the time of the petition there was no evidence that the wife was leading an adulterous life, though there was evidence that the she had done so earlier.

Refusal to resume cohabitation. Another provision of the act which is often taken advantage of is non-compliance with a decree restituting conjugal rights for two years or the lapse of the same period after a decree of judicial separation. One of the grounds for judicial separation is desertion provided it is 'without reasonable cause'. In interpreting 'reasonable cause', the judiciary has often exhibited their inability to appreciated the socio-economic changes and the Constitutional right to equality.

Whenever conjugal rights have come into open conflict with the woman's right of equal opportunity in education or employment, the attitude of the judiciary has often been rather ambiguous. Instead of guiding the conflicting parties towards a rational adjustment to the process of social change, the judiciary has either evaded the issue or thrown its weight on the side of the traditional view of the husband's authority. Two illustrations will suffice to demonstrate this tendency:

(a) A husband's demand for his wife to resign her job as a teacher in a city away from his place of employment, to join him, was upheld by the Punjab High Court, which ruled that it was the duty of the wife to remain under the 'roof and protection and submit obediently' to the authority of the husband.

(b) In a similar case, the Allahabad High Court took a step forward by opining that the concepts of protection and society are "inelastic and rigid rules which cannot be interpreted in the context of present day conditions and needs of society.... In view of the altered social and economic conditions both husband and wife many think it necessary to work and contribute to the family chest". The court, therefore, conceded the right of deciding the question to the wife where "in cases of economic stress... for the sake of the family and children" the wife genuinely thinks it is necessary for her to work. The judgment, while conceding the right in cases of genuine economic necessity, totally evades the issue of the individual women's right to decide whether to work or not.

We are of the opinion that difference in the place of work should not be regarded as ground for a case of desertion or restitution of conjugal rights.

Cruelty and desertion. Cruelty and desertion have not been made grounds for divorce thought they are recognized as grounds for a judicial separation. It, therefore, follows that in these cases the innocent party to the marriage, agains whom there has been cruelty, or who has been deserted, has to wait for two years before he or she can get a divorce. Uttar Pradesh has given the lead in this and amended their law to make these grounds for divorce. *In our opinion these should be added as grounds for divorce in the Hindu Marriage Act so that persons are not compelled to follow the present circuitous route and undergo the expense of going to court twice.*

Muslim Law

Under Muslim Law a husband has an absolute and unlimited right to repudiate the marriage at his will. This is known as Talaq. A Muslim wife has no such right to dissolve her marriage. Unwritten and traditional law tried to ameliorate her position by permitting her to seek dissolution under the following form:

(a) *Talaqi Tafwid.* This is a form of delegated divorce. According to this the husband delegates his right of divorce in a marriage contract which may stipulate that *inter alia* on his taking another wife the first wife has the right to divorce him. The courts have upheld these pre-nuptial and post-nuptial agreements as not opposed to public nor against the spirit of Muslim Law. The Assam High Court has strengthened this right by declaring that such a power of Talaq given to the wife is irrevocable.

(b) *Khul.* This is a dissolution by an agreement between the parties to the marriage, on the wife's giving some consideration to the husband for her release from the marriage tie. The terms are a matter of bargain and usually takes the form of the wife giving up her dower.

(c) *Mubarrat.* This is divorce by mutual consent.

According to Hanafi Law the inability of the husband to maintain his wife does not give her the right to dissolve the marriage. Following the Hanafi Law the court in India had refused the wife the right to dissolve her marriage in the ground of non-payment of maintenance. The Shafi and the Maliki Laws, however, allowed the wife to obtain divorce on this ground.

Dissolution at Muslim Marriages Act, 1939. This Act took advantage of the law as enunciated by the Maliki and Shafi Schools and recognized the right of a wife to dissolve the marriage on the following grounds.

(i) that the whereabouts of the husband have not been known for a period of four years;

(*ii*) that the husband has neglected or has failed to provide for her maintenance for a period of two years;

(*iii*) that the husband has been sentenced to imprisonment for a period of seven years or upwards;

(*iv*) that the husband has failed to perform, without reasonable cause, his marital obligations for a period of three years;

(*v*) that the husband was impotent at the time of marriage and continues to be so;

(*vi*) that the husband has been insane for a period of two years or is suffering from leprosy or a virulent venereal disease;

(*vii*) that she, having been given in marriage by her father or other guardian before she attained the age of fifteen years, repudiated the marriage before attaining the age of eighteen years; provided that marriage has not been consummated:

(*viii*) that the husband treated her with cruelty....

(*ix*) on any other ground which is recongnized as valid for the dissolution of marriage under Muslim Law.

Muslim women have benefited by the Act. The provisions that have been resorted to most frequently are the 'option of puberty' and failure to provide maintenance by the husband.

Option of Puberty. According to traditional Muslim Law, when a minor girls had been given in marriage by the father or the father's father, the marriage was valid. She could, however, repudiate the marriage if she could show that the guardian had acted negligently or fraudulently. But if the minor had been given in marriage by any other guardian, she had the right to repudiate the marriage on attaining puberty. The present Act has modified the traditional law permitting her to exercise the right irrespective of who was the guardian who gave her in marriage. The courts in India have interpreted this right very liberally, often invoking the principle of equity and justice in favour of the girl. They have not rigidly applied the letter of the law in regard to the time when this right could be exercised. It has been held that a minor wife did not lose her right to repudiate the marriage within a reasonable time after she came to know of her right and not necessarily when she attained puberty. In such cases, they have even waived the condition of non-consummation when such consummation was by force or before she attained the age of 15.

Right of the wife to dissolve the marriage on ground of failure to maintain. This right has been interpreted in two ways. One group of decisions, basing itself on the traditional 'fault theory', has denied the right to a wife to divorce where her conduct was such as to absolve the husband from his duty to provide maintenance. The other group has tended to uphold the right irrespective of the wife's conduct.

These two groups of decision clearly indicate that legislation alone cannot eliminate rigid traditionalism, with its desire to preserve the status quo. Without supporting judicial interpretation, even the policy of the law is negated. The decision of Justice Krishna lyer is, therefore, significant as he has focussed his observation of the right of the Muslim wife to divorce when her husband has failed to provide her maintenance for two years. He has used his erudition to support the theory of dissolution when the marriage his broken down, irrespective of the relative faults of the parties.

> "There is no merit in preserving intact the tie of marriage when the parties are not able to and fail to live within the bonds of Allah, that is to fulfil their mutual marital obligations, and there is no desecration involved in dissolving a marriage which has failed. The entire emphasis is on making the marital union a reality and when this is not possible...., the Quran enjoins a dissolution.... This secular and pragmatic approach on Muslim law of divorce happily harmonises with contemporary concepts in advanced countries."

We recommend that the right of the wife to divorce, on the failure of the husband to maintain her, irrespective of her conduct which may be the main or contributory cause, should be clearly spelt out.

Muslim Law had always recognized that in some cases the wife may be able to get a divorce. To the uncodified law the Dissolution of Muslim Marriages Act 1939 has added further grounds. But the power of the husband to pronounce talaq unilaterally remains, and has is no way been curtailed either judicially or through legislation. As long as this absolute and unlimited right remains, the position of the Muslim wife will remain insecure and her status cannot be raised. We totally disagree with the view that with Justice Krishna lyer's judgment and her right to obtain divorce by 'Khul', a Muslim women's rights "are brought into approximation with those of the man." While the judgment is undoubtedly a great step forward, it has to be remembered that she still has to wait for two years without maintenance before getting her release. Also, a right to buy her release, as provided in the Koran can hardly be regarded as approximating the unilateral right of the man.

Legislation is the only instrument which can bring the Muslim divorce law into line with not only the needs of society but with the prevailing law in other Muslim countries. Turkey and Cyprus have completely prohibited unilateral divorce, while in Tunisia, Algeria, Iraq and Iran the husband has to apply to a court. In Pakistan Legislation has restrained the freedom of the husband to dicorce his wife. He has to inform the Arbitration Council which will try and bring about a reconciliation. The husband's pronouncement of 'talaq' without informing the Arbitration Council has been declared to be an offence.

We recommend immediate legislation to eliminate the unilateral right of divorce and to introduce parity of rights for both partners regarding grounds for seeking dissolution of a marriage.

Christian Law

All Christians are governed by the Indian Divorce Act, 1869. Under the Act both husband and wife can obtain a divorce, but there is a great difference between the rights of the husband and the wife. The husband can obtain a divorce if the wife has committed adultery. The wife can seek a divorce on the following grounds.

- *(a)* husband's conversion from Christianity and marriage another woman.
- *(b)* incestuous adultery.
- *(c)* bigamy with adultery.
- *(d)* marriage with another women with adultery.
- *(e)* rape; sodomy or bestiality.
- *(f)* adultery with cruelty.
- *(g)* adultery with desertion.

Thus the wife has to prove two offences by the husband before she can obtain a divorce.

The law is so outdated that the need for revision has been felt for quite sometime. The Government, realising the need for reform, referred the matter to the Law Commission in 1960. The Commission prepared a Draft Bill. The Christian Marriage and Matrimonial Causes Bill, 1960, contains almost all the grounds included for divorce under the Special Marriage Act, 1954, such as desertion, cruelty, adultery, leprosy, venereal disease, conversion to another religion, and willful refusal to consummate the marriage. Further, either party to a marriage can also obtain a decree of judicial separation on any of the grounds mentioned for divorce.

We regret that in spite of these preparatory steps, no action to enact this measure has been taken by the Government so far and *recommended that no further time be lost to reform and amend this law on the lines suggested by the Law Commission.*

Parsee Law

The Parsees are governed by the Parsee Marriage and Divorce Act, 1936. Both the parties to the marriage can initiate divorce proceeding on the following grounds·

- *(a)* continuous absence for seven years without information to those persons who would naturally have heard of him or her.
- *(b)* non-consummation.
- *(c)* insanity.
- *(d)* adultery, bigamy, rape on an unnatural offence.
- *(e)* causing grievous hurt or venereal disease.
- *(f)* imprisonment for seven years or more.
- *(g)* desertion for three years.
- *(h)* non-resumption of co-habitation following a decree of judicial separation or restitution of conjugal rights.
- *(i)* conversion.

(In addition to these common grounds, the wife can obtain a divorce if she has been completed by her husband to prostitution. The husband has the right to dissolve the marriage if the wife was pregnant by some other person at the time of marriage).

Jewish Law

The Jews in India are not governed by statutory law but by their customary law. Originally, the ghet was the only form of divorce. In India, however, dissolution of the marriage can be done through the court on grounds of adultery or cruelty. The marriages are generally monogamous excepting in certain specific cases. Because they are a small minority, no effort has been made to codify or reform this law. *We feel that this should be undertaken now and the principle of monogamy as well as the normal grounds for divorce as provided in the Special Marriage Act should be adopted for the community also.*

Special Marriage Act 1954. This Act provides for a secular form of marriage which can be taken advantage of by all persons in India irrespective of their religious faith. Persons who marry under this Act will be governed by the provisions of the Act and not by their own personal law, with respect to their matrimonial rights and remedies.

The grounds on which divorce can be obtained by either party to marriage are adultery, desertion for a period of three years, cruelty, unsound mind for 3 years, leprosy, venereal disease, continuous absence for 7 years without information to those persons who would naturally have heard of him or her, non-resumption of cohabitation for one year following a decree of judicial separation or restitution of conjugal rights. In addition to these, the wife can obtain divorce on the ground of rape, sodomy or bestiality. A special feature of this act is that the parties can also dissolve the marriage by mutual consent. All that the parties need do in order to obtain divorce under this provision is to present a petition to the court that they have been living separately for a period of one year or more and that they have not been able to live together and that they have mutually agreed to dissolve the marriage.

Conversion as a ground for divorce. In the field of personal law and particularly in divorce, the existence of various legal systems create a peculiar situation. The Constitution recognizes the right freely to profess, practise and propagate religion. Conversion, therefore, from one faith to another is an individual's right and the motive for the conversion is or should be beyond judicial scrutiny. But when such conversion impinges on the right of another persons, the question poses a problem. In India today as a legacy of the multiple systems, a person by his or her conversion also acquires the right to be governed by a different set of laws. Even after the Constitution, the codified Hindu Marriage Act has mentioned conversion as a ground for divorce. Is conversion then to be treated as a matrimonial wrong? Under statutory Muslim Law a woman converted to a faith other than Islam or renouncing Islam has only the right to divorce if the husband has committee a matrimonial wrong conversion per se does not affect the validity of the marriage and is in no way a bar to its continuance. On the other hand, a man converted to Islam for another religion has the right to be governed by his new personal law, including the right to marry more than once. This is so even when his first marriage was a monogamous marriage. He is also entitled to claim that his new faith does not permit his to remain married to a Hindu and he can, therefore, proceed to divorce her by uttering 'talaq' three times. The Indian Divorce Act does not recognize conversion as affecting the validity of the marriage unless it is followed by the marriage of the husband to another woman. The Converts Dissolution Act permits the convert to Christianity to dissolve the marriage provided the marriage has in-effect broken down as a result of the conversion. It requires to be proved clearly that cohabitation has been discontinued because of the conversion. Under the Parsee Law, conversion is a ground for divorce provided the suit is brought within 2 years. This thorny question is dealt with in many ways, but the problems remains of reconciling the right to freedom of religion with the possible impact of conversion on marriages. It has been suggested that the question of marital rights on conversion should be governed by principles of equity, justice and good conscience. The other is that no converted person can, for a period of two years at least, be able to affect any marital right by resorting to the new relation. While the second suggestion has the merit of deterring people from easy conversion to solve their matrimonial problems, *in our opinion conversion should not be a ground for divorce as it offers an easy way of evading matrimonial obligations.*

Divorce by mutual consent. Our review of the different laws governing divorce indicates that both customary laws and the secular law, *i.e.* the Special Marriage Act, 1954 recognize mutual consent as a ground for divorce, but this conspicuous by its absence in any of the statutory laws governing different communities. On the other hand, the religious laws and judicial interpretations of them have generally tended to emphasize the fault theory, being particular to prevent the party guilty of a matrimonial wrong from obtaining a dissolution of the marriage. This leads often to the use of perjured evidence. As there is even today an indirect way of getting divorce by mutual consent, by registering one's marriage under the Special Marriage Act, after celebration according to religious rites, *we recommend that this ground should be recognized in all the personal laws so that two adults whose marriage has, in fact, broken down can get it dissolved honourably.*

Prostitution as a ground for divorce. The provision in the Parsee Marriage and Divorce Act, 1936 which enables a wife to obtain a divorce if her husband has compelled her to prostitution, in our view, is a very desirable protection. *We recommend inclusion of this provision in all other Personal Laws.*

As a general principle, we recommend parity of rights regarding grounds for both husband and wife. This already exists in some of the personal laws, and in our view is essential to guarantee equality of status for both partners. It may be noted that the findings of our survey on this question shows an overwhelming opinion in favour of party. "74 per cent of the respondents (72.9 per cent males and 74.37 per cent females) have stated that the grounds for divorce should be the same for both husband and wife.

V. ADOPTION

"Adoption is the institutionalized practice through which an individual belonging by birth to one kinship ties that are socially defined as equivalent to the congenital ties. These new ties supersede the old ones either wholly or in part." It is the act of a person who takes upon himself the position of a parent to a child who is not in law his own child.

The origin of the custom of adoption is lost in antiquity. It has, however, been recognized in India for centuries and is also recognized in other South Asian countries, such as Burma and Thailand. Adoption forms the subject matter of personal law. In India the only personal law which recognizes adoption in the true sense of the term is Hindu Law which regarded adoption as the taking of a son as a substitute' in case there is no male issue.

Muslim Law

Even though Muslim Law does not recognize adoption, in India previously the law had permitted this right to Hindu converts to Islam, who had enjoyed this right prior to their conversion. This customary right was, however, partially abrogated by the Shariat Act under which a Muslim could make a declaration that he and his sons would in future give up all customary rights including that of adoption and be governed by the Act.

But the custom of adopting sons was in vogue in Arabia at the time of the Prophet Mohammad. The word *adia* used in the Holy Quran means adopted sons. Justice Ameer Ali held that a family Waqf could be made not only for the benefit of descendants of the founder but also of dependents, which would include an adopted child who has resided with the settler as a dependent relation. The Lahore High Court held the word *'family'* to include an adopted child who had resided with the settler as a dependent relation. All these clearly indicated that adoption was not unknown among Indian Muslims.

Islam never gave any special significance to an adopted son, as it does not to a natural son. Islamic religion, unlike the Hindu one, does not associate a son, or any other relative, with the performance of the last rites of a deceased Muslim whether male or female. It, therefore, does not recommend adoption of a son or a daughter for a person dying issueless, nor does it absolutely prohibit it. The Quranic verses having a bearing on adoption did not lay down a specific negative rule.

Parsee Law

For the Parsees, there is no law of adoption as such or is adoption recognized by custom. However, the widow of a Parsee dying issueless can adopt a *Palak* on the 4th day of the deceased's death, for the ad-hoc purpose of performing certain religious rites for the deceased. This adoption is only for a limited purpose and does not confer any proprietary right on the Palak.

7

Women and Social Change : An Overview of Islamic Society

More than 850 million people profess Islam. Muslim societies are found from the Atlantic in the west, throughout North and West Africa, to the Middle East. There are Muslims in the Balkan area and in the Soviet Union, where they represent a large and widely-spread Iranian and Turkish-speaking population. The latter live as far north as the Baikal Sea and extend eastward spoiling over the Chinese border into China proper. Islam is the dominate religion in Pakistan and Bangladesh. It embraces Malaysia as well and reaches our to the southern Philippines and Indonesia.

Muslim societies have increasingly attracted world interest within the last decade concurrently with their growing impact on the general economic and political situation. The economic influence that some Islamic countries exert *via* their control over large portions of the total world production of crude of and the consequent impact on trends in world prices, international trade relations, and on the socio-economic development of the world, have raised attentiveness about and provided incentives to understand Muslim social systems, values and beliefs. These inclinations have been further stimulated as Western countries are facing greate difficulties in fully understanding the recent political developments in a number of Islamic states, especially as regards the role of religion in these changes. This applies for instance to the Iranian revolution, which replaced the Shah regime with a politico–religious government headed by Ayatollah Khomeini. It applies also to the events in Afghanistan, where the Saur revolution in 1978 and the subsequent military intervention by the Soviet Union has met dogged resistance, which to some extent is cast in religious idioms and motivated by religious beliefs. Or one may think of the politics of Colonel Ghaddafi, which can be understood only in its specific Islamic setting. A growing need has also been felt for further insight into other aspects of Muslim culture, specifically those regarding family life and Muslim attitudes toward behaviour between the sexes, to marriage and love relationships, *i.e.* for further insights into the structures and values that influence the situation of Muslim women. This interest has neen spurred by various incentives, one of which is the fact of differences in values in respect of domestic life and sex-roles. In Western societies numerous problems arise from a lack of understanding of the way of life of Muslim immigrant workers and their families, and the resulting tension may cause major grievances and even lead to conflict. For Westerners who live in societies where marriage partners are sought and chosen by the individual, ideally on the basis of mutual love, and where such love matches are idealized and made objects of glorification in numerous ways as, for instance, by the Hollywood cinema industry, it is bewildering to be confronted with alternative views and attitudes on these matters. It may even be shocking to face the fact that not only are such values not shared, and that love relationships may be socially condemned, but that under certain circumstances, for instance in Saudi Arabia, the social condemnation may take the form of capital punishment. The differences in values may even become highly politicized, as was the case when the British television production, 'Death of a Princess', became an international hot issue and caused many diplomatic headaches.

The Islamic world embraces an overwhelming complexity of social forms and cultural ways, and Muslim societies are found at all levels of techno-economic development. There are Muslims who make their living as agriculturalists by the means of but a simple hoe, others as highly specialized rice-cultivators, while still others make use of the most advanced agro-technology, managing farms in accordance with modern agricultural methods. There are still Muslim societies that maintain their existence as pastoral nomads with flocks of sheep, goats, and camels, or with cows. But an ever-increasing number of Muslims are becoming urbanized and integrated at various levels into the industrial sectors or within administration, business or military sectors as a part in the process of rapid modernization that is taking place in Muslim states today. Muslim women therefore live under widely different conditions, and their position and the influence they can exert over their own lives changes considerably from one society to the other.

Islamic laws and traditions are frequently evoked to account for behaviour among Muslims, particularly behaviour between the sexes. This may be so, as pointed out by Emrys Peters with regard to the Middle East (Peters, 1978), because so much of our knowledge of these societies until recently has been drawn only from literary sources. This may have furthered a far too simplistic but widespread opinion in the Western world, namely that Muslim women occupy a position of absolute subjugation; that they are completely under the domination of men, controlled within the family by their fathers, brothers or male cousins, and later in marriage by their husbands. Furthermore, it is believed by many that they have but little knowledge of and no influence on the wider workings of their society. They appear to be without a say in public matters, unable to take action in politics, and prevented from doing so in the religious field, as Muslim women cannot hold religious office. Muslim women are thought of as almost non-existent within the public sphere, kept out of sight in confinement within the protective walls of their homes or 'invisible' when, heavily veiled, they move outside these.

Sociological and anthropological investigations of the social organization and the behavioural patterns even within the core area of the Islamic world demonstrate however, that the status of women, their rights and duties as regards their control over property, over their own body, the degree of seclusion and veiling, etc., vary considerably, as eminently demonstrated by the papers of this volume. It is a fact that even among more traditional societies in Saudi Arabia there are striking differences with regard to women's influence in domestic and political affairs. Anthropological studies reveal, moreover, that Islamic laws do not necessarily determine the behaviour of the sexes and the position of women. It is rather a complex picture of the relationship between Islam and the actual life situations of Muslim women that emerges, when we take a closer look at Islamic social systems, and one is confronted with a considerable range of interpretations of laws and traditions within these. Comparative examinations of specific practices as regards, for instance, women's inheritance of property show that there may be greater differences in such practices within communities that declare themselves adherents of a particular Islamic school of law than between communities belonging to different schools. The variability in the position of Muslim women is even more conspicuous when we move outside the core area of Islamic civilization to African and Asian Muslim societies. Here Islam and its laws were adopted by cultural and social systems totally different from those in the Middle East in which the religion arose. Especially among these, actual social practice and the working out of women's rights and women's social standing in general, may be inconsistent with the laws of any Islamics school.

This is not to say that Islam is not a force in the behaviour of people. Nowhere do Muslims question that their particular way of acting, their handling of social matters, their interpretations of Islam, are in accordance with the will of Allah as laid down in the holy book, the Koran. *To the Muslim world Islam is more than a set of beliefs and ritual practices. It constitutes a complete system of thought and rules of behaviour codified to envelop Man in all his relations.* The Koran contains God's will and his commands, revealed to man through Muhammad. As such these commands are divine, they are given once and for all, and no human being can change them, nothing can be added nor subtracted. However, God's will is also expressed in the Sunna, containing the traditions about and the sayings of the Prophet Muhammad, and the Canon Law or *Shari'a* is composed of the Koran as well as the Sunna. It is the Sunna that provides for interpretations of the Koran and for an adaptation of its commands and norms to existing and ever changing social systems.

The interpretation and transmission of the *shari'a* has always been in the hands of male lawyer-theologians. Already in the eighth century A.D., barely a hundred years after the death of the Prophet, the split between the two major Islamic schools of thought, the Shi'ite and the Sunnite, was a fact, and the latter was further divided into four major law-schools, the Hanafi, Maliki,

Shafi'i and Hanbali. Moreover, it is well to remember that historically Islam arose in a tribal society in Arabia, organized along patrilineal principles of descent, inheritance and succession.[1] In a very brief period of time after its rise in the seventh century it developed into the Islamic civilization moulded upon traits that were prevalent in ancient Arabian and other Middle Eastern societies, which then spread with the Arabs through North Africa to other parts of this continent and eastwards to Asia. The Islamic civilization was not able to expect traditional cultures and replace matrilineal and bilateral forms of social organizations in all parts of the world, where the population becomes Muslims. Rather these social systems incorporated aspects of the Islamic culture together with its faith and ritual practices.

Here we shall not dwell in the historical context in which Islam was formulated,[2] nor on the processes during which the *shari'a* has been interpreted and modified, and the highly different sexual politics that rusulted in various social categories and groups as well as in modern Muslim states. Faced with the diferences in interpretation of the *shari'a* and with the considerable variance in social practice as regards the regulation of women's lives in the hundreds of social systems that proclaim the Muslim faith, one of the intriguing questions to be asked is: *what is it in Islam that can be used to justify specific kinds of interaction between the sexes, and what are the symbolic qualities of Islam in this respect*? Some scholars have suggested that at least part of an answer to this question can be found in the Muslim concept of sexuality.

Social orders regulate sex in highly different ways, and the integration of sexuality and religion takes many forms. The differences between Western and Eastern societies in this respect has often been stressed (cf. Bousquet, G. -H.: *La Morale de I'Islam et son Ethique Sexuelle*). In Western Christian experience sexuality itself has been disdained and at times severely attacked by the Church. In the Middle East on the other hand sex, sexual powers, and the sexual act have at all times been highly valued. Sexual hospitality has been a widespread custom back to pre-Islamic times from North Africa to Baluchistan. Even among some of the South Arabian tribes a perfect host would provide his male guests with female companions for the night (Robertson Smith, W., 1907 and Patai, R., 1960). Inherent in Islam are concepts of the biological order, of the individual and its instincts, of maleness and femaleness, concepts that are basic to Muslim views on women and their place in the social order. These concepts are the main components of the rational of the sexual politics of Muslim societies. To the Muslim, sexuality as such poses no danger. Sexuality is seen as positive factor with vital functions not only in that it is necessary in order that the Muslim community shall perpetuate itself on earth. Sexual satisfaction is considered to give men a foretaste of the delights secured for them in Paradise, where it has been promised that: 'therein shall be agreeable and beauteous damsels . . . Having fine black eyes, and kept an pavilions from public view . . . Whom no man shall have deflowered before their destined spouses nor any genius. Therein shall they delight themselves lying on green cushions and beautiful carpets' (The Koran, 1955). Sex encourages men to strive for the coming perfect world and hence to obey Allah's will while being in this one. Sexual desire thus serves God's will and the interest of the individual at the same time.

In her fascinating book, *Beyond the Veil*, the Moroccan anthropologist Fatima Mernissi has argued that Islam offers a kind of double image of sexuality. She claims that the prevailing contemporary view is that men are active in their interaction with women, while women are passive. But underlying this notion is a view of an active female sexuality casting woman as the hunter and man as the passive victim. This concept is formulated in the classical interpretation of the Koran by Imam Ghazali, who sees women as powerful and dangerous beings due to their ability to deceive and defeat men, not be force but by cunning and intrigue. Women exert a fatal attraction which erodes the male's will to resist her and places him in a passive and pliable role. This power is seen as the most destructive element in the Muslim social order, because men become distracted from their social and religious duties. The man has no choice, he can only give in the attraction of women, whence an association of females with what in Morocco is termed *fitna* which means chaos as well as a beautiful woman. Whenever a man is faced with a woman *fitna* may occur. Women must therefore be controlled so that they do not tempt men, says Ghazali. According to Mernissi, Muslim organization of social interaction and spatial configurations of the sexes can be understood in terms of this concept of female sexuality. Curbing active female sexuality is at the basis of many of Islam's family institutions. Society can only survive by creating institutions which foster male dominance through sexual segregation. Islamic laws are therefore saturated by a notion of the eminence of men over women, and they include numerous rules to regulate women's lives. The rules that Mernissi thinks of are found especially within what in Western legal practice is codified as family law, first and foremost within marriage and divorce regulations. (Although marriage as such is not institutionalized by means of religion but considered a private agreement between the two parties or rather their families, the content of the agreement is subject to legislation). Islamic law codifies the duty of the man to provide for his wife materially and physically but also his right to repudiate her unilaterally, while women can only obtain a divorce under specific circumstances and only following a court decision. The custody of children goes to the man with certain reservations only with respect to the age of the child. The right of the man to marry up to four wives is established here as are inheritance rules according to which women, get but half the shares of men inheriting from their parents, and the rule according to which the testimony of a woman is worth but half that of a man. The supremacy of men comes out in numerous ways, openly or slightly disguised. We learn that women must show respect to men and that they are in need of male guardians to see them safely through life. Contrary to Western culture however, where sexual inequality is based on a belief in women's biological inferiority, where women are the second sex, as argued by Simone do Beauvoir, the Islamic system is based in an assumption of an active female sexuality. Mernissi claims that it is an ideology in which females are not considered inferior, but that Islamic laws and custom do secure that women remain subjugated to the authority of men. What is attacked in Islam is not sexuality but rather the woman as the embodiment of destruction, as the symbol of disorder. The woman is *fitna*, chaos, a living representative of the dangers of sexuality and its disruptive potential.

It can perhaps be called in question whether Mernissi is right in claiming that Islam does not base its views on women on a belief in her biological inferiority. It is clearly stated in the Koran, for instance, that 'Men shall have pre-eminence above women, because of those advantages wherein God hath caused the one of them to excel the other, and for that which they expend of their substance in maintaining their wives' (The Koran, 4:35), while it is furthermore explained that the male has this dominant position due to a superior understanding and strength. In accordance with this, the privilege of holding high social positions and of conducting war in defence of God's true religion has always been reserved for men. Mernissi's argument, however, that a pivotal idea in Islam is that of an active female sexuality is interesting. It seems worthwhile to pursue the question and to try to find out whether Muslim sexual politics can be explained in close relation to this concept of an active female sexuality that must be kept under control. It may thus be possible to delineate to what extent the image of women as based on this concept has influenced and provided a rationale for the position of women in various Muslim societies.

Another important question regarding an understanding of the position of Muslim woman in general is generated by the fact that Islamic legislation regarding rules that influence and control woman's lives has been maintained more rigorously than other parts of the Islamic law-complex in modern times. The fields of domain and the interpretations of the *shari'a* have, as mentioned, been changing ever since Muhammad's time. At the level of state legislation various sectors of social life have been withdrawn from the control of religious laws in the course of modernization within the last century. This has happened due to the impact of Western culture of the direct interference of western colonial powers. The extent to which civil law has replaced the *shari'a* varies from one Islamic country to another. It is noteworthy, however, that *only in Turkey has the Islamic family law been completely replaced by a civil one.* This has made a number of scholars ask why it is that precisely the family and personal aspect of Islamic legislation and culture have been held on to most tenaciously, while penal laws, taxation, constitutional laws and laws of contracts and obligations have generally been replaced by civil laws. Mernissi sees an explanation in the fact that most Muslim states have been unable to generate a genuine modern ideology capable of coping with social change and the problems of modernization. As a result, these turn to the only coherent ideology available, that of Islam. In their search for a Muslim way and a genuine Muslim identity the Islamic traditions are drawn upon and the *shari'a* becomes a symbol of the Muslim uniqueness. This has repercussions on the women's situation. As the very same *shari'a,* besides religious duties, deals to a large extent exactly with matters that concern women and their rights, their fight for liberation is up against a set of obstacles, different from those in the West. And whenever these societies face political problems in their efforts to cope with modernization, restrictive tendencies are intensified, as this releases a necessity to reaffirm traditional Muslim values with immediate effects on the relation of the sexes (Mernissi, 1975). The present situation in Iran comes readily to mind as an example. Beck and Keddie on the other hand try to explain the same phenomenon by setting in focus the situation of Muslim men. They maintain that the limits imposed on male freedom by religion and tradition and by the modern power of employers, government institutions and Western incursions, may encourage men lacking wealth an power to keep control of the only area they can, that of women and children. Changes in the family law with its codes on personal status are therefore not considered an advantage but a loss of rights and powers, and to a great many as an encouragement to marital infidelity and the sexual freedom of women (Beck and Keddie, 1978). Rahbek gives a related explanation in her paper, when she describes how the Palestinian men became highly concerned about the behaviour of women in the refugee camps, so that the latter suffered a set-back in independence after their internment in 1948 as compared to their situation in Palestine previous to that. She suggests, following Soraya Antonius, that this happened because the Palestinian men in the camps has lost everything that gave their life meaning except their honour, and as men's honour is intimately linked to the behaviour of women, the latter fell victims to further restrictions. Or one can think of the fate of the Algerian women. According to Rezig, who cites Fanon, the Algerian reaction to the French colonial politics of emancipation and its fighting of the veil, which to the European is a striking sign of oppression, was to keep women more isolated behing closed doors than ever. To the Algerians the veil was given new significance during the revolution as a national symbol. Although Algerian women played an active role in the revolution they had to realize that the new state, although it proclaims itself to be a modern socialist country, nevertheless stressess 'tradition' in its effort to preserve or find an identity, with the very same consequences for women's liberation as mentioned above.

This volume is an outcome of the growing interest in Muslim societies, and , in particular, of the emergence of a concern about women, a concern that swept through academic disciplines within the humanities and the social sciences in the wake of the women's liberation movements in the late 1960s. The volume is the result of a conference on 'Women in Islam' held by the Scandinavian Institute of Asian Studies in Copenhagen in November 1979. The idea of the conference was to bring together for the first time Scandinavian scholars of all disciplines and schools of thought who held an interest in Muslim women, in order to further research within this field. Only a few Scandinavian scholars had, till recently, dealt thoroughly with the conditions of Muslim women. The two prominent exceptions are the Finnish anthropologist, Hilda Granquist, whose book, *Marriage conditions in a Palestinian Village, is* a classic in its field, and the Danish anthropologist Henny Harald Hansen, who has written two major publications on Muslim women, *The Kurdish Woman's Life and Investigations in a Shi'a Village.* The participants in the conference were not asked to write on any particular set of issues, but to present whatever research they had been or were working on. As a result, this publication explores a wide range of subjects and demonstrates great differences in methodological and theoretical approaches. It neither provides the reader with a regional coverage of the Muslim world, nor with a systematic outlook on the conditions of Muslim women today. To do so would have required much more attention to the situation of women in the core area of the Islamic world, that of the Middle East, and to the millions of Muslim women in the Indian subcontinent. Had that been the case, the rapidly growing number of women in urban settings should also have had to be dealt with more extensively. In the Islamic world as elsewhere in the third world the effects of modernization force women irreversibly out of the domestic sphere and into school and from there into the labour market, to offices and to the many other jobs that industrialization demands. From a purely quantitative point of view this volume has an imbalance of papers dealing with women in the periphery of the Muslim world or with women in traditional settings. The Contributors do, however, explore a wide range of factors influencing women's lives in a general historical and /or socio-economic perspective as well as in more specific sets of circumstance. Taken as a whole the contributions to this volume offer an insight into the manifold conditions under which Muslim women exist, the problems they have to face and the nature of their struggles as a result of the intricate historical processes during which Islam and Islamic culture were adopted by and adjusted to various social systems. Moreover, the very fact that a fair number of papers focus on these peripheral societies highlights the diversity in sexual behavioural patterns in the Muslim world and thus strongly suggests that any generalization about the position of Muslim women should be advanced with caution.

References

1. Whether matriliny prevailed in Arabia in pre-Islamic times as Robertson-Smith, McLennan and others claimed, has been argued intensely but repudiated by a majority of modern scholars.
2. At the time of the Prophet it seems that the rights and duties of women were functionally interrelated with the traditional socio-economic pattern in Arabia, where the creation of marriage alliances through the exchange of women were crucial to the establishment of obligations and hence to the functioning of the political system.

Bibliography

Beck, L. & Keddie, N. 1978, Introduction, in *Women in the Muslim World,* (eds.) L. Beck & N. Keddie, Cambridge, Harvard University Press.

Bousquet, G.H. 1953, *La Morale de L'Islam et son Ethique Sexuelle,* (Bibliotheque de la Faculte de Droit D' Alger xx) Paris, A. Maisonnauve.

Granquist, Hilda, 1931 & 1935, *Marriage Conditions in a Palestinian Village, I-II,* Societas Scientiarum Fennica, Commentations Humanorum Litterarum III & VI), Helsingfors.

Hansen, Henny Harald, 1961, *The Kurdish Women's Life, Field Research in a Muslim Society, Iraq,* Nationalmuseets Skrifter, Etnografisk Raekke 7, Kobenhavn 1968, *Investigations in a Shi'a village in Bahrain,* Nationalmuseets Skrifter, Etnografisk Raekke 12, Kobenhavn.

Mernissi, Fatima, 1975, *Beyond the Veil, Male-Female Dynamics in a Modern Muslim Society,* London, Schenkman Publ. Co.

Patai, R. 1960, *Family, Love and the Bible,* London, MacGibbon & Kee.

Peters, Emrys L. 1978, "The Status of Women in Four Middle East Communities", in *Women in the Muslim World* (eds.) L. Beck & N. Keddie, Cambridge, Harvard University Press.

Robertson Smith, W. 1907, *Kinship & Marriage in Early Arabia,* London, Adam and Charles Black.

The Koran, London & New York, Fredrick Warne and Co.

Von Grunebaum, G.E. 1961 (1955), *Islam: Essays in the Nature and Growth of a Cultural Tradition,* London, Routledge & Kegan Paul Ltd.

8

Female-Headed Households and Family

Is migration of the male instrumental in the upward social mobility of the family? Is migration the only alternative to cope with the problems emerging from rapid social change? These are some relevant questions that may be difficult to answer within the scope of this study but have been kept in mind in the analysis of the data presented below on the family in the village.

The total population of our selected 97 families is 650 persons, the average size of the family being 6.7 persons. The sex ratio is disproportionate (308 females for 342 males) in spite of the migration of several males. The imbalance is observed in all but the age-group 35-60. A little more than a quarter of all the females are below 14 years. The largest group is between the ages of 14 and 35 years. The dependent (non-working) female population (girls below 11 and women above 60 years of age) form 26.6 per cent of the total female population, the corresponding figures for males being 29.5. This indicates that the women start working an early age and continue to work longer as compared with the men. Only 4.8 per cent of the women are literate. But male literacy, at 25.7 per cent, is higher than the state average. Only seven girls are in school, as compared with fifty boys at different educational levels. None of our female respondents (wife/mother of the migrant) has ever gone to school. The structure of the selected families shows three variations:

Type one: Incomplete simple family made up of wife and unmarried children only, the husband having migrated to the city and remaining there for the major part of his life.

Type two: Incomplete extended family with migrant's wife and unmarried children as well as married sons and their families.

Type three: Incomplete extended family with migrant's wife staying with own children as well as his parents, brothers and sisters.

A single family may belong to any one of the three types during a particular phase of its formation and fission, and change into another type with changes in role relations, responsibilities and obligations. Thus, these family types may be viewed as changing units, adapting to the requirements of male migration. When the migrant leaves for the city, he is young and his wife and children are left in parental custody or in the care of other relatives in the lineage group. The wife helps in coping with the situation by being an earning dependent. As her children grow older and the husband gets more security in the urban job, she becomes more independent of the extended family. When her sons become the primary earners she may have a simple incomplete unit and relegate herself to the background, assuming a dependent status. The next stage is of the growing-up of another unit with the marriages of sons and addition of new members in the family. If the son is also a migrant, he too needs the support of his mother to help his wife and children. Thus the extended family type is highly functional for migrants and their families.

In our sample, 32 per cent of the families are of type one. The females are in late middle age with married daughters and sons separated with their families. Some of these families (one-third of them) have very young females with small children. Even if a simple incomplete family has a physically separate residential unit, it is very much a part of the kinship network with its associated obligations and rights. This is best observed during marriages, festivals and situations of crisis. Every family has an average of 2.5 earners, with 1.0 female and 1.5 male earner per family. In the selected families, the largest number of persons is engaged in agricultural labour (57 per cent of the females and 36.5 per cent of the males). Those who combine cultivation with wage labour are 33.8 per cent of the males and 18 per cent of the females. Cultivation as the only means of work is reported by 25 per cent of the females and 22.3 per cent of the males. Finally, 7.4 per cent of the males are in regular service.

The position regarding the female respondents reveals that nine of them do not work at all: they are either too old or the economic improvement of the family led to their withdrawal from the work-force. Those who live by agricultural labour are 37 per cent and those who combine it with other kinds of labour and cultivation are 46 per cent. Only 13 per cent report working on their own holdings. The remainder are engaged in traditional occupations (washer-women, grain-perchers). None of our respondents has any other skills.

Employment in the village is not available throughout the year. During the peak season, as in sowing (one month) and harvest of paddy (fifteen days) and wheat (fifteen days), work is available for about sixty days. During the rest of the year, they may work at weeding, hoeing, cleaning food grains, grinding spices and plastering floors and walls with cowdung. The maximum they earn is Rs. 5 a day and that during the short harvest period. On an average, they earn around Rs. 2.50 a day. The employers claim that they pay Rs. 5, the minimum wage fixed by the state, but the women workers deny this and report that the wages in terms of grain have not changed at all.

Material Possessions

All the families own houses, which are 'Kutcha' (made of mud and thatch) with the exception of one 'Pucca' house made of cement and brick. Sixty-two per cent of the house have only one room. The total area covered is rather small. Every house has a small courtyard and/or verandah where food is cooked, cattle are tied and a dozen daily chores are performed. A separate kitchen is reported by only 30 per cent of our respondents. The remainder have no separate place to cook. A corner of the courtyard is used for this purpose. In the rainy season, cooking is done inside the room. None of the houses has electricity. Counting the material possessions of the families, one is struck by an extremely low standard of living. The only items they possess are bicycles (65 per cent) and transistor radios (30 per cent). It was observed that it is only after at least ten years of working in the city that a migrant is able to purchase such items. In several families, with males living in the city for twenty years, hardly any luxury items are visible. Items such as a cycle, transistor of watch are purchased for the use of males. There is very little evidence of transfer of the urban way of living to the families of the migrants.

Except for three families that have a hand pump each, all families obtain water from a common well. Women have to fetch water from the wells for cooking, washing of utensils and drinking and for cattle. This involves considerable physical labour. A large portion of the cash income is spent on such essential items as edible oil, kerosene oil, salt, spices, pulses, clothes, etc. The average expenditure on food is Rs. 63 per family per month. This may very from Rs. 10 to Rs. 100 per month, depending on the total farm produce and the mode of payment in the case of wage employees. Food-grain requirements are largely met from their own farm produce or collected through wages paid in kind. The next basic need is clothing, on which the minimum amount spent is Rs. 40 and the maximum is Rs. 400 annually by a family, the average being Rs. 122 per annum per family. Clothes are usually brought from the city. The average expenditure on medicine is Rs. 23-40: on postage it is Rs 2.45 per annum per family. In 80 per cent of the families, travel to the city costs between Rs. 60 and Rs. 70. There is no external help employed, as the amount of land is so small that it can be cultivated by family labour alone.

The purchasing power of these families is low, yet they borrow money towards the purchase of such items as jewellery, since silver ornaments are essential for a wedding. Twenty families reported having purchased jewellery, all except two belonging to the families of the EM category. Expenditure is reported by twenty families on items like bicycles, construction or alteration of a house and the purchase of cattle. The lowest-caste migrant families raise goats.

Cash savings, if substantial (i.e. more than Rs. 1,000) are spent on the purchase of cattle. This is a high-priority item, but is optional compared with such exigencies a celebrations of a marriage or the birth of a son, and events like the death of an old parent; all these call for a feast for the castemen. In spite of poor economic resources, social ceremonies have an important place in their life. They even borrow money for these events. Fifty-five per cent of the families report having celebrated ceremonies, the average expenditure coming to over Rs. 600 per family per annum. It is reported that only 40 per cent of the expenditure comes from the family's own resources, the rest is borrowed. The females arrange this loan with the prior permission of the migrant or other important members of the family. The rate of interest varies from 75 to 100 per cent per annum. They never borrow from an institutional source, but mostly from a money-lender, who is a big landowner in the village. Such loans are easily available, as a migrant has a regular source of income and the money-lender can also pressure the family to send someone to work on his fields on his terms. Sometimes the male migrant arranges for a loan in the city. Though they avoid borrowing from a relative, since this brings loss of prestige, a neighbour or a friend may be approached for small sums.

The majority of the rural-based families (73 per cent) receive some remittances from the city regularly, while a few (27 per cent) do not. Some families have more than one person (our selected migrant) working in the city and sending remittances. On an average the amount sent home by male migrants is Rs. 94 per month, the minimum being Rs. 25 and the maximum Rs. 250, depending on the earnings of the migrant. Those who earn less than Rs. 200 cannot afford to send any money at all. Beyond that is their surplus from the bare minimum standard of living they maintain in the city.

The women in the village do not count the distance to Delhi in terms of kilometres, but in terms of time. The nearest of the sample villages is 624 km and the farthest 762 km from Delhi. They know that it takes one night and a few hours more to reach there. Asked to say when the male migrated to the city they recall events like the birth of a child, or a marriage in the family, or some natural catastrophe like a flood or drought, but not the exact year. Some women said their husbands were already working in Delhi when they got married. Thus no specific replies were given. They are more sure about their replies regarding what the men were doing before they went to seek employment outside the village. While a negligible number had been studying in the village before going to the city, nearly half of them had been trying to support the family by combining cultivation of their own small plot of land with whatever other alternative was available, such as share-cropping and agricultural labour. More than one-third tried to survive on their own labour, but work was not available throughout the year. One-tenth were engaged in providing services to the village at the dismally low customary payments in kind. For example, a washerman gets 5 kg of good-grain twice a year, at the time of the harvest, from the family or families he works for. He may work in this way for ten to fifteen landowning families. There is no cash payment for any kind of labour or service. On computing the value of payment in grains, the wage received was equivalent to Rs. 1 to Rs. 1.25 twenty years ago. Today it is Rs. 2.50. The payment varies from 15 'chatak' to 6 'pao' (less than 1 kg to 1.5 kgs.) The price of food-grains has gone up, and in that ratio the wage has increased. There is, however, higher payment for the 'harwaha' (ploughman), who may get Rs. 4 and some food at the start of the day, as well as a small piece of land. This has to be surrendered when he ceases employment with the landowner.

In the initial years of struggle in the city, a migrant does casual work and thus going home means the loss of daily wage. It is only when they obtain regular work that the migrants start visiting the family, at least once a year. Holi (a festival in which people play with colours) marks the end of the harvest season and offers an occasion on which most migrants pay a visit to the village. A little after Holi is the wedding season; so they combine the two occasions. Since the female respondents were interviewed only two months after the festival, 65 per cent reported that the husband/son had visited them a couple of months before. The visit may last from fifteen days to a month. Those who have permanent employment come once a year but for a longer period. Those whose employment is not secure come more frequently but stay for a shorter periods. Death of a relation, a major illness of a member of the family, a serious quarrel with a neighbour, a summons from a court of law, necessitate an emergency visit. These are reported by only nine respondents.

Women expect the migrants to bring presents for the family. They like to show off all that is brought. It is the measure of the migrant's success in the city. One-third of the women said that their men bring clothes when they pay a visit. They also bring utensils, perfumed soap, oil, plastic buckets, etc., from the city. Five per cent reported that the migrant never brought any presents with him when he visited the village, as he was still struggling to get a decent salary.

There is a discrepancy between male and female reporting about remittances. While one may expect differences in the average amount of remittances there is no such scope for those who did not send or receive any money at all. Whereas only seventeen migrants stated that they do not remit any money home, twenty-seven of the females reported that they have never received any money. The migrants may have purposely misinformed the researcher, as the social expectation from a male is that he should maintain his family. It cannot be easy for them to admit that they are not able to fulfil this obligation. There are also differences in the two versions about the amount remitted. Whereas thirty-eight migrants reported sending Rs. 50 per month. Only twenty-four females mentioned receiving that much. But more females than males report that the remittances are between Rs. 50 and Rs. 100. Again those women who reported having received more than Rs. 100 are less in number than the migrants who reported thus. This may be due to the fact that in many cases the money is not received by the females at all, and their information is only second-hand.

Attitude Towards Migration

Male migration is viewed as unavoidable, and the women are reconciled to it, especially as it means regular employment for the man and a cash income for the family. One-third are positively unhappy about the arrangement and half of them regret the long absence of the male members of the family. Tradition bars these women from expressing personal emotions towards the husband. It is in fact considered shameful and immodest to express love for the husband and to complain of loneliness in his absence. Yet 43 per cent said they felt lonely. They feel helpless in this situation, as they do not have any prospects of joining the husband or of his coming permanently to the village, as long as he is fit to work in the city. There were, however, 21 per cent who were positively happy that their husbands were in the city; they entertained the hope that some day they too would migrate to the city. At least one case was reported of a young bride who refused to the city. At least one case was reported of a young bride who refused to return to her husband's home from her natal village; her husband has not visited his village for the last three years. None of the women complained of men's faithlessness in spite of their long residence in the city.

Adjustments

In half of the families, the females, in most cases the wife of the migrant, shoulder the major responsibility of taking care of the children. They manage the several minor and some major crises in the family, sometimes single-handedly. Though agriculture is a familial activity, there is sexual division of labour for various agricultural activities. For example, preparation of soil, ploughing of land, arranging inputs for land and other purchases are undertaken by males, while transplanting, hoeing, weeding, husking and winnowing of food grains and storage are typically female activities. Men and women work together during harvest. Produce is carried to the house by males. Tending cattle is shared with females, males look after bullock, and females take care of milch cattle. The repair of houses and equipment is undertaken by males, while females cook the food, wash utensils and clothes and fetch water for domestic use and for cattle, in addition to arranging fuel and fodder with the help of children. In the absence of males, the work-load for women and children is increased, as they have to take over many male-specific activities.

Because of lack of security and credit-worthiness, only nineteen families reported having obtained credit. This was usually arranged by a male member of the family; only four females took the initiative in doing so. To supplement their meagre resources, the peasant families have been talking land on lease from bigger landowners. At the time of our inquiry, only seven families reported having taken some land on lease. There is some degree of underreporting regarding the amount leased either for fear of the landowners refusing to renew the contract for the following year or because there is an actual decline in the amount of land being offered for lease. The fields are generally irrigated by rainwater, though some families irrigate their land either by private wells or by purchasing water from rich cultivators' tube-wells, or from the state canal.

Women seldom decide what crops are to be sown. This is

done by the men in view of the availability of irrigational facilities, the needs of the family and the availability of family labour. Since most families keep cattle, chaff-cutters are a common implement in these families.

None of our selected respondents are members of any village organization. In fact, there were no women's organizations in any community. This does not mean that they have no occasions for coming together. There may not be any specific purpose, but women do tend to sit together and exchange gossip during, as well as after, work. Numerous social ceremonies also provide occasions for coming together. There is increasing emotional interdependence and physical co-operation between neighbours.

Problems

Since most of the male respondents left the village family early in life, the females cannot recall if they had ever helped in taking care of the children. Home remedies and medicines are used to cure minor ailments. A doctor may be consulted for more serious problems, and for this a distance of 3 to 10 km may have to be covered. The commonest problem cited by our respondents is financial. They somehow cope with the problems regarding household, children and others. But coping with poverty is a major problem and to overcome it they borrow from the cultivator-money-lender on his terms.

There is, however, mutual help extended between neighbours, kinsmen and relatives, since so many families have a male member in the same city. Yet a migrant who is better off then others may be the cause of jealousy, and his family may then face much hostility in the neighbourhood. By and large, there is a common sympathetic bond between families in which male migration has taken place.

Decision-making

There are hardly any material possessions in these families. The major worry is physical survival. When the family can afford it they may buy clothes, utensils or other articles of necessity and, if they are lucky, cattle. Even items like kerosene oil and spices are considered a luxury. Since the decisions are forced on women by circumstances, they are hardly significant of their position. In the absence of males, women have control over what they earn in kind, but it is doubtful that they gain any substantial power in the family. More often it is the male who decides the expenditure on different items.

Women take great interest in match-making for marriages. It is the daughters-in-law and the married daughters who suggest eligible bachelors in their respective families. But here, too, the decisions regarding the amount of expenditure on marriages the amount of money to be borrowed are taken by the males. Distress loans for food are negotiated by the females. They borrow food-grain too, and pay off with their wages or when the migrant remits money. Thus the long absence of these men does not perceptibly alter the authority structure of the family.

Time Budget

Working outside the home, whether on one's own or another's farm, means an early start. Before beginning work outside the home (by 7 a.m. in summer and 8 a.m. in winter) women have to make some arrangement for food for the family. The day begins for them at 5 a.m. when they have a breakfast of parched gram or rice and some salt. Sometimes left-over bread from the previous evening is eaten with pickles. They work in the fields for four to five hours. In the afternoon, they go home and cook rice for the family, which is eaten with some lentil soup (dal), or with salt and pepper. Those who work at a distance from their home cannot go home; for them food is brought to the fields by some member of the family, usually a women. The main meal is cooked in the evening, which is again rice and/or 'chapattis' with lentils (rarely a vegetable) and/or salt and chillies. Older girls look after younger siblings when the mother goes out to work. Younger daughters-in-law do the bulk of the housework. Young boys take out the cattle for grazing. Girls help the mother inside the home while the boys work outside. Other males work as labourers if they are from landless families, or on their own landholdings when they have any. During the slack season one can see clusters of men, women and children languishing in the afternoons.

The male migrant is home for a fortnight or a month. He too helps in the fields, especially during harvest time, which is in fact

Table 8.1
Summary View of Responses Given by Female Respondents

	Number of magrants	Years in the city			
		up to 5	5-10	10-20	above 20
Purchase of food (Rs. per month)					
No expenditure	8	6	2	—	—
Up to 50	43	9	18	12	4
50-100	34	—	9	13	12
100 and above	12	—	—	5	7
Total	97	15	29	30	23
Purchase of clothing (Rs. per annum)					
Up to 50	16	9	5	2	—
50-100	35	6	17	1	11
Above 100	46	—	7	27	12
Total	97	15	29	30	23
Travel (Rs. per annum)					
Up to 50	23	—	11	10	2
Above 50	54	—	13	20	21
Total	77	—	24	30	23
Education fee (Rs. per month)					
Up to 5	15	1	5	7	2
Above 5	6	1	2	2	1
Total	21	2	7	9	3
Stationery					
Up to 5	26	1	9	10	6
Above 5	13	—	2	9	2
Total	39	1	11	19	8
Postage (Rs. per month)					
1 to 3	36	1	3	19	13
Above 3	17	1	2	9	5
Total	53	2	5	28	18
Health and medicine (Rs. per annum)					
Up to 20	44	8	17	13	6
20-30	16	1	2	6	7
Above 30	14	1	3	4	6
Total	74	10	22	23	19

the period when the migrants visit their families. They seldom help in the household duties, though they all do their own cooking, washing, cleaning, etc. in the city.

DIGGING DEEPER : CASE-STUDIES

Let us have a closer look at one of our selected village communities and a few families with a view to understanding the social and economic setting from which a male migrates, the coping mechanism of the family left behind, and the position of women in these families.

The Village

The village of Amawan Kalan is located in Sohita Kalan Community Development Block of Shahganj Tehsil in Jaunpur District, Uttar Pradesh. To reach the village one has to get off at Shahganj on the Lucknow Mughal Sarai railway line. Shahganj is 740 km from Delhi and is connected directly by rail to it: the village is 29 km from Shahganj. From Narender Patti, one has to go in the Ramanagar Road for a distance of about a kilometre, turning right on the Kutcha Road near the state tubwell. It takes about 18 hours to reach the village from Delhi. Leaving in the evening, one reaches home the next day by noon.

The village consists of a core settlement and three hamlets. The core settlement is inhabited by upper castes and service-caste families; the three hamlets are single-caste settlements; almost all the Chamar families stay together in one hamlet called 'Chamroti' Koirana' is inhabited by Koiris (peasants); and 'Ganderan' by Ganderis (herdsmen).

The 1951 census recorded the village population as 730 persons, of which 347 were males and 383 females. During the decade 1951-61, the village population increased to 911, of which 473 were males and 438 were females. It may be noted that while the total population increased at an annual average rate of 2.5 per cent, the female population increased by only 1.4 per cent, the male growth rate being almost three times that of the female growth rate. The 1971 census placed the village population at 1,129 of which 604 were males and 525 were females. The annual average growth rate during the decade 1961-71 works out to 2.4 per cent for the total population 2.7 per cent for males and 1.9 per cent for females.

The total population in 1951 was divided into 113 households, the average size of a household being 6.5 persons. In 1961, the number of households increased to 155, which resulted in a decline in household size from 6.5 to 5.8 persons. The present population comprises 183 households, and the average size is 6.2 persons. The caste-wise distribution of households is given in Table 8.2.

Table 8.2
Households in the Village of Amawan Kalan

Caste	*Number of households*
High	62
Peasants	20
Service castes	38
Scheduled castes	56
Muslims	1
Total	183

Sixty per cent of the total population was categorized as non-workers in the 1961 census; two-thirds of the women and half the men did not participate in any gainful activity. By 1971 many more women had left the labour-force an joined the category of non-workers. At present, only 25 per cent of the women participate in economic activity, as against 43 per cent of the males.

Only about 4 per cent of the total population was recorded as literate in 1951, all of these being males; 139 persons or 15.3 per cent of the total population was recorded as literates in the 1961 census. Of these, 116 were males and 23 were females, the percentage of literacy being 24.5 for males and only 5.3 for females. At present, though nearly one-third of the total population is literate, female literacy is still at about 9 per cent. It is important to note that members of the higher caste attribute the utmost importance to literacy and make it a point to send their children, particularly the males, to school, even though no school is located in the village and the children have to cover a distance of over a kilometre to attend the school. The members of the lower caste, though they realize the benefits that education can bring them (notwith standing the fact that the lone graduate among them is employed as an unskilled worker in Delhi), are not in a position to send their children to school, for various reasons. Their children have to help them in their economic activities, such as looking after cattle, goats and even assisting their mothers and also looking after the younger children. A high rate of school drop-out is caused by lock of guidance at home, humiliation in the school on account of low ritual status, failure to do homework or answer questions in the classroom, ill-treatment at the hands of the school-teacher, and lack of books, stationery and other equipment. Thus, not only is the male-female literacy ratio and educational attainment disproportionate, the gap between the high and the low castes is also wide.

Agriculture is the mainstay of the people, occupying in 1961 census, 91 per cent of the total work-force. Household industry (weaving) engaged about 6 per cent and the remaining three per cent were engaged in providing services like transport, etc. A faster population growth rate and its non-absorption in the village economy on account of lack of occupation diversification has forced a sizable number to migrate in search of employment. Thus many people belonging to the upper castes have migrated to places as distant as Bombay, Surat, Nagpur, Calcutta, Ludhiana and Delhi. They take up jobs in cotton mills and other industries and also take up small-scale dairying or petty business in these cities. Those who have acquired higher education seek employment as teachers, supervisors, etc. Members of the lower caste, who cannot find regular employment in the village, migrate to Delhi and seek jobs as gardeners, *chowkidars,* loaders, coolies, etc. Fifty-two persons belonging to the higher-caste and thirty-five belonging to the lower-caste communities have migrated during the last two decades.

9

Sons and Daughters : Sociology of Fertility

'Food is man's life and clothes afford protection.
Gold gives him beauty, marriages bring cattle;
His wife's a friend, his daughter causes pity;
A son is like a light in highest heaven.' (*An anonymous Indian writer 600 B.C., quoted by Williamson, 1978*).

'I want five boys and one girl. The boys will take care of me, but the girl will take care of her husband.' (*An anonymous Bedouin wife 1970, quoted by Sebai, 1974*).

Sex Preferences

Boys start life with a great advantage over girls because sons are more welcome than daughters. Preferences for children of a particular sex have been studied by demographers who are interested in impact of the desire for sons upon fertility levels. Much less attention has been given to the question of the impact of such preferences on children of the 'wrong sex'. 'Abu-banaat', meaning 'the father of daughters' is a common but nasty insult in Arabic. It represents just one of the countless ways in which Middle Eastern women learn that they are little valued. Around the world congratulations to parents depend upon the sex of the new born child.

In the majority of the world's cultures there is a strong preference for the birth of sons rather than daughters. This is especially true of Moslem, Chinese and Indian cultures. Even where there is no special preference for sons, very few cultures actively prefer daughters. In her worldwide survey, Williamson (1976) only found five small groups of Aboriginal populations in Australia, New Guinea, Assam, California and Peru where fathers would rather have daughters than sons. In all the other cultures studied parents either preferred to have a clear majority of sons or wanted an equal balance of the sexes.

One cross-cultural study found:

(i) Clear son preference in South Korea, Taiwan, India, Ankara (Turkey), Mexico City and amongst Chinese populations in Thailand;

(ii) A mixed pattern in which the preference depended upon the measure used and was not firmly in favour of sons in Jakarta, East Java, the Philippines and among Thais in Thailand and Malays in West Malaysia;

(iii) A firm desire for at least one child of each sex in Europe and North America (Freedman and Coombs, 1974).

All cultures influenced by China exhibit a strong preference for sons. Thus in Korea amongst women with three children, 76 per cent of those with at least two sons want no more children, while only 32 per cent of those with one son, and 15 per cent of those with no sons would be prepared to cease childbearing (Freedman and Coombs, 1974). Statistics on women in mental hospitals show a very significant excess of sonless women amongst the patients (Chung *et al.*, 1974; Rhi, 1977). Here sons play such an important role in society and in proving that a woman is a 'good' mother that women equal men in their preference for sons. In Thailand where strong sons preference is largely confined to the Chinese population, Thai husbands are much more eager to have sons than their wives and there is thus a sex differential in family building preferences (Knodel and Prachuabmoh, 1976). Where the social structure makes women as eager as men to have more sons than daughters then a vicious circle is formed. Because females are devalued they are allowed to play only unimportant roles in development and because they are only considered to play unimportant roles they are further devalued. One reason why centrally planned economies can be much more effective in raising the status of women and in lowering fertility levels is because they can enforce radical changes in the roles allocated to women and the public valuation placed upon their services.

Sex preferences will only have an impact upon fertility levels where there is already a considerable degree of fertility control. This is why Repetto (1972) failed to find evidence of sex preference in the childbearing patterns of women in Northern India, Bangladesh and Morocco. Re-analysing the Bangladesh data, Ben-Porath and Welch (1976) where able to show that there is a relationship between the sex composition of families and the mortality of girls living in them. In Bangladesh 'girls born into families where girls are in the majority are significantly more likely to die before age five than girls born into families with more boys than girls'. In the absence of a technique for selecting the sex of the baby in advance, parents influence the sex composition of their surviving children through the lesser care given to sick female infants.

Where there is little deliberate family size limitation, parents of many sons rejoice in their good fortune and prospective wealth, while parents of many daughters keep desperately trying to secure sons. Birth intervals after sons are likely to be longer than the intervals after daughters (Halder and Bhattacharya, 1970). Where family size limitation is common, then sex preferences may constitute one major barrier to further fertility decline. In America where there is a preference for a balanced sex distribution, 1970 Census data clearly show that the chances of having a third child are higher for couples whose first two children were both male or both female than for couples who had one of each sex (cited in Ben-Porath and Welch, 1976). Interestingly, in the United States, where parents can choose the sex of the child they elect to adopt, there is a preference for adopting girls (Kirk, 1964). Even this may not indicate high status for females since it may just reflect the fact that men are reluctant to pass on their names to a child who is not biologically their own. Alternatively, since it is wives who are most eager to adopt a child, it may be felt that there should be a girl for the mother.

In cultures where there is strong son preference this is often reflected in the practice of putting up daughters for adoption or even sale as in traditional China. Boy preference would still appear to be a major obstacle in the way of achieving the two child family ideal and reduced fertility levels in modern China. Thus in 1975 Chinese officials launched a direct attack upon son preference which paralleled the promotion of one-child families with special benefits for the parents of such families (*New York Times* 8.9.1975). All the available evidence would suggest that the strength of the preference for sons declines with spreading education and urbanization, whatever the original level may have been. There are sound reasons for this. Parents wish to have large families and many sons for substantial economic reasons. When economic circumstances and the structure of wealth flows within the family change, then the motivations for large families and son preference decline together. Programmes designed to reduce sex preference will have some impact if they increase the visible economic contribution of women relative to men. Certainly moral arguments alone will not be sufficient. One factor in the decline in son preference in Singapore and Hong Kong's Chinese populations has certainly been the financial contributions made by unmarried female factory workers to their parents.

There are some high fertility populations where there is little evidence of son preference: examples would be the Yoruba of Nigeria, and the Javanese and Balinese of Indonesia (CAF Nigeria, 1974; WFS Indonesia, 1978). Although both the Yoruba and the Javanese are predominantly Moslems, they are also distinguished as groups where women make significant economic contributions to their families through trading and agricultural labour. In the case of the Yoruba, there is evidence to suggest that the desire for sons may actually be increasing in the urban areas because of the lesser opportunities for women to find well-paid employment in modern sector white collar occupations (Ware, 1981).

Sex Selection

Much attention has been devoted to the question of what would happen if parents could easily select the sex of their children (Winston, 1932; Goodman, 1961; Etzioni, 1968; Markle and Nam, 1971; Jones, 1973; Westoff and Rindfuss, 1974; Rosenzweig and Adelman, 1976). At present the only certain method is to determine the sex of the foetus at 12-16 weeks through analysis of the amnotic fluid and then to abort those of the undesired sex (Cederqvist and

Fuchs, 1970; Rinehart, 1975). Shettles (1970) maintains that it is possible to influence the sex of the child by detailed attention to the time and position of coitus, but the results obtained are not very impressive (cf. Guerrero, 1975; Allan, 1975; Kerr, 1971).

Obviously the effects of a simple and certain sex selection method would vary greatly with the levels of sex preference and fatalism in an individual society. Evidence available to date suggests that Chinese and Chinese influenced populations would be the most strongly affected since they are strong in both son preference and willingness to take action in this area. In one Chinese experiment, in which sex determination and abortion in the first three months were offered to 100 couples, 29 of the 30 who chose abortion chose to abort female foetuses (Tietung Hospital, 1975). The authorities in China, who had favoured the experiment as pointing the way to an overall reduction in fertility levels, were less enthusiastic to follow it up when it became clear that almost all of those wishing to take part in the experiment were seeking to have sons.

Data from an Indian hospital show that, in a sample of 700 women, all women who were told that they would have sons chose to continue the pregnancy while only 4 per cent of women expecting daughters did not have abortions (Ramanamma and Bambawale 1980). Even seriously defective male foetuses were accepted while almost all healthy female foetuses were rejected. Not surprisingly, the Indian authors entitled their report 'The Mania for Sons" (cf Pakrasi and Halder, 1971).

The social effects of deliberately breeding a majority of boys would certainly be dramatic although it is not clear whether they would result in higher or lower status for women (Campbell, 1976; Postgate, 1973; Keith-Spiegel *et al.*, 1974). However, the real question is whether breeding for males would prove to be more than a short-term phenomenon. All communities can already select the sex of their children if they are prepared to practise infanticide. Surprisingly few societies have chosen to do so. Although most communities which have practised infanticide on a regular basis tended to kill more girls than boys, there is at least one society, the Rendille of Kenya, which kills boys so as to have a surplus of marriageable girls to exchange with their polygynous, bride-price paying neighbours (Douglas, 1969; Spencer, 1965). If there was really a great advantage to be gained from having more boys than girls then one would expect more societies to use infanticide to create an excess of males.

Since the early 1970s intensive family planning programmes in Chinese or Chinese influenced cultures have begun to reveal the effects of family size limitation in societies where there is a strong preference for sons (Heer and Wu, 1975). In Korea, Park (1978) has shown that for couples who had their third child after 1964 (*i.e.* after the introduction of the intensive national family planning programme) only 40 per cent went on to have a forth child if they already had three sons, or one daughter and two sons, but 70 per cent went on to a fourth child if they had three daughters or one son followed by two daughters. Others researchers have failed to find a stopping-rule effect because they looked too early, before family size limitation became a widespread reality.

Korea provides an excellent example of a society where the introduction of a practical form of sex pre-selection would have really radical effects. A 1971 nation-wide survey of two thousand wives showed that the average ideal number of children was 3.6, while the ideal number of sons was 2.2 (Chung *et al.*, 1972). This would yield a sex ratio at birth of 160 males to 100 females in a perfect-contraceptive, sex-predetermined Korea (Lee and Lee, 1973). In contrast, in the Philippines there is a desire for a balance between the sexes in the capital but a strong son preference in the rural areas and especially in Moslem rural areas (Stinner and Mader, 1975).

Although great stress has been laid upon the effects of sons preference in supporting high birth rates (Sheps, 1963; Heer & May, 1968) the effect is only really marked when parents insist upon having more than one son and cannot predetermine the sex of their children. Talwar's (1975) model shows that the Indian birth rate would fall to 22 if all Indian couples stopped after three children whatever their sex ratio, but would only rise to 26 if each couple insisted upon having at least one child of each sex who would survive to age five.

One family planning programme has experimented with the provision of sex selection, this is reported in an 'Evaluation of an unsuccessful sex preselection clinic in Singapore' (Williamson *et al.*, 1978). The clinic failed because the Shettles rhythm and douche sex selection method proved to be too difficult to use and did not produce the desire results. The women attending the clinic had a total of 403 living daughters and 58 living sons, and only 6 per cent of the women were actively seeking to have a daughter. The authors conclude that the Singapore government should instead concentrate upon designing 'public policies to enhance the opportunities and status of females and encourage the early demise of boy preference. At present, this approach is more practical than sex preselection' (cf. Valenti *et al.*, 1972).

Whilst sex preselection would almost certainly become an issue of greater importance to women than to men, it is very far from being a practical possibility for the great majority of the world's population (Rinehart, 1975). In contrast, the practice and technology of fertility regulation already has a much stronger impact upon women than upon men.

Birth Control as a Feminist Issue

With all the attention given to official family planning programmes it is easy to forget that many families are successfully planned without any help from such programmes. It is notable that fertility decline in the West was well underway long before the promotion of birth control became even a half-respectable activity (Micklewright, 1961). When public clinics were finally opened in the twentieth century they were designed to help poor women, for it was assumed that the middle classes had already succeeded in controlling their fertility. Nineteenth century feminist movements were generally concerned with issues remote from sexuality such as winning the vote, the economic plight of unmarried ladies and the property rights of unhappily married women. The link between feminism and birth control came later after family size limitation had become widespread and after respectability had ceased to be so important to women that they would make every sacrifice to maintain it (Bank and Banks, 1964).

The major motivation for the adoption of birth control in the West began with middle class men's awareness that, with changes in family structure, they could no longer afford to have large families in an industrialized society (Banks, 1954). Middle class wives were not directly involved in earning money. Although they might, together with Queen Victoria, the high status mother of nine children, regret the burden of repeated childbearing, they left the decision to adopt preventive measures to their husbands who had to bear the financial burden. As the practice of deliberate family size limitation spread to factory workers and skilled artisans, observers at the time attributed this trend.

> Chiefly to the spread of education among working-class women, to their discontent with a life of constant ill-health and domestic worry under narrow circumstances, and to the growth among them of aspirations for a fuller and more independent existence of their own. This change implies, on the part of both husband wife, a large measure of foresight, deliberateness, and self-control which is... difficult for the very poor, especially for the occupants of one-roomed houses (S. and B. Webb, 1897(2).

We know surprisingly little about the motives of those who are now just beginning the practice of family size limitation in the rural areas of the developing countries. The great majority of studies involving these innovators and either surveys of knowledge of, attitudes towards, and practice of contraception (KAP studies) or examinations of fertility differentials. These studies certainly show where fertility is being limited but they do not show why, and they do not show whether women or men are the primary innovators in this area. These are very important failures for wrong assumptions on these points will result in undesirable action programmes.

It is now almost universally accepted that family planning programmes should be integrated with maternal and child health and welfare programmes. Any remaining debate on the question reflects concern that the amalgamation may result in the downgrading of the importance of family planning. The question as to whether making family planning a 'women and children's' issue is a wise decision is rarely discussed. There are a number of little heard arguments against such a decision. Firstly, where population growth is negatively viewed, it places the whole blame for the barrier to progress upon women. Secondly, it alienates the interest of men in the subject and downgrades the importance of male methods of contraception. Thirdly, it makes it difficult for young unmarried women, divorcees and widows to have access to contraception although their needs are especially pressing. It also runs against the possibility of encouraging the postponement of the first birth to married women. Yet such a postponement might be one of the most important factors in opening up new roles beyond motherhood to a new generation to women. Women themselves should perhaps be suspicious of the fact that while in every other sphere men are very reluctant to give responsibility to women, in this case they appear to be only too eager to do so (Rose and Hanmer, 1976).

While administrators are keen to make family planning a women's issue there is little evidence of organized women's movements being eager to take up the cause. Where women's movements do because involved it is because family planning is the one 'women's issue' for which it is reasonably easy to secure funding. Divisions within the international women's movement create grave problems. The Women's Liberation Movement in the developed countries often seems to be largely restricted to middle class women and middle class interests. In the developing countries, women's groups are often either elite organizations with a charitable interest in the poor or offshoots of male political parties. Interestingly, in Guinea, where the women's party organization has real influence, one issue which divides women from the men is the need for fertility control which is denied by the men but pressed by the women who wish to increase their autonomy. In most cases however, elite organizations favour birth control while poorer women stress that high fertility is the consequence rather than the cause of poverty. The right to abortion is one feminist issue which might unite women. However, there are often religious divisions in which the elite women find it easier to maintain their principles, or class divisions in which the law makes it much easier for educated women to obtain legal abortions.

In the case of contraception there is also a conflict between the needs and concerns of women at different levels of development and wealth. In the West there is a movement towards barrier movements by women dissatisfied with the health risks associated with hormonal contraception and desiring to have greater control over their own bodies (Bruce and Shearer, 1979). The greater availability of safe legal abortion has made it easier for these women to choose marginally less reliable methods. In the developing countries women should certainly be offered a genuine and broad choice, but in the absence of safe abortion facilities and given the practical and cultural constraints upon the poor, condoms have more to offer than diaphragms.

Birth Control and Status of Women

Abortion is an experience restricted to women, but there are both male and female methods of contraception and male and female methods of sterilization. Although much research effort has been devoted to recording the levels of usage of each individual method, surprisingly little attention has been paid to the question of the relative preference for male or female methods and the reasons why couples choose a male or female method (Khoo, 1980).

Sterilization

Sterilization is probably the most widely used method of fertility control for the world as a whole. Male sterilization is an extremely simple operation which can be performed almost anywhere (in India there are vasectomy rooms on railway stations) and which has no long-lasting physical side-effects. Female sterilization, even with the improved modern techniques, is still an operation which requires considerable skill and usually, a short period of hospitalization (Population Report, 1978). Yet more than three-quarters of all sterilization operations are performed on women rather than men and the proportion is increasing (Sardon, 1979).

The proportion of sterilizations which are female ranges from 100 per cent in Tanzania, Tunisia and Jamaica to 25 per cent in India. Only three of the 23 countries for which statistics are available have more male than female sterilizations, whilst 18 of these countries are countries where 80 per cent or more of all sterilizations are female. There are a number of reasons for this inbalance. Programmes concentrate heavily upon women; men fear that the operation might affect their virility and women feel that the family bread-winner should not be exposed to any risk of ill-health. It is difficult to tell what the relative proportions would be in the absence of the bias of the programmes. In Thailand men are increasingly paying to be sterilized even though the operation is free for females. In Latin America men are beginning to adopt vasectomy despite their legendary concern with their 'Machismo' or masculine image. In South Korea the proportion of female sterilizations has risen from 28 per cent in 1975 to 77 per cent in

1977 owing to changes in the systems of bonuses provided for doctors performing sterilization operations (Sardon, 1979). It is difficult to give a cultural explanation which will account for 28 per cent of sterilizations being female in Bangladesh in contrast to 87 per cent in Pakistan. This appears to be a clear case of the sex of the method adopted depending upon the services offered. Where the government pays much higher fees for female sterilization operations there is a clear temptation to sterilize women rather than men.

In the United States the proportion of female sterilizations has risen from 20 per cent in 1970 to 51 per cent in 1976. This rapid change over is said to constitute a part of a world-wide shift to female sterilization resulting from the development of new female sterilization techniques which have resulted in the availability of female sterilization as an out-patient procedure, greater interest by physicians in performing female sterilizations and a general relaxation in age and parity requirements for females to be sterilized (Population Report, 1978).

It is an interesting question whether male or female sterilization is associated with higher status for women. The choice of male sterilization shows that males are willing to share the burden of birth control and risk their masculine image. On the other hand, female sterilization gives women direct control over their own fertility, and liberates women who wish to have a variety of sexual partners (Newman and Klein, 1978). Much obviously depends upon the social setting. In village Indian women accept sterilization for themselves because they believe that the male operation damages the man's working capacity, and because their men refuse to accept the operation for themselves from fear of being weakened.

Contraception

The most effective contraceptives available, the hormonal pills and injections and the devices placed in the uterus, are all female methods. The most effective of the male methods; the condom or penis sheath is only effective when used by highly disciplined individuals. The great bulk of all research on new contraceptive methods concentrates upon female methods (WHO, 1979). This is partly because it is biologically much easier to prevent the production of one egg per month in a female than the production of billions of sperm (Bremner and Kretser, 1975). However, it is also true that there is much less interest in controlling male fertility (Djerassi, 1979). Just as, in traditional societies, the woman is almost always blamed when the couple cannot have children, so too, in modern societies, it is the woman who is held to blame for excess fertility.

In the development of modern contraceptives in the United States feminist pressure from women who wanted control over their own bodies played a major role (Goldzieher and Rudel, 1974). Men can have control over their own bodies without the need to control their fertility. Thus they have an in-built biological autonomy which women have only acquired in this century and which is still denied to many women in the developing world (Rozenzweig, 1973).

In policy terms it is essential that both men and women should be able to control their fertility and to share the risks and benefits associated with contraception and sterilization. Given the present bias towards female methods in both programmes and research, the need is for more emphasis upon the masculine half of the equation. While some women wish to retain control for themselves, there are also many others who would rather share the responsibility for family planning with their mates. In traditional societies one would expect a male contraceptive injection to be highly popular, especially if it were believed to increase masculine potency. It is a sad example of the way in which contraceptive research is directed towards the needs of the wealthy and developed countries that research on a possible chemical for a male pill was terminated when it was found to react unfavourably with alcohol – possible use by Moslems who do not consume alcohol was of no account. (Jackson, 1970).

Radical Feminism and Reproduction

This book is principally concerned with options which are currently available or could be made available in the near future. However, it is also important to be aware of more radical visions for the next century. Amongst the radical feminists who believe that true equality for women can only be achieved after a social revolution there are three major campaigns concerning human reproduction.

Firstly, there is the belief that women who become pregnant can never be equal and therefore that the whole process of reproduction should be taken over by machines which would be responsible for the whole process from the uniting of sperm and egg onwards (Firestone, 1971). Secondly, there are those who believe that women cannot be equal so long as they have relationships with men, and therefore argue that men should stay away from women except where the women desire to become pregnant (Rivolta Feminile, 1970). This group argue that the invention of effective contraceptives has actually lowered the status of women because it has made it possible for men to treat women simply as sex objects, and society no longer has any interest in regulating the process since no children result. The third group argue that women should seek to control the research, development and use of fertility control technology (Dalla Costa and James 1972). All three groups share a common belief that women should control their own bodies and that birth control technology is not sexually neutral but favours the sex that controls it.

Up until the present feminists have fought for the right to control their bodies, to prevent pregnancy and to have abortions. In the future, if population pressures become more severe and governments become more authoritarian and more concerned with breeding from the right stock, women may find themselves fighting for the right to reproduce,. the right of every woman who wishes to have at least one child in her life. (In the 1930s 24 of the United States of America had compulsory sterilization laws for the 'feebleminded, criminals and paupers' which removed women's right to reproduce Pickens 1968).

Women's Status and Access to Contraception and Abortion

One clear interaction between the status of women and fertility which is generally ignored relates to the provision of contraceptive services for unmarried women. To deny contraceptive services to unmarried women is to deny them control over their own lives; to encourage early marriages (often forced into being by unwanted pregnancy); and to lose a valuable opportunity for showing that sexuality and childbearing are not invariably linked. In New Guinea in 1979 the Minister for Health, after a storm of protests from women nurses and other women's groups, revoked his threat to prevent pills and other contraceptives being supplied to single women and wives not proving their husbands' approval (Canberrra Times 12.10.1979). Usually this issue is never debated in public and the decision is left to male administrators.

It is often claimed that to provide contraceptive services for the unmarried and for wives who do not have their husbands' consent are liable to risk a backlash which no family planning programme should be asked to face. Such an argument says a great deal about the relative power of men and women in society, but it is also quite unwarranted. Any programme which refuses services to women who ask for them is, in fact, saying, 'we do not believe women have rights, we do not really believe in contraception, we do believe in women being forced to have children they do not want'. Aggressive publicity of services for single women may be unwise in cultural conditions where there is little demand for such services but they should always be discreetly provided. Certainly there is a clear demand for contraception by the unmarried in such widely separated contexts as urban Nigeria and South Korea (Ware 1976; Chui 1978).

Any country which does not provide safe legal abortions for all women who want them is discriminating against women. Some countries may decide on moral grounds that they wish to exercise such a discrimination in which case they should perhaps be prepared to carry out a women-only referendum on the issue although it is still debatable what right women have to force other women to carry pregnancies which they do not want and to bring into the world unwanted children when there are such limited resources even for children who are wanted.

Male Fertility

Throughout the broad range of demographic studies from the statistical studies of fertility levels to the surveys of knowledge, attitudes and practice in relation to contraception, fertility is treated as an almost exclusively female attribute. At best there is a glancing reference to male attributes and opinions. At worst the treatment would suggest that women are solely responsible for bringing children into the world. Yet one of the very few studies which does examine male roles in fertility has argued that in Sierra Leone, amongst the Creoles, males are the ones who determine fertility levels (Steady, 1978).

There are a number of practical problems associated with attempt to assess the relative weights of male and female contributions to the maintenance of high fertility levels or the onset of family size limitation. One problem relates to the nature of social structure. In an ideal experimental design there would be four groups: husband and wife of equal, high status; husband and wife of equal low status; husband's status high, wife's status low; and wife status high but husband status low. In almost all societies marriages where the wife is of markedly higher status than the husband are so rare as to make the last group so atypical as to be of little use as a control. The result is that the focus is concentrated upon the contrast between marriages where both partners are equal and marriages where the husband is of superior status to the wife. Even here remarkably little has been done. Almost all studies contrast the behaviour of uneducated and educated wives without making the distinction between uneducated wives with equally uneducated husbands and uneducated wives whose husbands have been educated. Equally most studies of husband-wife interaction are concerned with a situation in which there is agreement between spouses; surprisingly little is known about cases in which there is a conflict of interest. We do not know what happens when the wife wants more children and the husband does not, nor do we know how common such cases are. One isolated Iranian study suggests that continuation rates with oral contraceptives depend, not on the wife's motivation but upon that of the husband. Where only the wife was interested only 12 per cent of women stayed with the method for longer than 6 months. However, where the husband was in favour 93 per cent of women continued on the method, irrespective of their own opinions on the matter (Momeni, 1975). Iran may be a special case, much of the anecdotal evidence focuses upon husbands who refuse to let their willing wives practise contraception. Thus injectable are popular in Kenya because, unlike the IUDs, husbands fearful of infidelity cannot force their removal. There are no data to show how common it is for husbands or other family members to pressurise unwilling wives into accepting contraception or sterilization.

Overall, the history of the modern development of birth control provides a good example of the way in which women, and especially Third World women, remain on the periphery even when their interests are central. Thus it was a very long time before the issue of appropriate contraception for breastfeeding women was raised (IPPF, 1979). Even now human rights issues involving women's control over their bodies and their sexuality are amongst the most controversial. In many cases, the freedom which control over fertility can give to women is regarded as a negative attribute by men who are the people who design family planning programmes and population policies.

10

Tradition and Female Identity : A Study of Women and Home in Bangladesh

In the development plans of Bangladesh in the past, very little importance was assigned to the problems of women, and no significant effort was made to involve them in the development process. They remained as it were in the background and continued to suffer from the traditional neglect. For this reason, there is a real lack of data regarding the specific problems related to women, in the absence of which no planned development is possible. Awareness of this situation is recent and efforts are now being made to fill this gap through the collection of basic data and research focused on women.

Various groups-social scientists, policy planners, national and international welfare agencies-entered the filed of research on women, and a fairly large volume of studies and research documents was produced in the latter half of the 1970s. Mahmuda Islam (1979a) classified the existing published documents into the following categories general studies, status in family and society, role in production, education and fertility. One flaw in the trend of research on women is the lack of co-ordination among the agencies, groups and individuals working on women. Owing to the absence of any supervisory body or an institutional arrangement for assessing and identifying fields in which information needs to be gathered, there is considerable duplication of effort. There are several studies that are shallow and have been perfunctorily handled. On the other hand, information is lacking on many important spheres of activities that affect the role and situation of women. Migration is one such field that has suffered comparative neglect.

Less developed countries pursuing development goals are going through a process of rapid urbanization. Bangladesh is no exception. Migrants from the rural countryside constitute a large portion of the urban population. Villagers migrate to the towns and cities for a variety of reasons. The come in search of high-earning opportunities, for better living conditions, for educational facilities, or even for personal security. A sizable number of the migrants come in search of jobs, because they have no land on which to subsist, or the family farm is too small to accommodate all the members of the family.

The overwhelming majority of the job-seeking migrants are males, and many of them come to the town alone, leaving all other members of the family at their village home. These male migrants live singly in town and from time to time visit their wives, children and other members of the family in the village. They go home either on week-ends, or on long holidays, and for religious festivities, or when an emergency arises. The rest of the time they remain absent from the home.

The absence of the male head of the family from the household for some length of time is a new development in the existing patriarchal family traditions. Traditionally in Bangladesh it is the male who leads the wife, children and other female members of his family and is a constant presence in the household. He is ready at hand to give decisions on all matters and to handle any exigency: the wife always plays a passive or a marginal role. The withdrawal of the male head of the family from the family home evidently reduces his ability and authority to control and decide, and the wife is likely to step in to fill the gap. To what extent the absentee migrant can still retain his control and how far the functions, role, authority and status of the wife undergo change in the new phenomenon of absentee head of the family is a matter worthy of investigation. The purpose of the present study is to identify the repercussions of absentee male migration on the female members of the family left behind in the village home. These repercussions will be studied in the context of the family, community and society.

The locus of the study is four contiguous villages situated 50 miles from the city of Dhaka, capital of Bangladesh. The investigators made a house-to-house inquiry to discover families in which male migration had taken place more than a year before, with the ostensible purpose of securing an income-earning occupation, and ninety-five such families were identified in the four villages. These families constitute our sample population.

The central female figure in each family (the woman who, next to the male migrant, wielded greatest authority among the female members) was interviewed through a structured schedule. The female field-workers read out and explained the questions to the women and obtained verbal replies that were recorded by the interviewer. The field-workers were scrupulously chosen on the basis of their experience in handling rural illiterate women interviewees, and their records of interview in this study may be considered an authentic reproduction of the feelings of the village women.

The field-workers' task, however, was not easy. Villagers are not accustomed to strangers, particularly young women from town, without any male escort. A section of the villagers, therefore, looked down on the women interviewers as sinners against modesty and feminine virtues. But the interviewers had the support of a few literate villagers who had been exposed to city life. The villagers, on the whole, were apprehensive of the interviews. They generally held the view that these interviews would yield them no tangible benefit and would mean a waste of their time. Some villagers even demanded payment for being interviewed. The apathetic attitude of the villagers towards the research workers appears to be the outcome of the general feeling of stagnation and lack of faith or hope in any imminent change in their wretched existence. Many rural women were reluctant to give much time for the interviews. They were sometimes advised by their menfolk not to talk much or talk freely. In some cases interviewers faced extreme views such as that the interview would result in the disadvantage of the interviewees; it might be a prelude to a new tax or a new land law. On the whole, women interviewees were found easier to handle when alone and in the absence of menfolk.

The male migrants of the ninety-five sample families were traced to Dhaka city and were also interviewed. Establishing contact with the migrant males proved rather difficult. Many had no fixed address and were continually on the move. They usually lived in the slums and in temporary hutments. Some of the migrants had no fixed working hours and could be contacted only at very odd hours and that, too, after several visits. It speaks highly for the sincerity and patience of the female interviewers that they ultimately met all the migrants. The environment in which the migrants were living was uncongenial for young women, and the migrants themselves were ill-accustomed to come in contact with and talk freely to educated young women. The migrants, however, acquitted themselves well, and no insurmountable difficulties arose during the interviews and field work.

The method applied in selecting samples for the study was not the only course open to the researcher. An alternative course would have been to identify migrants in the first place in Dhaka city and to reach their families in the villages through them. But that course was fraught with almost insurmountable difficulties. Seeking out the adequate number of migrants in Dhaka city is in itself an uphill task. It was decided at an early stage that a sample of about a hundred respondents would be necessary to do justice to the study. Not only was finding 100 migrants in Dhaka difficult for women workers but it was also well-nigh impossible to get an adequate number of adjacent villages. Intensive scrutiny and investigation would suffer if the respondents were scattered over a large area consisting of a number of villages. In view of the social and geographical situation, the number of villages had to be kept at a bare minimum and a contiguity of the villages were intended to facilitate intensive investigation. After an unsuccessful preliminary search in Dhaka for an adequate number of migrants coming from a few contiguous villages, the field work in Dhaka was abandoned and the alternative procedure was adapted to identify the families in the selected villages from which migrants had gone to Dhaka.

In selecting migrants, an attempt was made to respect certain criteria but not always with complete success. As far as practicable, married migrants were chosen. It was, however, found that many young people had migrated to the towns at a comparatively young age and were not yet married.

Our migrants had left behind all the other members of the family in the village home. This criterion restricted the scope of the study to the relatively poor. More often than not, the families do not migrate because the migrants do not earn enough to maintain their families in the cities, where the cost of living is higher than in the villages. To take a simple example, wholesale migration involves a rental expense, which is high because of the scarcity of urban housing. Many migrants have to sustain parents and younger brothers and sisters and find it difficult to maintain two establishments—one for parents at home and the other for wife and children at the place of work. It is only the relatively well-placed migrants who take their families to the place of migration.

All migrants in our study have stayed in the city for more than a year. Persons who have gone to the city for higher studies, and migrants who are unemployed have been excluded. All the migrants in the sample have jobs in the city.

The four villages chosen for the study are administratively part of one police district, namely Kapasia in the subdivision of Gazipur within Dhaka district. The villages are situated at distances of 8 to 20 km from the police station, which is the smallest administrative unit in Bangladesh. Three villages—Dawna, Bhulashar and Barrhar—are almost of the same size, extending 5 km in length and 1.5 km in breadth. Their population varies from 1,500 to 2,500. The fourth village, Buraich, is a little larger in area and population. All the villages are socially and economically alike. The population in these villages is predominantly Muslim. Agriculture is the main source of livelihood, with little industrial activity. People are in general poor. Each village has a primary school. Only Buraich has a secondary school, which serves all the four villages. The inhabitants of the villages are more or less tradition-bound. Very few people except the migrants had been to Dhaka. Communication with Dhaka is tedious and costly. Ordinary people walk to the police station. The relatively well-to-do use a man-driven rickshaw to reach it. Kapasia is connected to the sub-divisional headquarters by an all-weather road served by an irregular bus service. From Gazipur, Dhaka can be reached both by train and bus. The fare, however, is beyond the reach of many.

The migrants from the four villages work in Dhaka. Besides Dhaka city, Chittagong and Khulna are two major port-cum-industrial centres which also attract migrants from villages. But none of these places if comparable with Dhaka in respect of population and urban amenities. Dhaka has the largest concentration of migrants from all over the country, as is revealed by the figures given in Table 10.1. Although our sample villages are only 80 km from Dhaka city. The weak communication links make the impact of the distance much more substantial. The researchers made a personal exploratory tour of a number of villages in three adjoining districts of Dhaka city and found the police district of Kapasia the most suitable area for the purpose of this study.

Table 10.1
Net Migrants by Districts in 1974, Base Year 1961

Gaining population		*Losing population*	
Dhaka	+579000	Comilla	-358000
Khulna	+228000	Noakhali	-261000
Dinajpur	+132000	Faridpur	-253000
Sylhet	+131000	Patuakhali	-184000
Chittagong	+91000	Mymensingh & Jamalpur[1]	-111000
Rangpur	+62000	Pubna	-99000
Rajshahi	+61000	Tangail	-97000
Chittagong H.T	+53000	Bogra	-16000
Jessore	+40000	Bakerganj	-14000
Kushtia	+19000		

1. During the 1974 census Mymensingh and Jamalpur constituted one district. Separate figures are not available.

Source: Population census, 1974.

COUNTRY PROFILE

Geography

Bangladesh is situated approximately between 20°75' and 26°75' N. and 88°3' and 92°75' E. The country covers an area of 143, 993

km^2 and lies in the north-eastern part of the South Asian subcontinent. Except for the Bay of Bengal to the south and a narrow border strip with Burma in the south-east, India is its neighbour on all sides.

The greater part of the country is a flat plain criss-crossed by innumerable rivers. Two of the largest rivers of Asia, the Ganges and the Brahmaputra, pass through the country into the Bay of Bengal. They have branches and tributaries all over the country and provide a river transport system, a silt-rich soil, and a storehouse of fish. In between the rivers arable lands stretch for hundreds of kilometres, interspersed with villages, nestling amidst bamboo clusters, mango and jackfruit gardens and trees.

Bangladesh is within the tropical monsoon zone. Tradition divides the year into six seasons, but the rain-soaked summer stretching from April to October dominates the weather. Winter is brief, but pleasant and dry. Rainfall is abundant but is concentrated in the summer. Mean annual temperature varies from 14 to 44°C. The climate is temperate because of heavy rainfall in the summer, which varies from 100 to 250 cm and reaches 500 cm in some areas. During the transition from summer to winter and from winter to summer, changing monsoon winds bring storms and cyclones causing widespread devastation. On the other hand, rain-water from the Himalayas carried by the rivers causes enormous floods, inundating and submerging the plain. Thus rivers, in and monsoon dominate the life of the people of Bangladesh and bring about its alternating fortunes and woes.

Political Structure

Bangladesh declared itself independent on March 26, 1971 but finally emerged as an independent country on December 16, 1971. Though comparatively young, the nation has a long colourful history. The people are a mixture of Austro-Asiatic, Dravidian, Tibeto-Burman and Aryan stocks. Before the Aryans migrated to the subcontinent, Austro-Asiatic and Dravidian had their settlements in the region. Around 1300 B.C. a Dravidian civilization flourished and continued unbroken into the seventh century B.C. Aryans, who had started coming to India around 2000 B.C. settled in northern India. They did not make any organized excursions into distant Bangladesh, which consequently succeeded in maintaining a unique culture of its own.

Politically, the region did not become a homogeneous entity before the birth of Bangladesh. The Dravidians, the Hindus and the Buddhists exercised political powers over different parts of the region until Muslims established their supremacy in the thirteenth century A.D. Although officially Bengal was under the Great Mughals, they never succeeded in establishing a firm hold in the region, which was ruled for all practical purposes by the local princes. In the early eighteenth century a local Muslim Sultanate established suzerainty over the major part of the region. Muslim rule, however, was supplanted by British rule in 1757 when the Nawab of Bengal, as the country was then called, suffered defeat at the Battle of Plassey at the hands of Lord Clive. The British ruled the country for 200 years, making Bengal a province of British India. At the partition of India in 1947 the Muslim-majority areas of the province of Bengal opted for the new state of Pakistan. Pakistan had a peculiar geography. Bangladesh, in the eastern part of the subcontinent, was separated from West Pakistan in the western part by a vast tract of Indian territory. Due to geographical, political, economic and cultural differences, tension soon arose between the two parts of Pakistan and, after a massive armed conflict in 1971. Bangladesh was born as an independent nation with linguistic, ethnic and cultural homogeneity. People of the country speak Bangla as their mother tongue, profess mainly the Islamic religion and have a unique, indigenous culture.

Bangladesh at present has a constitutional government headed by a president directly elected by the people. He is the chief executive of the government and is assisted by a council of ministers selected by him from among the members of the National Assembly. The members of the Assembly are elected by the people on the basis of universal adult franchise. The Assembly is the supreme law-making body, limited in its power only by the constitution. The country has an independent judiciary deriving its power from the constitution and not answerable to the president or the parliament. The form of government is thus presidential with reasonable separation of powers among the executive, the legislature and the judiciary.

Demography

Bangladesh is small in area but large in population with a density of 535 persons per km^2 . Accordingly to the 1974 census the population of Bangladesh was 76.4 million, but due to an annual growth rate of 2.52 per cent, the population in 1978 has been estimated at 84 million, and is expected to reach 121 million by the year 2000. The population explosion thus is a problem of very high priority in Bangladesh, and an intensive family planning campaign is under way to contain the population within 100 million by the end of the century.

Males preponderate by a ratio of 108 males for every 100 females. People live mainly in villages. Only 8 per cent of the population lives in the urban areas. The country is therefore basically rural. More males than females live in urban areas. In the urban population, age-groups 20-24 and 25-29 have a clear edge, while people in the age group of 44 and above live mainly in the villages. In other words, the towns are inhabited by comparatively young people—a factor that indicates that town life is a comparatively recent innovation.

In the social life of Bangladesh, marriage is a universal institution. Mean age at marriage is 24 for males and 15.9 for females. The fertility rate is also high: the average number of children born alive to a married woman is 3.83. Among the urban women, the fertility rate is lower, and it declines with the increase in the level of education. Crude birth and death rates per 1,000 are 48.3 and 19.6 respectively.

The population of Bangladesh is comparatively young: 46 per cent of the male population and 48 per cent of the female population is aged 15 years or less; 32 per cent of the total population is less than 10 years old. The result of this exceptional proportion of children and adolescent are a very high dependency ratio of 104 as against dependency ratio of 85 in South Asia and 57 in Europe.

Economy

Bangladesh is one of the poorest countries of the world. A preliminary estimate for 1978-79 places gross domestic product at 6,330 million taka and per capita income at 729 taka (One U.S.

dollar = Tk 16 roughly.) Though there has been persistent growth in the GDP, the country continues to remain poor, owing to the high rate of population growth. Large-scale poverty is thus the primary characteristic of the country. The economy of Bangladesh is overwhelmingly agro-based. Agriculture contributes 55.23 per cent of the GDP and absorbs 78 per cent of the total labour force; 90 per cent of the total foreign exchange is earned by agriculture. Main crops of Bangladesh are rice and jute. Rice is the staple food of the people. But the country is always in deficit in rice production and is heavily dependent on foreign aid for its basic food needs. Jute is the main cash crop. It is exported both as a raw commodity and in the form of goods made of jute. In the year 1978-79, 71.11 per cent of the total foreign exchange earnings came from jute and goods made from jute.

Although agriculture is the main source of income, it is still in a backward state. Agricultural production is low, in fact one of the lowest in the world. Cultivation is carried out by people who are illiterate and who use traditional tools. Agriculture continues to depend on the vagaries of nature. Drought, floods and cyclones largely determine the production. Flood control and irrigation systems are yet to be developed.

In 1978-79, only 8.80 per cent of the GDP came from manufacturing industries. Before the emergence of Bangladesh the country was dependent on West Pakistan for its essential consumer goods. Industries which existed in Bangladesh were damaged during the liberation war. The country is therefore heavily dependent on imported goods. Because of this dependence on imports, Bangladesh is faced with a continuous deficit in the balance of payments, giving rise to the need for foreign aid and assistance.

11

Women Left Behind: A Case Study of Some Effects of Turkish Emigration

During the last few years we have studied the effects of emigration to Europe from two villages in the province of Konya in Central Anatolia, Turkey. The two villages exhibit strikingly different patterns of emigration, especially with regard to the active participation of women. There are but few women among the emigrants from one of the villages, called Alihan, whereas there are about as many women as men among the emigrants from the other villages. In both cases, however, the decisive factor for or against the emigration of women is one and the same: the pronounced will of the men. In the one village most of the men decided that the women should remain the village whereas the men in the other villages chose to bring their women along.

In this article my interest is focussed upon the women left behind in the village of Alihan with proportionately few women among its emigrants. Alihan is situated about 100 kilometres south of the town of Konya.[1] When the emigration to Europe started in the middle of the 1960s, Alihan had an estimated population of 650. Up until 1977, 135 adults had left for Europe. Among these emigrants, however, there were only 15 women. Thus the village experienced a mass exodus of young and middle-aged men with a majority of women remaining behind. This created a situation in which most families in the village were spatially split up. The decisions as to whether the women should go or be left behind were made by the men and not by the women themselves. The great majority of the women wanted to accompany their husbands to Europe but most of the men disagreed. It is therefore, of interest to analyse whether the emigration has brought about any great changes in regard to the women's traditionally subordinate positions in general, and in regard to major decision-making in particular. Has the prolonged absence of the men from the village scene increased, decreased or left no effect on, the traditional social standing of the women as compared to that of the men? And have the men's experiences of women's position in western cultures altered their view of the role of women?

Observers of Turkish village life agree that it is common throughout the country for the men to have the ultimate right to make all decisions.[2] At the same time men usually leave a large part of decision-making concerning the daily running of the household and the raising of children to women. Decisions concerning communal affairs and relations to the world outside the village, as well as decisions concerning major changes to be made in the family and in the household, however, are considered the business of men. Not surprisingly, however, it is often found that women have ways of influencing their men, even in those spheres. Yet the last word is left to the men so as to make it appear that they are the decision-makers.

Even before emigration, the life-spheres of men and women in Alihan were quite distinct, yet they existed within a common framework. Emigration breaks this framework and the gap between men and women grows wide. The women find that most of the time they have hardly any means to bridge this gap, and the majority of men exhibit a greater loss of interest in trying to bridge it. It is obviously far more difficult for the women to exert any influence upon men who are thousands of miles away or who are only at home on holidays or a few weeks of the year, or every second or third year.

Most of the Alihan women have great difficulties writing letters. Many of them, especially the older women, are unable to write themselves and have to ask someone to do this for them.

Very few letters do in fact generally pass between an Allihan husband and his wife even if the husband is away in Europe for a considerable length of time. The men in Europe tend to communicate with some male relatives back home rather than directly with their wives. In fact, a young man who writes directly to his wife expresses 'too much interest' in her and is considered to be a somewhat suspect person; what a man has to say to his wife should be said via the patriarch. Even if there is some communication by mail it is obvious that most letters contain very little direct information and hardly any personal thoughts but are to a large extent made up of different kinds of elaborated phrases of greetings. Thus mail is hardly a way for the women really to communicate with their husbands and still less a way of exerting any influence upon their men. Yet as long as men and women are spatially separated there is hardly any other means open to them.

With the majority of men away in Europe, some of the women have gained in importance in that they function today as the local head of the family household while the men are away. This is, however, mainly within the women's traditional spheres of influence, that is, the daily household chores and the upbringing of the children. Rarely does it involve direct influence over the family's agricultural resources as the men usually leave this responsibility to a male relative or to a close male acquaintance in the village.

In former times most business with the outside world was handled by the men; the women rarely left the village and in no case did they do it without a male escort. Today the women sometimes go to town on major shopping expeditions; on such occasions, however, they are usually accompanied by some male relative young or old. If no male relative is at hand and they still have to go to town for some reason they will try to go in company with some other women; never will they go to town on their own. This is not only a question of security but also an awareness of the fact that without a male to do the business or a male in company to look after their interests women often find themselves in weak positions in town as most of the businessmen, specialists and authorities may be men with little regard for a village women. Major business transactions are still mainly cared for by the men, either when they are at home on visits or through some arrangement with a male relative.

Most of the women in the village certainly have far more money today than ever before, money that they can handle themselves, yet the money they are entrusted with is almost entirely spending money and not money that they can invest at their own will. Some of the men abroad seem not to realize or seem not to be willing to realize the enormous rise in the cost of living in Turkey during the last few years due to an extremely high inflation. The men often remarks that the women do not know how to handle money properly. They are said to spend far too much money living at great ease, fed and clothed by the men's money coming in from abroad, while the men themselves have to live under strained conditions working ever so hard to provide for themselves, their families and a better future. Attitudes of this kind do not make it easier for the women to gain standing towards men.

The women have come to be regarded as consumers of the men's production rather than as vital parts in the production itself. It is said that in earlier times and at the beginning of the century men and women worked about equally hard in the fields. In the twenties when horses replaced oxen as draught-animals, however, it appears that the men took over a larger share of the agricultural work. Money made abroad during the past decade has brought tractors to the village and with an increasing mechanization of agriculture, the part played by women is steadily decreasing. The primary sources of income for the village households today are agriculture, in which the women take an increasingly smaller part, and work in Europe, in which the women have no part. Nowadays the women's realm of work is almost exclusively concentrated upon household chores which do not directly provide any money. Besides, most of the men are not present in the village to enjoy and benefit from the work of the women in the home. The men in Europe have to perform their own household tasks, which they certainly do not seem to enjoy or be happy about, as they regard such tasks as women's work and thus beneath their own dignity. Or they have to arrange for someone where they live to do the household tasks for them. Thus, the traditional complementarity of the work of men and women have to a large degree been destroyed, and this in a way that does not strengthen the position of the women.

Besides, many of the items produced by the women such as embroidery, hand-knitted woolen socks, home-made clothes and the like which earlier were regarded as important for the household and its pride, are today looked upon with scorn by most men. Nowadays the men prefer nylon socks and ready-made clothes and tend to regard this part of the women's work as of little practical value, as something for the women to occupy themselves with for lack of other important tasks.

Another matter which tends to weaken the position of women in the eyes of their men is the growing number of problems with the upbringing of the sons at home. In former times most of the fathers seem to have had no great difficulty in demanding and receiving respect and obedience from their sons. The father-figure was an imposing, stern person of great authority with obvious means of punishing a disobedient son. A boy would not leave the village territory without his father's permission, and within the village there were many eyes to watch him and his behaviour. Today most of the boys are growing up with a very remote father-figure. In earlier days the boys learnt their roles as men by listening to and learning from men of all ages in the village's male common-rooms[3]. Today there is only one such room left, the one next to the mosque, which is frequented almost exclusively by the oldest men in the village who stay there between their prayers in the mosque. Most of their talks deal with religion and the young boys do not care to spend time in their company.

Exaggerated reports and stories of the pleasures of life abroad, make life in Europe appear so much more thrilling to the boys than life back home in the village. They tend to regard village life with the same attitude as that expressed among the emigrants, that is, as a quiet but backward form of life, a form of life which they are not happy to conform to. Many of the boys spend an increasing share of their time away from the village, most often in the town of Konya. In town they visit cinemas with American and European films and get an even more biased view of the realities of life outside the village.

The boys are taught that they are to function as superiors to females; yet, in most cases, the one locally responsible for their upbringing is a female. No wonder that they often choose to go their own ways. In connection with all this, they do not tend to be 'good boys' and obedient sons, as earlier. The men often tend to blame the women for this development, rather than to acknowledge that the rebellious behaviour among the boys may be seen as resulting from confusion created by too sudden changes in values and ideals and their own absence as father-figures and male ideals. Thus it comes to appear that the women are not managing very well in their traditional role of bringing up the children, yet another factor lowering their esteem in the eyes of the men.

The right of decision-making among the men in a household is by tradition largely a matter of relative age. The patriarch, the oldest male, is the functioning head of the family. Before emigration it was the patriarch who had the economic resources on which the younger men of the family were dependent for their work and their livelihood, an arrangement of utmost importance for the older men's social control over the younger men. The patriarch's strong position of authority and power was especially pronounced in matters concerning marriage arrangements for the younger men. Being dependent upon the patriarch's paying the requested bride-wealth and his continuous supplying cases created a reverse situation. In these days many of means of livelihood, the younger men usually accepted the fact that the patriarch had the ultimate word in the choosing of the bride. In regard to financial dependency, emigration has in many of the older men are financially dependent upon their sons, especially in regard to the raising of the bride wealths.[4] In this new situation the younger men often succeed in exerting quite an influence upon the patriarch's choice of bride, sometimes even to the extent that the girl chosen is not to the satisfaction of the patriarch. During the first years of married life a new family lives in the household of the patriarch. Partly in return for the bridewealth the new bride is in some sense brought into the patriarch's family as a servant. As long as the daughter-in-law is the choice of the old man himself, he usually shows concern that her staying in his house will work as well as possible. A woman who has only reluctantly been accepted by him as a daughter-in-law can hardly count upon a similar show of concern for her welfare. The young men usually return to Europe shortly after their marriage and may not be back for several years. In this way many of the young women find themselves as new members of families in which the head is not particularly interested in making life easy for them and this in a situation in which their husbands are not present to protect or further their interests. Thus, many a young woman finds life in her new family even harder than it used to be and her possibilities of influencing her own situation sharply reduced by the absence of her husband.

It did not take long for the women to learn that emigration has brought not only geographical separation but even greater distance in the realm of experiences. Having tasted life in Europe many of the men now tend to regard life in the village as more or less backward and look upon those who have not been abroad as persons of less knowledge and experience than themselves. The women who have stayed behind are in this way identified with a stagnant pattern of life while the men who have been abroad regard themselves as dynamic actors with wide perspectives on life.

As long as a man has his family living in the patriarch's house he is regarded as being under the authority of the partriarch and is expected to hand over his savings to the patriarch. In older days a son would usually live a good part of his married life in his father's house. Nowadays most of the men who have their own earnings seek to establish themselves in independent households as soon as decency allows. The majority of the men who have been abroad do not plan to settle down in Alihan after their return but in the nearby town of Konya where they hope to open some small business of their own. In the last ten years, more than half of the village families have left Alihan to settle down in Konya. More than 90 per cent of the families who have left the villages are families of emigrants. The majority of men working abroad will use the better part of their savings to get a house in Konya. As soon as they have arranged for a house they move their family there. Having thus established themselves as heads of their own households the men usually return to Europe for further periods of work. Does such a move to town establish a stronger position for the women? To some degree yes, but not to the extent that perhaps could be expected. Almost all the Alihan houses in Konya are situated in one and the same area on the outskirts of town next to the road that goes to Alihan. The women are free to move around to visit people they know in this area but are not allowed to go to other parts of the town on their own. Many of them being without what is regarded as proper male protection can in fact be seen as more limited in freedom of movement and action than they were back in the village.[5]

The men visiting on holidays often consider themselves experts on how to live in town and have very little appreciation for the women's traditional village ways. While not allowing their women to adapt themselves to the ways and fashions of town women, which the Alihan women themselves as yet show little interest in doing, the men who have been in Europe often seem to be somewhat ashamed of and irritated by their women's old fashioned village-like appearance.

While abroad, many of the men have been in close contact, or even on intimate terms, with European women, a fact which most of them rather tend to boast about than try to conceal. The men's experiences with European women seem to have produced a double image or ideal of what a woman should be like, one for what she should be like as a mistress and another one for what she should be like as a mother. It certainly would be next to impossible for any women to combine the two ideals, it would seem, without developing many conflicts. Many of the men appear to be more or less enticed by the idea of having a western type of woman as a sex partner, at least that is the idea which they convey to one another and to those around them. Yet much of what they tend to find exciting and thrilling about European women as companions in fun and sex are attributes which they would never accept being displayed by their own women. In the eyes of the men, the emancipation of western women has created disorder in family life and in society as a whole, and has resulted in ways of behaviour on the part of the women which are not morally acceptable for a decent woman. It appears that experiences abroad in regard to women's emancipation more often have had the result of convincing the men that it is their duty to hinder such a development at home rather than to further it. Yet they obviously enjoy the company of European women.

While it is common knowledge that most Alihan men have love-affairs with other women while abroad, the Alihan women must of course be careful never even to look at other men. They have not much choice but to accept years of involuntary separation and sexual abstinence. The wives of emigrants do not usually express regret about their husbands having brief affairs with other women. But they often express worries that their men will not be satisfied with them as women and they fear that their men will become engaged in permanent love-affairs with European women. Most often they feel that they are competing with western women for the attention of their men on quite unequal terms, they themselves being in the weaker position, being absent and being less educated and experienced.

According to tradition it is quite easy for a man to divorce his wife; in earlier times, however, the bridewealth to be paid by a man to acquire a new wife functioned as a substantial hindrance to many a divorce. A divorce is regarded as a catastrophe for a woman. There is no socially accepted sphere for single women in this society. In case of divorce a new marriage will most likely be arranged for the woman but in most cases on less favourable terms. Today most of the men would have no great difficulty in raising a second or even a third bridewealth.

The villagers allege that before emigration there were no cases of divorce in Alihan. During the last few years, however, there have been three cases of divorce in the village. All three cases involved an emigrant who divorced his wife in order to marry another woman whom he had met while abroad. One of the divorced women has since been married off to a far-away village, another has been placed in her older brother's household while waiting for him to arrange a new marriage for her, and the third woman has had to leave her younger daughter with her old widowed mother while she herself was married off to an old widower with no less than six children in a small town nearby.

Events like these demonstrate to the Alihan women their vulnerable position as wives of emigrants. Many women worry constantly about their own future, for which they certainly have obvious grounds. Emigration has most often not only widened the pre-existing gap between men and women in the community, but has done it in such a way that the women today appear to be in a much weaker position in relation to the men than they were when their complementary roles were enacted within the traditional framework.

What has been presented here is but a glimpse of a very complex matter. Yet the examples given are suggestive of a general trend of the effect of emigration to Europe on the social standing of the women left behind in the village of Alihan. It is yet to be seen whether this is a picture which is also applicable to other villages with similar emigration patterns, and similar social and cultural backgrounds.

References

1. The name of the village is invented. Further details on the community are found in the author's dissertation 'The Force of Tradition: Turkish migrants at home and abroad', Engelbrektsson, 1978.
2. Men's superior position in decision-making in villages and small towns is reported in a number of studies from various parts of Turkey. For example, from the Kuzova region by N. Erdentug, the Konya region by J. Hjarno, the Ankara region by D. Lerner, the Balikesir region by P. Magnarella, the Kaman region by J. Pierce, the Bodrum region by F. Mansur and the Kayseri region by P. Stirling.
3. For details on male common-rooms, see for instance, B. Beeley's article, 'The Turkish Village Coffeehouse as a Social Institution', 1971.
4. It has been reported by P. Magnarella and others that the bridewealth practice in Turkey has been virtually discontinued in the cities while its frequency is decreasing in rural areas. The decrease in rural areas is seen as resulting from the spreading influence from the cities. Paul Magnarella writes, 'Many villagers believe that city customs and practices are culturally superior to their own, and there has been an effort by an increasingly large number of them to imitate these urban ways of life.' (Magnarella, 1969: 152). Yet the Alihan emigrants, who live or have lived in European cities in which there is no practice of bridewealth among the local population, not only continue the practice of bridewealth, but do give it added significance.
5. In his article, 'Cause, knowledge and change: Turkish village revisited', Paul Stirling reports similar observations in the town of Kayseri. He writes, 'Village women resident in town are not allowed to go out to work. Indeed, they are not allowed to go out at all, not even shopping, and it is my impression that although the new situations in which women find themselves vary enormously, mutual observation and gossip relationships between women neighbours develop very rapidly. I was struck by the fact that village-born women with village-born husbands are more restricted, housebound, segregated and socially isolated when they move to town than they were in the village.' (Stirling, 1974: 213).

Bibliography

Beeley, B.W. 1971, The Turkish village coffeehouse as a social institution, in *Ekistics* 187, June, 1971.

Engelbrektsson, U.-B. 1978, The force of tradition: Turkish migrants at home and abroad, Reissue 1982, Goteborg: Gothenburg Studies in Social Anthropology, Acta Universities Gothoburgensis.

Erdentug, N. 1959, *A study of the social structure of Turkish Village,*

Ankara, Publications of the Faculty of Languages, History and Geography.

Hjarno, J. 1971, *Fremmedarbejdere.* Kobenhavn: Nationalmuseet.

Kolars, J.1964, *Tradition, season and change in a Turkish village,* Chicago: University of Chicago, Department of Geography.

Lerner, D. 1958, *The passing of traditional society,* New York: The free Press.

Magnarella, P.J. 1969, The Turkish bridewealth practice in transition. In *The Muslim World* 59, April, 1969.

Magnarella, P.J. 1974, *Tradition and change in a Turkish town,* New York: Halsted Press.

Mansur, F. 1972, *Bodrum, a town in the Aegean,* Leiden: E. J. Brill.

Pierce, J. E. 1964, *Life in a Turkish village,* New York.

Stirling, P. 1974. Cause, knowledge and change, Turkish village revisited. In Choice and Change (ed.), J. Davis.

Stirling, P. 1965, *Turkish village,* New York: Weidenfeld and Nicolson.

12

Women in a Tribal Community

Status, in this context is considered as the ascribed position of an individual or section of the community on par with the necessities arised out of the ecological and traditional conditions. The role is the actual behaviour of the person as expected by him or her in a given social framework. Conseptually, though both are separate, often they overlap each other especially in closed societies like that of tribals.

An attempt is made here to see the status and role of women in a particular tribe through their inter-relations with men. For the purpose, the Minyong of North-Eastern Region is selected. The major reason for this is, the Minyongs are not primitive and isolated and experiencing a transistional phase. For that matter, no tribe is left as a real tribe and each one is at a different stage of development and Minyong is of no exception to the concept.

The North-Easter Region, until recently was mystery for outsiders. The sensational stories of colourful cultural costumes, gruesome brutalities of head-hunting and interesting descriptions of military expeditions were available only through the written documents of British Officers and later on by some well-known Anthropologists. Though the situation never remained same, the part of the mystery still prevails as certain areas continue to have restricted entry for outsiders.

The North-Eastern Region comprise seven states viz., Arunachal Pradesh, Assam, Manipur, Meghalaya, Mizoram, Nagaland and Tripura. The total geographical area is 255 sq. kms. with a population of 26,607,199 (according to 1981 census), which is 7.7 and 3.88 per cent of the India's area and population respectively.

Minyong is one of the major tribe of Arunachal Pradesh, occupying most of the South-Eastern parts of East Siang district. According to 1971 census, the total population of Minyongs in the State was 19,146 with 9,456 males and 9,690 females (1981 census figures are not available). The earliest mentions of Minyongs (Dalton, E.T. 1872, Hamilton, A: Millington, P, 1912) give an account of them as a branch of Abors, and in recent decades because of their separate identity and growth in population, they are recognized as a separate tribe by the Government. Most of the discriptions provided by British Officers brings out the fact that Minyongs were one of the most dangerous and brutal stock. The famous Bower's Abor expedition of 1911 (Hamiltion, 1983) resulting the crushing defeat of Abors, who comprise a number of clans including the Minyong was because of the gruesome and treacherous massacre of two British Officers at the hands of Abors. But the present situation represents a complete reverse of the old. Equal rights to all through constitutional provision, and exposure to the developmental inertia have eliminated the internal feauds and rivalary, and now they are the most peace loving people of the area.

Demographically, though they are spread throughout the district and neighbouring areas, their main concentration is found in the Pangin and Boleng administrative circles of Pangin block to Pasighat sub-division. As the purpose of the paper, is to study the status and role of women among Minyongs, certain characteristics were identified as the indicators of the concept. These are: *(i)* the work participation, *(ii)* control over the resources and *(iii)* decision-making.

According to the legend, the group is originated from a common mother, who had two sons, one a brave and honest and the other a cunning craftsman. In due course the mother migrated to the west and the second one left with her as he was her favourite. And the legend goes that along with him, he carried all the art, implements of agriculture and arms, leaving the inferior things to the brave and honest brother. Minyongs claim to be the direct descendent of this lady through the brave and honest son and attribute their low level of technology and backwardness to this legend. This has also contributed to the attitudes they possess towards the women in general. Though not the women are highly respected, they are treated on par with men. Husbands are very considerate to the wives, which is a rare phenomenon in other tribes of the area who are rude in this aspect (op. cit Dalton, E.T., 1872).

Minyong is an endogamous group. Next to clan is the sub-clan and lineages which are exogamous. Polygamy exists but very rare and fast disappearing. Marriages are occasionally arranged, otherwise mostly young girls and boys arrange these affairs themselves. Even when it is arranged, due weightage is given for girls consent. Divorce is permissible, pre-marital courting also tolerated. Though the group is patriarchal, the girl's get their due share in marriage in the form of Mithuns, pigs, fowls and all the mother's jewellery she inherits. The only difference between boys and girls are, the boys get all immovable property and girls get movable one, but the share will be equal. This freedom in marriage and equal share in the property is based on the notion of equality and in recognition of their individuality and capacity.

In the economic sphere the Minyongs are a simple agricultural community, practising shifting and terrace cultivation supplemented by hunting and fishing. Work participation in the form of labour is equally shared by both sex, but sometimes more by the women. The statistical figures of the both Pangin and Boleng circles, where the whole population is of Minyongs, will show the trend Table 12.1.

The work participation trend shows, that the males are slightly more than the females in the main workers category.

Occupation-wise classification shows, there are more number of female cultivators than the male, which indicates their increased role in the productive activity. The reason for this is more than one. The land tenure system among the Minyong is still community based and each individual/family is provided land for cultivation according to his/her capacity and resources. The most powerful motive among them is the possession of land they till. It not only provides the basic economic security but is an economic heritage, provides recognition to her individuality and from which she draws socio-economic and psychological security.

Table 12.1
Distribution of Workers Sex-wise

	Main workers	*Culti- vators*	*Agril. labourer*	*Other workers*	*Marginal workers*
Male	2.670	2,360	54	253	41
	(51.6)	(48.9)	(75.0)		
Female	2,490	2,460	18	19	122
	(48.4)	(51.1)	(25.0)		

Source: Census of India, 1981.
Series: 25—Paper 2 of 1982. Primary Census Abstract of S.C. & S.T. (Figures in Parenthesis are percentages).

The second reason is of historical one. During the days of inter-tribal feauds and rivalary, most of the men were pre-occupied in defending their territory and people—hence majority of their time was consumed in non-productive activities like fighting etc., and females were forced to take up productive activities such as agriculture, animal husbandry and horticulture. Till today the hunting, fishing and cutting timber for construction etc., are considered as masculine activity and all other, including agricultural activities are under female's domain.

The diversification of occupation by men towards other fields like trade and commerce, construction and government services are other reasons for increasing role of females as cultivators. This diversification trend is more clear as the persons in "Other Workers" and "Agricultural Labour" category is increasingly pushing the female towards cultivation.

Another interesting observation is, the men folk have become lethargic and easy going. Majority of their time is spent on gossiping, chewing betelenut, consuming home brewd 'Apung'. The major factor for this is the increased responsibility, the female carry on their shoulders including the food production and marketing leaving little scope for men.

The other field, where women's participation is conspicuous, is the handicraft like weaving and bamboo work. Though the Minyong women are not as good as Mishmi's of the neighbouring area, the young girls produce good amount of materials for commercial purpose apart from domestic consumption. They are never seen idle and busy in some activity even while they are resting. It is observed that since young age, the girls are provided separate patch of land in the backyard to grow cotton, which they use for weaving purpose. These girls after attending the family core, attend to their cotton, cultivation and weaving work. Whatever the product they manufacture like shawls and jackets (which are of typical Minyong pattern) marketed in nearby towns of Along and Pasighat. Sometimes they also travel up to Lakhimpur in a group of 4-5 girls for the purpose. The money earned thus are kept for their requirements and the most important is the habit of self-reliance is inculcated since the childhood.

Coming to the second indicator, which directly affects her status, is the control over the resources. As already seen, the women's participation is not of limited field among the community. As a major contributor to the economic production, her control over the resources is more substantial than men. The resources include the land, the agriculture production, the family labour and the income. She is also in control over the resources brought from her parental house like cattle and jewellary. It is also observed that in many cases women also exercise control but also to the functional control which is well reflected in the sphere of decision-making process.

The decision-making process among Minyongs is at two levels, one is at community and the other is at family. The Community has a council of elders known as 'Kebang' which look after the community level affairs. So, it is the second level structure, where the decision-making power affects the individuals status. This is the structure where family as a unit including its members are decision makers. To see this Power at the familial level observations were confined to only four fields. They are: *(i)* selection of the crops to be grown, *(ii)* labour utilization, *(iii)* marketing the surplus commodities and *(iv)* education of children.

The Table 12.2 shows the ratio of women's role in different decision-making areas. Only in the first category of crop selection both male and female share the responsibility equally. In this field some activities are masculine like felling and chopping the trees etc., where men's contribution is required. Other than that, it is the women, who is more knowledgeable about the type of soil, the method of rainfall and climatic conditions etc., and their decision carries the weight. All remaining categories belongs to the women's domain and men has little say in it. The reason are the women's more knowledge in the respective field and secondly the notion of women's capabilities.

Table 12.2
Decision-Making, Sexwise

(Percentages)

Category	*Male*	*Female*
1. Crop selection	50.0	50.0
2. Labour Utilisation	35.0	65.0
3. Marketing	21.0	79.0
4. Children education	28.0	72.0

(N=40, in two villages).

In the field of community festivals too, the women's role is equal to that of men. These are occasions for both the sex to display their skills through dance and hunting or other such activities. The women attire to their best and enjoy to the maximum. The only area where women does not have any role and their participation is restricted, is the rituals. Women's restriction on these occasions are based on two criteria. One is that the women are thought as ritually impure and proximity causes impurity. Second one is, most of their rituals surrounds the ancestral workshop and women have less knowledge about this as they have come from different families and villages, hence their involvement is less. Even under such circumstances, it is observed that during ancestral worship, the male members seeking advice from families elderly women regarding achievements and wishes of the dead etc.

The above analysis supports that status is an ascribed position of an individual/section of the community on par with the necessities arised out of the ecologial and traditional conditions and the role played by the individual is controlled by the social situation and inter-relationship with fellow individuals.

Minyong women's entrepreneurship and their role in the economic productivity are the positive indicators which helps directly the developmental process. Even in other communities, the women may possess the similar characteristics but their relative status enjoyment may not be the same. So, whereever the status is better, the potential for general development increases proportionately and the role expectation will also be of higher order.

Bibliography

Dalton, E.T. 1872, *Discriptive Ethnology of Bengal,* Calcutta, Government Printing.

Hamilton, A. 1983, *In Abot Jungles of North-East India*, Delhi, Motilal Publications 1983 (Originally printed in London, 1912).

Millington, P. 1912, On the track of the Abor, London.

13

Dilemma of Liberation : A Study of Palestinian Women

There are many reasons for dealing with the Palestinian women: From a social-anthoropological point of view we can find among Palestinian women representatives of all the different social strata in the Arab world and among Arab women: the beduins, the peasants, the artisans, the female workers, the traditional middle-class housewives, the modern educated women and the bourgeois women. From a sociological point of view it is especially interesting to study how the objective situation, *i.e.* the situation of colonization and expulsion and the state of war, has influenced the situation of women within the different social classes and in their different places of residence. From a humanitarian point of view we are confronted with women who have suffered for decades and whose fate cannot leave one unaffected once confronted with it. From a political point of view we know that these women and their fellow men are important determinants of the situation of world peace. From a personal point of view I have met representatives of most of the above-mentioned groups, and I have been inspired by their culture and their courage and I hold them in high esteem and deep respect. The latter fact does not necessarily make research more biased, but it stimulates curiosity and makes the approach more committed.

These are my reasons for having chosen the Palestinian women as the theme, in addition to the fact that by focusing on the world of (Palestinian) it is possible to encompass the past, the present and the future. This is so because women not only represent the present, but in most societies—including the Palestinian—they are carriers and transmitters of culture and traditions. We can also see what future they, as primary agents of socialization, are preparing the children to form, and in the revolt of many Palestinian women we can see glimpses of a future that implies Fundamental changes in both the private and the public sphere of the society.

Palestinian women can be divided into various groups, such as age groups, social classes and the like, but I prefer here to use a division which is at the same time geographical, social and political. That means that I will divide them into territories, those who live outside the camps in the various Arab countries and those who live in the refugee camps.

Common to all Palestinian women is that in one way or another they are affected by the establishment of the state of Israel in the land of Palestine, the expulsion of the majority of the Palestinian people and their resulting statelesseness. One of the reasons why this has affected the situation of Palestinian women is that the family was one of the few institutions, if not the only original Palestinian one, that survived the Palestinian disaster in 1948. The family thus gained an enormous importance as a protector of Palestinian identity, and as this identity had lost several of its material elements, the trend to stress more idealistic values such as solidarity, family relations and the concept of 'honour' became intensified. This was even more so the case, as in the wave of war, terror and panic, assaults on women's honour (*e.g.* rape) were if not often carried out, at least deliberately used as a threat. The protection of the wife and daughter(s) is still today, according to many older Palestinians, the reason for fleeing their country. According to Barakat and H.P. Daw (Y. Haddad, 1980) 'the fear of having their women assaulted by Israeli forces was the primary reason for 30 per cent of those leaving the West Bank in 1967'. I am well aware of the fact that bombs and massacres are at least as convincing, but I do believe that the other threat has left its deep imprints on the consciousness of many Palestinians.

As was also the case in Algeria during the war of liberation, a defensive family structure was found among the Palestinians in Palestine, now Israel, as well as in the diaspora. After having been bereaved of their country, their land, their profession and not least their honour (not being able to protect their land) the men made of the family their last fortress. This could be seen both among villagers who remained in Palestine and in the refugee camps that were often built as displaced villages in the sense that people from the same village would try to settle in the same quarter of the camp and in that way make it a collective of villages. This has been extremely important as to strenghtening and maintaining the collective memory, and the national identity. But it has also meant that high priority was put on the reproductive functions of the women, namely sexuality and the reproduction of new and old labour, *i.e.* childbearing and taking care of the male members of the family through traditional housework. All these functions are controlled by the men and thus work against equality.

The Palestinian Women in Israel and the Occupied Territories

In Israel this tendency has been enforced and strengthened by the expropriation of Palestinian land which has turned hundreds of former productive villages into what is called 'sleeping hotels' (Since the establishment of the state of Israel 384 out of around 500 Palestinian villages have 'disappeared', *i.e.* been erased, and the Palestinians of which the great majority were peasants are left with all together 50,000 ha. of land which is about one-tenth of a ha. per person. (H. Lebrecht, 1979). In the remaining villages the vast majority of men are working outside – as there is no more land to cultivate – and the majority of women are cut off from their former participation in the productive life of the village.

However, a certain proletarianization of Palestinian women does take place. This must be viewed as an extension of a general proletarianization of Palestinian men which again is a result of the depeasantization which, as already mentioned, is not (only) the result of an industrial development, but primarily due to land expropriation. According to Don Peretz (1977), two-thirds of the Muslims in Palestine (they made up around 80 per cent of the Palestinian population) were farmers (or peasants) at the end of the Mandatory period (the late forties). In 1974 only 30 per cent of the refugees in Gaza and 21.6 per cent of the Gazan non-refugees were employed in agriculture the same year. According to the same source it is estimated 'that Arabs (about half Israelis and half from the occupied areas) provide nearly a quarter of the labour in Israel's "productive industries". Arabs supply half of Israel's workforce in agriculture and building and more than ten per cent in industry. About half of all un-skilled workers in manufacturing and "virtually all farm hands" are Arab' (*ibid*, 1977).

The Palestinian women who have entered the Israeli work force are mostly to be found within textile and food-processing industries and as agricultural labourers. To a certain extent their wage-labour is thus an extension of their domestic work which in the meantime also has become less labour-intensive due to the various commodities and due to the dissolution of the extended family system which finds no material basis in the 'sleeping hotels' (Amal Samed). Another reason for this proletarianization – which hardly exceeds 10 per cent of the Palestinian women – is the victory of economics over tradition. The concept of honour, which also presumes that a man does not sell his female labour to strangers, has had to give in under the pressure of material needs. The Palestinian community has been forced into the conflict-ridden Israeli capitalist system where salaries – especially those of Arabs – in no way can keep pace with the rise in prices and the rocket-like inflation.

As is the case in most Arab countries, this female workforce is formed primarily by young unmarried women (and some needy divorcees and widows). This has several effects: As to the father, it means that he can control the income of the daughter and channel it into the family budget. As to the Israeli authorities, they might have though it beneficial in fulfilling their dream of reducing the Arab fertility rate by postponing marriage. (The father will be less motivated to give his young daughter in marriage.) As to the women concerned, it means that wage-labour does not lead to economic independence, the idea of which is further eliminated by the low wages and the high prices.

The ideological impact of this female wage-labour is complex. On the one hand, one could imagine the development of a class consciousness that could lead to solidarity and common struggle with Jewish female workers. But on the other hand, the Arab women often take over jobs left by Jewish women who have been promoted into better jobs in the public sector and the service sector; this leaves no ground for common struggle. Another and even stronger reason for this lack of common struggle is the superiority feeling of the Jewish women, created and backed by the Zionist ideology. Furthermore this situation the proletarianization – is considered a symptom of the Palestinian tragedy, which ideologically means that female work is connected with the establishment of the state of Israel and the resulting misfortunes. And it is – rightly or wrongly – seen as a contradiction of the good old days, and values, and family honour which did not allow female members to sell their labour to strangers.

Education

Education is one of the factors considered to possess a certain emancipatory force for women. After the loss of their country and their material basis for existence, education presented to the Palestinian people one of the few possibilities for finding a way out of their misery, a way to at least individual dignity and survival. This possibility as presented by UNRWA (United Nations Relief and Work Agency for Palestinian refugees), the Arab countries, the socialist and some Western countries, has been used to such an extent that today the Palestinians are one of the most educated (as to the ratio of university graduates to population) peoples in the world: 11.2 Palestinian university students out of 1,000 compared to 30 in USA, 18 in USSR, 9 in France and 8 in England (N. Badran, 1980).

At the end of the British Mandate, the educational situation for the Arabs of Palestine was as follows: Altogether about one third of the school-age population went to school with 85 per cent in the towns and 20 per cent in the rural areas where almost 80 per cent of the population lived. 65,000 pupils attended elementary public schools, 37,000 in the rural areas with 7 per cent girls, and 26,000 in the urban areas with 42 per cent girls. Another 40,000 attended private educational institutions. The discrepancy between the percentage of girls in the rural areas and those in the urban areas is not only due to a different and often more progressive attitude to girls' education among urbanites, but also due to the fact that the 20 per cent of the Palestinian population which was (is) Christian was mainly concentrated in the cities. Another forceful factor that limited the attendance of rural girls was that 95 per cent of the villages had no school for girls (50 per cent had no schools at all). Secondary education was almost entirely limited to Jerusalem and a few other cities, and it was mainly in the hands of foreign (often religious institutions that favoured the Christian minority.

Today – 32 years later – the situation has, of course, changed. According to Israreli statistics (Women, 1980) 90 per cent of the 'non-Jewish' girls in Israel attend primary (elementary) schools compared with 98 per cent of Jewish girls. This is in agreement with 'a leading member of the democratic Women's Movement in Nazareth' (R. Sayigh, 1980) who, however, continues by saying that in Nazareth only 75 per cent of girls *finish* elementary schools and only 20 per cent *finish* secondary. According to the above Israreli statistics, 37 per cent of 'non-Jewish' girls attend secondary schools as compared to 72 per cent of Jewish girls. The Israeli statistics wisely stop at the secondary level, for otherwise we would have learned that less than 2 per cent of the Arabs in Israel go to university (1974-75 figures, T. Zayad, 1976). A more recent figure is 'below 3 per cent' (G. Toubi, 1980). Rosemary Sayigh (ibid) estimates that only 5 per cent of these Arab students are girls.

The education of Palestinian girls in Israel has several objective barriers to overcome: one being a lack of school buildings and facilities, another the unequal distribution of secondary schools between urban and rural areas, and a third the lack of financial support for Arab students in universities which amount to a mere 0.33 per cent (T. Zayad, 1976) of all financial support to university students in Israel, where university fees are high. Actual figures on the educational level of Palestinians in the occupied territories are difficult to find, but my estimate would be that they are rather similar to those in Israel as to the elementary and secondary level, whereas it is well known that the situation at the university level is much better due first of all to access to the universities in the Arab countries.

The above-mentioned leading member of the Democratic Women's Movement in Nazareth summarizes the situation of Palestinian women in Israel in this way:

Arab women are part of the whole population, and face the same general problems: first, neglect of Arab towns and villages, and discrimination between Arab and Jewish localities. The Ministry of the Interior gives three times more to Jewish than Arab municipalities. For example, Afuleh with a population of 14,000 gets a budget of 1-£ 250 million, while Nazareth, with 45,000, has just had a budget of 1 £ 80 million rejected. Jewish cities the same size as Nazareth, *e.g.* Tiberias and Safed, get 1 £ 450 million.

In the so-called mixed cities (Akka, Haifa, Yaffa, Lydd), the situation is even worse, because the Arabs actually live in separate quarters, and are starved of municipal funds. They can't develop, can't build schools and kindergartens, or sports centres. It's the same in the villages. Children are learning under trees, without equipment, without even lavatories.

It's the same story with the Ministry of Health, medical facilities for Arab areas lag far behind. The Histadrut gives health insurance to all its members, but their clinics exist only in Jewish centres, and Arabs, especially from the villages, can't always reach them. In a recent epidemic of measles, many children died because their mothers couldn't reach the clinics. Here in Nazareth there are small private and missionary hospitals but no government or Histadrut hospital – we have to go to Afuleh. We have only four mother and child care centres, subsidies are inadequate, equipment inferior. Government clinics in the villages usually open twice a week, for a few hours.

Women's Reaction to Their Situation

The reaction of Palestinian women to their situation of being caught between the chains of the family and tradition on the one side, and the socio-economic and cultural deprivation enforced on them by the Zionist state on the other will vary according to age, class, education and political affiliation.

One reaction, and one that seems to be the most dreaded by the Israeli authorities, is the maintenance of one of the highest fertility rates in the world. This could be considered a reaction and not just a passive and traditional act, because experiences from most other places in the Third World show that a growing educational level and increased participation in wage-labour lead to a decrease in the birth rate. But among Palestinians it is considered almost a national duty to give birth to as many children as possible to fill the places left by the martyrs. The attitude of the Israeli authorities to this fertility rate can – apart from outright discriminatory statements – be seen from their changing legislation.

> To encourage families to get many children it was agreed upon that the state according to the 'Law of national Insurance' should give a certain allowance per child. But also the Palestinian families with many children benefited from this. That was not the intention. The law was supposed to secure an increase in the Jewish population. The law was replaced by a new one, the 'Law of demobilization of soldiers'. This law combined child allowances with military service. And as the Palestinians have no access to the army, they cannot benefit from the child allowances (L. Johnson & N. Stockmar, 1980).

Another reaction is seen in a growing political participation in both nationalist groups and in the Communist Party of Israel that receives more than 60 per cent of the Arab votes. But for women the national feelings have mainly been channelled into and through social and charity organizations that mushroom in the area. Alone in East Jerusalem, West Bank and Gaza there are about 150 of them. These organizations carry out social, cultural, medical and educational activities. The leadership will mostly consist of (elderly) women from the more privileged and well-educated social strata, whereas the activities – as is mostly the case with such organizations – will be directed towards their less privileged fellow sisters. The ideology of these organizations will be mainly national and rarely feminist, that means that issues on women's liberation are not (or rarely) raised.

Women Prisoners

Before the occupation of the West Bank, East Jerusalem and Gaza in 1967, it was extremely rare to find Palestinian women in prison for political activity. But with occupation followed resistance which again was followed by repression. Soraya Antonius (1980) gives a list of 1,229 Palestinian women who during the period of 1967 to 1979 were arrested by the Israelis. To this should be added '150 names for which no details are available' and hundreds of women kept in detention camps plus many more involved in mass arrests. An example of the latter is that in the year 1976 some 33,000 men and women were detained and only 8,000 of them were charged.

The list of the women political prisoners gives an idea of various political activities of women although the grounds for the charges, in many cases, might be far from sound. The age-range is from 13 to the mid-sixties, but the majority will be teenagers and women in their twenties and thirties. The charges run from participation in demonstrations, membership of illegal organizations (mostly PLO and its organizations), to participation in military activities. It is interesting to notice that family ties can lead to sentencing and imprisonment: women are sentenced for not denouncing a son's, a brother's or a husband's alleged activities or for having helped in or known of the illegal activity of a family member. Women have even been tortured to make the husband confess, and in the case of Issam Abdel Hadi, president of the General Union of Palestinian Women (GUPW), her daughter was whipped bleeding and threatened with rape in front of her mother in order to make the latter confess. The mother was later deported without having been put on trial. (S. Antonius, 1980). The repression and the collective punishments (curfews, demolishing of more than 20,000 houses belonging to family members of suspected prisoners, etc.) are part of the daily life of Palestinian women in the occupied territories, irrespective of their socio-economic status.

It is sad to have to state that so far the only equality between Palestinian men and women both in Israel and in the occupied territories is the one found in prisons and chambers of torture.

Palestinian Women in the Arab Countries, Outside the Refugee Camps

A great number of the Palestinians with permanent residence outside the camps in the Arab countries belong to the middle and lower middle-class (to the extent that rigid class terms can be applied to the Palestinians), and it is, of course, also here the bourgeoisie should be found. This residential class division happened in two ways. First, when the Palestinians became refugees those who had managed to bring (and a precondition for that was, of course, that there was anything to bring), their jewellery and savings, and those who had contacts – family or professional – in the neighbouring countries and whose education or profession made it easy to find employment, would settle outside the camps, mainly in the cities. The big majority was absolutely destitute and had no such choice and had to accept being crowded together in camps made up of tents, later changed into sheds and now cement houses. Second, during the first-two decades of their diaspora there was a tendency to leave these refugee camps as soon as the money sent home from a son or a daughter in Kuwait or any other place allowed it. Today the camp population seems to be more stable in the sense that even people who economically could afford to move out prefer to stay with their country people.

It is difficult if not impossible to find any statistics showing the rate of education and work-participation of Palestinian women dispersed in the Arab countries. However, it is possible to state a few common features.

In the educated middle-class it was not unusual that women became the breadwinners of their families. They would mostly do that as teachers, secretaries and nurses. These qualifications were needed and in demand in the oil states in the Gulf area where the general level of education was extremely low and that of women hardly existing. As these states were, and are, also very sex-segregated, they needed female labour to teach girls in schools and to nurse women. Also in Lebanon with the much higher level of education the Palestinian middle-class girl or woman had advantages with her command of English at a time when Anglo-American interests in the country were increasing. In Palestine as everywhere else, the second language – if not the first – was that of the colonizers.

In the Gulf states these women often found themselves in a paradoxical situation. On the one hand, they had to work outside the home, in jobs that before had been carried out by men, and they even sometimes became the main breadwinner of the family (*e.g.* in the case of being the oldest child). On the other hand, they had to submit to restrictions on their personal freedom, restrictions hitherto unknown to them, such as veiling, and strong restrictions in mobility. However, the combination of their professional and economic positions gave these women a very respected position. Contributing to their situation of being more emancipated than most other Palestinian women, is the fact that the power of the (extended) family has been limited by the dispersal of the family and by the change in roles. This has again lead to a lower birth rate.

Bassam Sirhan (1976) concludes from a study entitled *Family and Kinship among Palestinians in Kuwait* that the Palestinian family in Kuwait is 'going through a transient stage from traditional to modern family, and that this transformation is going ahead, despite the prejudices still remaining in the minds of heads of family and dating back to the traditional society of the predisaster period.' He also states that 'there is a big transformation in its (the family's) values and behaviour, and in the distribution of authority within the nuclear family . . (and) . . . a great change has taken place as far as the woman in the Palestinian family is concerned.'

The Palestinian middle-class women have often played two important roles from a national point of view: First, they have enabled their families not only to survive, but they have also enabled their sisters and brothers to have an education while they never managed this for themselves; second, many of these women have worked as committed members of the GUPW and the PLO where they have been very important in the mobilization of women in the refugee camps. It should be added that everything indicates that these women of higher status outside the camps are in no way estranged from the national struggle of the Palestinian people.

Palestinian Women in the Refugee Camps

Those who are most directly involved in the daily struggle are, however, the women in the refugee camps. In their lives we can find emancipatory as well as oppressive factors.

When the Palestinians fled from Palestine it often happened that whole villages (or at least several families from the same village) fled together, and the mere panic of the flight meant that everybody went to the closest border. Thus it is not surprising that these people also settled together. In this way the refugee camps have retained a social structure from the villages in Palestine, a structure that most probably would not have survived a 'normal' development with industrialization. This means that the neighbour in the camp with great probability was also a neighbour in Palestine and thus to a great extent shares the same historic experience. Together they can talk about such concrete things as the olive trees, the orange groves; together they can strengthen their Palestinian identity, and together they can fight to return. In spite of the strong oppression from external forces the people in the camps have not been completely deprived of status. It still counts to come from a big family in Palestine, a family with the honour unquestioned, or to be a man or a woman of mature age and with life-long experience. This preservation of the old roles is only possible because the members of the community remember the way it was in Palestine, and this knowledge is transferred to the younger generations. The negative side of this is that there is no whitewashing for past wrongdoings.

This structure has also meant a strengthening of the Palestinian identity of women, but at the same time it has meant the maintenance of the patriarchal family and the establishment of a defensive family structure with rigid sexual norms. A Palestinian woman puts it this strongly: 'The Palestinian used to be much more advanced in his own country and women were independent and freer than women in Syria or Egypt or Iraq, but after 1948 this changed: in the camps the Palestinian became ultra-strict, even fanatic, about the 'honour' of his women. Perhaps this was because he had lost everything that gave his life meaning, and 'honour' was the only possession remaining to him.' (S. Antonius, 1979).

The Palestinians living in Lebanon in the camps are those who have been studied and described the most, and the following figures are also from there and are presented to give an idea about the framework around the daily life of Palestinian refugee women.

The average size of a nuclear family is 8-10 – the household may be much bigger. The average density of population is 6-7 persons per two rooms. 88.3 per cent of the homes have a total living space of less than $80m^2$. 40.4 per cent of homes have no form of heating; 35 per cent have no electricity; 20 per cent have no private toilets; less than 12 per cent have bathrooms; 60 per cent have no running water. (Bassam Sirhan, 1975).

The camp population is young (64 per cent under 20 years of age and only 8 per cent above 50 (ibid.). Neither poverty nor revolution has changed the attitude to marriage. It remains one of the most important goals to attain in life, a goal which is higher than that of work or education. The average marrying age is 24.5 years for men and 21.6 for women, but women are considered of marriageable age after 15. Divorces are rare and even more rare are unmarried adults.

Economic Situation

Only 3.2. per cent of the total female population work outside the home (ibid.). The percentage is 8.8 for women between 20-24 but drops to 3.7 for those between 25 and 29. The highest figure is to be found in the 65-69 age-group with 12.1 per cent, that is the generation of widows to whom it is not only a necessity but also more acceptable to work. Married women are expected to stay in their homes and so are the unmarried young girls whose chances of marriage do not increase with wage-labour (R. Sayigh, 1978). It should be remembered that what jobs are available to the majority of the camp women are jobs in dirty factories, or cleaning jobs in offices, or jobs as maids in private houses. All of it is often at 'black' prices; that means salaries below the very low official minimum salary, because many of the Palestinians do not have a work-permit. This is also the case for many of the men of whom 40 per cent are employed. According to a Lebanese Manpower Survey from 1971 (R. Sayigh, 1979) 58.4 per cent of the employed camp workers were still paid on a daily basis, and only 8 per cent had long-term contracts. 21.1 per cent were employed in agriculture, 13.6 per cent in building and construction, 11.8 per cent in industry, 2.4 per cent in transport, 14.4 per cent in trade and hotels, and 36.7 per cent in categories of 'other services' or 'unspecified'.

It is estimated (R. Sayigh, 1979) that around 80 per cent of working-class Palestinians earned (1977) less than 300 LL a month. The most poverty-stricken are, however, those who have lost their main bread-winner and who depend on UNRWA and the Resistance for help. The number of these destitute people has increased by tens of thousands after the civil war in Lebanon.

Educational Situation

The Palestinian children are not admitted to Lebanese governmental schools at any level, whereas they can attend public schools in most other Arab countries where they reside. This fact means that the Palestinian camp children in Lebanon have only had the UNRWA schools and later also schools established and run by the Palestine Liberation Organization. The result is that in 1971 (before the establishment of the PLO schools) only 64 per cent of Palestinians of school age in Lebanon went to school. Of these 88.4 per cent were 6-11 years of age, 67.1 per cent were 12-14 years and 37.3 per cent were 15-17 years. Girls form 47.5 per cent of the total school enrolment. Only 0.2 per cent of the camp residents in Lebanon hold university degrees (R. Sayigh, 1979). Considered that the quality of the UNRWA school education is very questionable, it is no wonder that the PLO puts a high priority on education at all levels from kindergarten to university.

The life of the camp is pre–occupied by the daily work of the women, a work that starts early at dawn and ends late in the evening. Rosemary Sayigh (1978) equates women's domestic labour-load in large families with that of a construction labourers. In the camps this work is 'aggravated by environmental dirt, poor housing, overcrowding, inadequate water and lack of equipment–poverty' (ibid). None of these factors serves for the women as— an excuse for not keeping high standards on cleanliness and food. According to the same source most women wash every day or every second day, floors are swept and washed every day. To this should be added shopping and the heavy job of bread-making as 'camp Palestinians regard bought bread as next to poison , and making their own has become almost a national identity symbol. Most families consume four or five kilos of bread a day so that women must bake two or three times a week, working ten to twelve kilos of flour at a time. Once ready, the loaves are carried to the local oven, marked by a queue of impatient women' (ibid. 1978).

Another duty is social visiting which serves several purposes. It keeps the community together and serves as a forum for an exchange of news of often vital importance to the members such as news about job possibilities or marriage partners. To this picture should be added the fact that for the last decade war and bombardments and threats of the like have been part of 'daily life' with all the anxiety and sorrow that these involve.

As can be seen from the above, the role filled by the Palestinian woman in the camp—and the role that she is expected to fill—is a very traditional Arab woman's role, namely that of a wife and mother. When traditions are invoked in the camp it is not for the emancipating features. Another force and another ideology is in operation, namely that of the Palestinian revolution which urges the women to take part in the national struggle.

In what way are the women moulded by these two ideological models? For the majority it seems that the national liberation struggle, being an integral part of their daily life and talks, does not – for those who have already formed families – change the set-up of the family and the daily life. The women will still work in the home and fulfil her role as a wife and mother, even if, besides the domestic work, she has to work outside the house as a needed wage-earner. The older generation seems satisfied with its position (which also does wield a lot of power and influence on the family level). It is the one that resembles the situation in Palestine the most. And, after all, the revolutionary ideology of women's liberation alongside the liberation of the land is only a decade or less old for the Palestinians.

But the young generation, the so-called *jeel al-thawra* (the generation of the revolution), how do they administer these two cultural fronts which, although not antagonistic, still pull in each their direction?

A Lebanese clinical psychologist, Sylvie Mansour (1977), directed a study of the self-conception of youngsters in the Palestinian refugee camp, Tel al-Zaater. This study has achieved a sad historical status, as the same camp a year and a half later was totally destroyed by the Lebanese rightist forces in one of the most bestial massacres in our time. This means that a great many of the young girls and especially boys interviewed in this study are buried under the ruins with bullets in their necks. Those who had expected a radical change in attitudes leading to a big gap between the generations will be disappointed, and it is still too early to say whether the small (verbal) attempts at protests and revolts can lead to a fundamental change or whether they just symbolize a youthful and wishful attitude.

Many of the girls (10 out of 16) envied the freedom of the boys and several made explicit protests against the inferior status of women. However, the majority of the girls agree with the majority of the boys that women's role in the revolution should be that a nurse. The most remarkable thing in the listing of women's roles in the revolution is that no girls (against three boys) include political work or work for the General Union of Palestinian Women. The political side of the revolution seems to be put in the background of concrete actions. This is, however, a realistic appraisal of the needs of the revolution at the time, and among the military martyrs in August 1976, 250 Palestinian women guerillas could be counted.

The girls admitted that however great their commitment might be, it would depend on their future husbands whether they would be involved in the revolution or not, and the boys supported the old idea that Palestinian women should participate in the Revolution, so long as it does not involve their own sister and wife. The majority of girls wanted to postpone marriage, but accepted arranged marriages. The preferred qualities in an ideal husband were; intelligence and a good education; after this comes attractive appearance and dedication to religious values as well as to the Palestinian cause. Wealth comes last, in spite of the prevailing poverty. The boys stated that the ideal wife should be intelligent, pretty, well-educated, dedicated to religious values and good morals, 'least important of all, she should be militant' (ibid.).

These young people are representatives of the camp that 18 months later became the symbol of Palestinian heroism, steadfastness and tragedy. It can be difficult to find the arrows pointing to the road of equality in their answers. One explanation is that the social structure of the camp has served as a conservator of the old village structure and of the old values. The artificial surroundings of a refugee camp have kept these values alive artificially, in spite of the fact that they are no longer adequate in the light of the new reality. Another explanation is that the oppression of the Palestinians as a people has been so tough that the main identity is the national one – expressed by both boys and girls alike – rather than the equality of the sexes. Consciousness about the oppressed role of women is not furthered by the fact that bombs hit indiscriminately. In the specific case of Tel Al-Zaater, the discrimination was to the 'benefit' of women: when the camp was 'evacuated' virtually all men and boys were executed by the attackers. Although Tel al-Zaater might be called an extreme case, it shows in all its horror the conditions under which the Palestinian women are becoming politically conscious. How and why should one teach these women to get fewer children in the name of personal liberation when they have experienced that, within hours, they can lose most of their children? (Bendt & Downing, 1980).

General Union of Palestinian Women (GUPW)

A study of Palestinian women would be incomplete if it did not include a chapter on the General Union of Palestinian Women. The political roots of the Palestinian women's organization go as far back as to 1919 when the first women's association was formed in Jerusalem. Then – as now – the major point of struggle was the national one.

When the Palestinian women on 27 February, 1920, took to the streets of Jerusalem together with around 40,000 others to show their anger against and rejection of the 'British Mandate and the Zionist expansionist aims in Palestine' (PLO) they were, according to S. Antonius (1979) 'heavily veiled and rode in closed cars'. This indicates that their class background was one of the bourgeoisie and the petit-bourgeoisie. It was also from these social strata that the attempt was made in 1921 to form a women's union in Palestine. This organization was to organize demonstrations and the like, but they never managed to attract the big masses of rural and working-class women. (This experience resembles that of the Egyptian women's movement as well as that of several European ones.)

The first Arab Women's Congress in Palestine in 1929, gathering around 200 women, was an important step towards a more organized movement and a movement with greater perspectives. The Congress adopted three resolutions (PLO, *ibid.*): '*(1).* The Arab women of Palestine should undertake a national awakening similar to that taking place in neighbouring countries. *(2).* The congress supports the decisions of the nation's preceding congresses. *(3).* National commerce and industry should be promoted by all means, and economic ties with Syria and other Arab countries should be enhanced.'

The Congress also sent several letters and appeals to international organizations, the King of England and British politicians, demanding the annulment of the Balfour declaration. The women first tried to present the petitions to the *wife* of the British High Commissioner, but as this was refused they had to go against traditions and present it to the *man* himself (S. Antonius, 1979). From this Congress emanated the first Palestinian Women's Union with Jerusalem as the headquarters and branches in the major cities of Palestine.

That the Palestinian women did not want to give the enemy any chance to play on sectarian (religious) issues was demonstrated in 1933, when a Christian woman first talked from the pulpit of the Omar Mosque in Jerusalem followed by a Muslim women, talking in front of Christ's tomb in the Holy Sepulchre (*ibid*).

In the revolution of 1936-39 the struggle of the Palestinian women gained a broader basis and took on new forms including armed struggle. The first Palestinian female martyr was Fatimah Ghazzal killed in battle in June 1936.

After the establishment of the state of Israel in 1948 and the subsequent dispersal of the majority of the Palestinian people, no formal organization of Palestinian women existed. In Israel it was (and is) forbidden for the Palestinians of both sexes to form political parties or organizations, and in the Arab countries the women who did work of a political nature did so through the local and the pan-Arab political parties.

With the establishment of the General Union of Palestinian Women in 1965, as a union under the PLO, a new epoch in the history of Palestinian women was ushered in. Branches were established in Jerusalem, Gaza, Lebanon Jordan and other Arab countries where Palestinian refugees lived. The June War in 1967 and the occupation of the rest of Palestine meant the closing up of GUPW's offices and branches in the occupied territories and the transition to illegality.

The catastrophic defeat of the Arab regimes in the war meant that all Palestinians lost faith in the capability of these regimes to confront the enemy, and the resistance organizations were viewed as the only possibility of a return to the homeland. This meant an enormous support for the resistance that now took the form of a mass organization. For the GUPW it meant that they now saw it as their major task to mobilize women for the revolution.

There are two ways of joining GUPW: either through one of the member organizations of the PLO or as an individual. The

Union offers many different kinds of activities: military, political and professional. Military training is compulsory for all members and it mostly aims at the defence (in the militia) of the camps, but for those who wish, it is possible to receive training courses in heavy arms and guerilla fighting. Several women have achieved a high status among the Palestinian people as courageous fighters (and martyrs) and as participants or even leaders of dangerous (next to suicidal) operations, but they are more symbols than representatives of the Palestinian woman.

Concerning the political activity, it will in the beginning mostly be of a receptive nature as new members participate in study circles arranged by the Union. Here they will discuss recent events and learn about the history of their country and the revolution. The Union prepares study material and will – among other things – stress the role of women in other revolutions. It has not always been easy for the women to be allowed by their men to attend such political meetings, not that they disagree with the message, but that they consider it the men's business. Thus the GUPW has often tried to mobilize the women through sewing courses and literacy course, which are considered more acceptable, and also through information given at the PLO clinics in the camps. Another side of the political work is international relations. To what extent the Palestinian women master this role was demonstrated at the Women's Conference in Copenhagen in 1980. At this event the Palestinian women delegation also made it clear that all talk about equality, development and peace without reference to their own reality, which is occupation and war, is futile.

The members of the GUPW are very conscious about the fact that women's participation in production is an essential factor for her liberation. But the women in the refugee camps are not only impeded by subjective factors but also by the objective lack of job opportunities. To meet this need the Union has establishment several workshops in the camps. The aim is to further the liberation of the women by removing or diminishing their economic dependence and by relieving the resistance movement of some of the economic burden of supporting all the families who have lost their prime supporter.

The workshops make clothes partly for the guerillas, and partly for selling at reasonable prices in the camps. Furthermore, there are workshops for the making of sculptures, jewellery, flags, badges, embroidery and toys. Besides the objectives of economic relief and personal independence, the workshops also serve to keep up the old traditions so important for a people which has lost not only its land, but also the right to a national identity.

All members of the Union have to take a first-aid course, the necessity of which should be evident. Furthermore, there are possibilities of receiving training as a nurse in the hospitals of the Palestinian Red Crescent. Other occupational possibilities are in the kindergartens of the PLO and the various member organizations. Today there are 31 kindergartens in the camps in Lebanon. In these kindergartens the pedagogues strive hard to compensate a little – for the fortunate ones who can enter – for the lack of activities and stimulation for the children of the overcrowded camps where there are no playgrounds or activity centres. The challenge of this work is tremendous: how to build small strong personalities with confidence in themselves and the world when bombers daily demonstrate how little the life of a child is worth.

So far there has not been established a proper training college for the pedagogues. Their training is confined to course of a few week's or months' duration.

Many members of the GUPW are working with organizational tasks, *i.e.* organizing and mobilizing women. This work requires patience and understanding of the living conditions of the fellow sisters. It might take dozens of visits to the home to convince a reluctant father or husband to let his daughter or wife play her role in the national struggle.

To sum up about the General Union of Palestinian Women, it could be said that national problems and questions are put above questions of equality of the sexes. The woman is, in the eyes of the Union, not so much a wife and mother as an important cog in the revolution. She is no longer judged according to her clean floors, her many children or her fine *tabouleh* (salads), but according to how she fulfils her role in the national struggle. But the above has shown that this is not how the rest of the society, including the majority of the women, look at things.

The work and struggle of the General Union of Palestinian Women is a reflection of the struggle of all Palestinian Women and of the whole Palestinian people: the dialectics between the national and the social struggle. On the one hand is the extremely difficult national struggle of the Palestinians which demands that all forces unite on the issue of liberating the homeland. That means that they cannot afford divisive social or feminist struggles. On the other hand, it is questionable whether it will be possible to achieve the national aim without a radical change in the social structure and thus also in the attitude to the role of the Palestinian women. But the problem is even more complicated than that, as there is no choice. There is no chance to take a deep breath, because in the meantime new settlements are built enforcing the Zionist character on the occupied territories, new families are made refugees in the South of Lebanon, New martyrs join the endless list and more children lose their parents. All of this has to be dealt with on both a day-to-day and a long-term basis.

The problem seems insoluble seen from the here and now, but a look back just a decade gives some ground for optimism. After each defeat, the Palestinians came up stronger with more women organized and active, and with fewer narrow-minded men. So may be the dialectics between the objective and the subjective forces can solve the problem of the dialectics between national and social struggle of women, at least to the extent that the Palestinian women in their future Palestine can continue their struggle from a better position and under more natural circumstances.

Bibliography

Antonius, Soraya, 1979, Fighting on Two Fronts: Conversations with Palestinian Women, *Journal of Palestine Studies* 31, Vol. VIII, No. 3.

Antonius, Soraya, 1980, Prisoners for Palestine: A list of woman political prisoners, *Journal of Palestine Studies* 35, Vol. IX, No. 3.

Bendit, Ingela and Jim Downing, 1980, *Vi ska tillbaka til var jord; Pälestinska lagerkvinnor i Libanon*. Stockholm: Prisma.

Haddad, Yvonne, 1980, Palestinian Women: Patterns of Legitimation and Domination, In the Sociology of the *'Palestinians, Nakleh and Zureik* (eds) London, Croom Helm.

Hallaj, Muhammed, 1980, The Mission of Palestinian Higher Education, *Journal of Palestine Studies* 36, Vol. IX, No. 4.

Johnson, Lone og: Stockmaar, Niels, 1980, *Palaestinenser i Israel*, Copenhagen, Gjellerup Media.

Lebrecht, Hans, 1979, Der zionistische Bodenraub, *Horizont* Sept.-Okt.

Mansour, Sylvie, 1977, The Sense of Identity among Palestinian Youth: Male and Female Differentials, *Journal of Palestine Studies* 24, Vol. VI , No. 4,

PLO : *The Women's Role in the Palestine National Struggle*, Lebanon, n.d.

Palaestinenserne i Israel (interview with George Toubi) *Palestine-Orientering* nr. 1, 1980, 2. argang.

Peretz, Don, 1977, Palestinian Social Stratification: The Political Implications, *Journal of Palestine Studies* 25, Vol. VII, No. 1, Autumn.

Samed, Aml, The Proletarianization of Palestinian Women in Israel, *MERIP Reports* No. 50.

Sayigh, Rosemary, 1978, Daily life in Palestinian Camps, *Spare Rib, London*, Jan. 78, issue 66.

Sayigh, Rosemary, 1979, *Palestinians: From Peasants to Revolutionaries*, London, ZED.

Sayigh, Rosemary, 1980, *Chains of Oppression, Links of Freedom*, Unpublished.

Sirhan, Bassem, 1975, Palestinian Refugee Camp Life in Lebanon, *Journal of Palestine Studies* 14, Vol. IV, No. 2.

Sirhan, Bassem, 1976, *Family & Kinship among Palestinians in Kuwait* (Primary results of a social research) Kuwait University, UNESCO.

Women, *a brief report on the status of women in Israel*, Israel Information Centre, n.d.

Zayyad, Tawfiq, 1976, The fate of the Arabs in IsrGarel, *Journal of Palestine Studies* 21, Vol. VI, No. 1.

Index